SHADOWS ROUND THE MOON

SHADOWS
ROUND
THE MOON

Caribbean Memoirs

ROY HEATH

COLLINS
8 Grafton Street, London W1
1990

William Collins Sons & Co. Ltd
London · Glasgow · Sydney · Auckland
Toronto · Johannesburg

First published by Collins
Copyright © Roy Heath 1990

BRITISH LIBRARY CATALOGUING IN PUBLICATION DATA

Heath, Roy A. K. (Roy Aubrey Kelvin), *1926–*
    Shadows round the moon: a Caribbean childhood.
    1. Fiction in English. Guyanese writers, 1945–
    Biographies
    I. Title
    813

ISBN: 0–00–215584–2

Typeset in Linotron Bembo at
The Spartan Press Ltd
Lymington, Hants
Printed and bound in Great Britain by
William Collins Sons & Co. Ltd
Glasgow

For Lloyd, the Storyteller

SHADOWS
ROUND
THE MOON

Contents

BOOK 1

'Knowest though thyself?
So little thou knowest of thyself!'
                    Eskimo poem

CHAPTER 1

The Family

Whilst still a small child I always felt that I belonged to a group larger than the family; or rather that the family was a larger unit than that represented by my mother, my dead father, my two sisters and absent brother. It included my mother's father – her mother was long dead and he had remarried – her half-sisters and half-brothers, her eldest sister's husband, Dolph – the sister had died some years back – and her unmarried sister, Clara, who was to remain a shadowy figure in our lives. This feeling of belonging, the notion of the larger family, was very strong and, as I know now, a source of confidence in case of destitution. Destitution and death were frequent occurrences, like the floods that devastated the coast from time to time in the wake of persistent rains.

The family on my maternal grandfather's side could be traced back to his father, who came from a small island in the northern Caribbean called St Martin. He emigrated to Guyana – then called British Guiana – in the 1850s and set up a wheelwright's business which thrived so well he was able to send his eldest son Aloysius to the United Kingdom to study law. Aloysius later acquired a reputation as the worst solicitor in the country, a notoriety he himself cultivated with some relish. He claimed that his ample office was better suited to entertaining his cronies than to practising law. Any legal affairs conducted there were accidental since he had not bothered to put up a sign. Friends and acquaintances called him the Affidavit Man because most of his income came from sworn affidavits. Swearing an affidavit, a matter of minutes, hardly interrupted the flow of an argument.

If Aloysius was not an enthusiastic lawyer, he was, from all accounts, a dedicated musician, and belonged to that old breed whose insatiable curiosity extended to the construction of the instruments they used. I saw an organ he had built with his own hands in the house of a barrister-priest, one Mr Peters, who lived in a vast mansion, the grounds of which took up the length of Drysdale Street, from Ketley to High Streets.

This same great-uncle who joked about his ineptitude as a solicitor was extremely sensitive to any comments on his organ-playing which were less than flattering. He had been largely self-taught and haunted St George's Cathedral in the evenings, where his practising attracted the attention of passers-by.

Aloysius also wrote a geography textbook, which was still in use when I attended school; and it is an indication of the family's curiously meagre concern with status that I only found out then that the Aloysius de Weever whose name appeared on the title page was none other than my mother's father's brother. In fact my mother fed me on unsavoury details about her male relatives long before I learned about their achievements, no doubt by way of a warning as to what lay in store for me if I did not lead an unblemished life. Leprosy – the affliction of her younger brother – was the wages of misconduct with 'bad women'. I have always believed that these strictures were the source of my interest in prostitution and my fascination with ladies who did not conform to a prevailing morality.

The same lack of concern for orthodoxy distinguished my grandfather. On the eve of Aloysius's departure for the United Kingdom he took his younger brother aside and berated him for his poor school attendance.

'You can't read at the age of twelve. You intend to be a porknocker★ or what?'

In creole families the foretelling of a future as a porknocker

★Gold- or diamond-seeker, usually from the most deprived classes or a shoemaker was often enough to galvanize a boy into action; but Peter Moses, apparently unmoved, went off with his slingshot to meet his fellow 'skulkers' from school. Four years later, on Aloysius's return, Peter Moses had already begun his apprenticeship as a pupil teacher at the age of sixteen. His apparent indifference to Aloysius's lecture had masked a profound feeling of shame at his illiteracy and, determined to show his brother that he was capable of educating himself, he had enlisted the help of an old man to teach him the secret of words. Nevertheless, his late start left him with an abiding inability to spell well. According to my mother, he always relied on his first wife – my mother's mother – to purge his letters of orthographic eccentricities.

Peter Moses became a head teacher and, later, the first principal of the Onderneeming school for delinquent boys in the Essequibo, where, in his opinion, he did his finest work. Being a new, experimental school – it was established at the turn of the century – substantial resources were placed at his disposal. He spent a great deal of money on musical instruments and agricultural tools. Each student had to keep a plot of land for which he was entirely responsible and to learn a musical instrument of his choice. My grandfather himself learned to play a number of instruments in order to teach his charges, and in the process read every musical manual he could lay his hands on. And this unpromising beginning spawned so many good musicians and agriculturalists that employers sought out apprentices from the Onderneeming school. Not only were they impressed by its reputation for excellence, but by the demeanour of the young men and their ability to turn their hands to anything.

The story of my grandfather's work at the Onderneeming has left its mark on my views about education theory. 'Everything begins with the hands,' he was often heard to say. He, a devourer of books, respected the hands. Yet, unlike his brother, who delighted in making things, Peter Moses was a teacher whose performance was often inferior to that of his pupils. His fascination was with ideas and the imparting of ideas to others. He believed teaching had less to do with the recognition of intelligence than with creating a perfect learning situation. 'We all learn a complicated language at an early age,' my mother never tired of saying, echoing her father's words.

These two remarkable brothers were the product of an assiduous migration between the islands and mainland territories. My father himself came to Guyana from Antigua, but had, in fact, been born in St Kitts, which his parents abandoned after it was devastated by a hurricane. Many Guyanese have Barbadian ancestors. Indeed, the lady Peter Moses first married was the daughter of a Barbadian minister of the church, who had been transferred to the diocese of British Guiana.

Nothing pleased my mother more than to contrast her two grandmothers: the paternal, a Guyanese domestic who 'went up in the world' by marrying the wheelwright from St Martin in the late 1850s, and the maternal, a Barbadian lady whose mouth 'hardly moved when she spoke' and who delighted in showing her collection of parasols with bone handles to visitors she entertained at the manse. Her prize possession was a parasol trimmed with white Paraguyan lace which, though prominently displayed in the hat stand, was never used lest it be soiled with dust thrown up by dray carts and carriages.

My mother's favourite of her two grandmothers, the ancient domestic, was invariably relegated to the low end of Peter Moses's family table at meal time and had to be content with chicken wings while her son, his wife and their children regaled themselves with the fleshier portions of the fowl.

I imagine these two grandmothers – my two great-grandmothers – at some celebration that might have brought them together, a wedding, an engagement or christening, one sitting at a discreet distance from the other in deference to the social gap separating them. My mother's maternal grandmother, with her fine manners, must have lamented the juxtaposition with a woman whose acquaintanceship with knives and forks was acquired through serving others! Such a scene characterized the 1860s, a world of women in long dresses and men attired in waistcoats and jackets entirely unsuited to a tropical climate; of anonymous letters informing their recipients of the unsuitability of a prospective bride or groom, written from malice or jealousy by middle-class ladies with maids to do their housework, who would have swooned at the suggestion that they should touch a broom or prepare a cup of chocolate for themselves.

My feeling of belonging – in the family sense – extended no further back than my maternal grandparents, even though my vicarious relationship to my great-grandparents seemed like a tapering shadow to a kinship with a vanished past. And as for the relations on my father's side, apart from my father himself, I had little desire to learn about them. My younger sister, Lynette, did go to Antigua once to look them up and came back with the illuminating piece of news that they were soft-spoken, that at table you had to bend your ear to catch their words.

My father – who died before my second birthday – married my mother, a teacher in St Andrew's school, of which he was the head teacher, after two years of courtship. Her recollections of him, wholesome nourishment to a young boy longing for a heroic father, were persistently romantic: he was a gentleman, she claimed, and would doff his hat if he passed her on the road in the company of another lady, 'as if we were not man and wife'.

'This was the proper way to behave,' she insisted, when I jokingly suggested that he might have been ashamed of her.

In fact, their marriage had followed the classic pattern of the ambitious lady who married a teacher in her late twenties as an alternative to enduring a life of celibacy under the watchful eyes of a host of relations. Her father, Peter Moses de Weever, had sent her and her elder sister to an exclusive convent school where the girls' rigorous preparation for life included the wearing of veils 'so that men would not see your faces'. The boredom of her education with those pale, sad-faced sisters was relieved by the brilliant lessons of a middle-aged nun,

who taught the older girls that well-to-do Roman women
were attracted to Christianity by the idea of a young man put
to death on the cross. Their sympathy with Christ's passion
prompted them to endow the Nazarene sect handsomely, thus
setting an example to women of every class in the Roman
Empire. Religion was passion if it was anything. The girls, of
course, subscribed enthusiastically to the teacher's interpretation which, nourished by the restrictions placed upon everything they did and said – their manner of taking a shower, of
crossing their legs, of addressing their superiors, of maintaining an irreproachable neatness in dress and habits – grew into a
dangerous interest in worldly pursuits. Two girls of seventeen, accused of attending a public dance on Old Year's Night
and allowing themselves to be kissed long and passionately
when midnight struck and all the other couples were 'at it',
were expelled. But the nuns became aware of a new mood of
insubordination among the pupils which, in turn, provoked a
reign of terror under a mother superior who had no doubts
where her duty lay. The middle-aged history teacher was
shipped back across the sea to Ireland and the rigorous Friday
examination of pupils' clothing became a twice-weekly
enquiry into morals and the state of all their accoutrements.
And thus was impressed on the minds of the young de Weever
girls that their youthful life, whether in the home or the world
at large, was a preparation for the restrictions of marriage.

I felt particularly at home in two households (both in
Queenstown): my grandfather's, which I associate with my
early childhood, and that of my Uncle Dolph. My grandfather's house, one lot from the corner of Forshaw and New
Garden Streets, had two verandahs, a luxury which impressed
me greatly at the time, since we lived in a modest cottage in
Jonestown, later to be renamed Agricola, a village on the east
bank of the Demerara River. The sun always shone in
Queenstown, I recall. Perhaps this really was so, for it was
usually during the long August holidays that I stayed in that

bustling house where the women were always preparing to receive visitors or go somewhere, on an excursion up the east coast, to a piano recital in a mansion on New Garden Street, to buy flowers for making a wreath on the very day a death and burial of an acquaintance were announced, or simply for an afternoon walk.

I worshipped my younger aunt, Beryl, my mother's younger half-sister, who, like the elder half-sister, Edna, lived with their parents. Children seem to possess an unerring skill in the judgment of character, arriving at their likes and aversions on the most tenuous evidence, an engaging smile or a moment of neglect. But perhaps we are fond of certain persons because they are fond of us, in a simple barter of affections initiated by some unpremeditated act. Beryl, and all those people whom I recall from those far-off days, were found, much later, to be as I had judged them then; her sister, Edna, moody and distant, her mother – my mother's step-mother – enigmatic, and her brother Hilton, likeable and supremely confident in his manner.

I recall one outing with my aunts Beryl and Edna particularly well, with that vividness memory endows so arbitrarily. I could not have been more than four years old when I accompanied them to a piano recital in a large house in New Garden Street, a few minutes' walk from their own home. I sat next to Beryl, while Edna had her place on the other side. After much fanning by the ladies in that large drawing room and much to-ing and fro-ing by two men until the artist took his place at the grand piano, silence descended upon the assembled listeners with, I thought, unusual suddenness. I imagined the pianist must be angry, because he brought his hands down on to the keyboard with a resounding crash. I looked up at Beryl, but as she did not seem to mind I felt reassured. I must have fallen asleep soon afterwards because I woke up to the sound of loud applause, oblivious to what occurred after that first thunderous chord. The recitalist, sweating profusely as though he had just breasted the tape at the end of a long-distance race, kept bowing to the audience, now to the north, now to the east, until he faced the point opposite the wall against which we sat, displaying a backside of alarming proportions. His posture had the effect of setting off a renewed round of applause. I remember looking about me at the expression on people's faces, being in the dark as to grown-up reactions, for I had not yet emerged from that childhood mist which made a mystery of so much around me. Having retained his threatening attitude for what seemed like a good half-hour, the pianist suddenly shot bolt upright and remained standing by the assaulted instrument, head thrown back and chest thrust forward. I decided there and then that I wanted to be a pianist when I grew up, to earn the applause of a drawing room full of people.

When I asked her later Beryl told me that the pianist had not been angry, but that the composer might have been. She showed me the programme she had kept and tried to explain why it bore the names of so many composers, while I listened attentively, though understanding nothing; for already I was burdened with the curse of the dissembler – I was far more interested in the warmth and closeness of her body, in the scent of some nameless flower emanating from her bodice.

Many of my August holidays were spent with my Uncle Dolph and his children, two boys and two girls, my first cousins. Alwyn and Horace were both older than me, the former by seven years and the latter by one year. Winifred and Enid were older than both boys, and although still in their teens they seemed like women to me. I quickly established the same contrast between the smiling and indulgent in one and the stern in the other. (Is there a tendency towards opposites in siblings?) Enid, who was always singing, undertook to teach me the piano, and corrected my mistakes by giving me the right note with her voice. Winifred, on the other hand, made no secret of her opinion concerning my musical gifts. Once, in a fit of anger, she advised me to take up boot-making. Enid protested that I was not yet seven, to which Winifred replied that the earlier I started the better. Put off by Winifred's disapproval I sat down at the piano only when she was out.

At first the two boys ignored me, no doubt impatient with my country ways and my age. Although only a year older than me Horace seemed to talk and behave with an extraordinary sophistication and, more importantly, had been to the cinema several times! But as I grew older we began to go out for walks together in the evening.

One night he and I set out for the Sea Wall along Vlissingen Road in Kitty. I had my slingshot with me. Why I should take a slingshot when out walking at night seemed senseless to Horace. There were no birds to terrorize at that hour and any target practice against a tree would have been futile in the dimly lit streets. In those days, the 1930s, every passing car attracted our attention; so that the appearance of a three-wheeled vehicle made us gape.

Without thinking of the consequences I pulled the slingshot from my trouser pocket, picked up a pebble lying at the roadside and let fly at the passing motor car. It braked and I fled. According to psychologists a runner travels at a greater speed in the presence of spectators. This may be so, but there are occasions when a runner travels even faster than he does in the presence of onlookers. Had the whole of Georgetown been watching I could not have flown as I did. I found myself so far from the Public Road when I ran out of breath that I was obliged to enquire of a passer-by how to get back to Vlissingen Road. I wandered round the unfamiliar district until I thought the danger was past, and then, trembling from head to foot, returned to my uncle's house, looking round continually to make certain that a three-wheeler was not creeping up behind me. I expected to see the vehicle parked in front of the house and my uncle standing at the front door, arms crossed in an uncharacteristically truculent posture. But Horace had denied that we were together and had refused to give the driver his address. According to Horace the man was taking his fiancée out for a ride and the noise of the pebble against the bodywork of the car had given her such a fright she was having a fit of

hysterics while he ran after me up the village street. Later I saw
the three-wheeler on several occasions and found it difficult to
resist an urge to shout at the driver that I had shot at his car; not
out of bravado, but from an irrational anxiety that he *must*
know it had been me, being a grown man and all.

Whenever I arrived at my uncle's house to spend those
interminable August holidays I would engage in a ritual with
which Winifred and Enid became familiar. I would ask for a
pencil and mark off the date of my arrival and that of my
prospective departure on a calendar hung up on the wall above
the piano. For several weeks after that I would cross out each
new day, counting the number left before I went back home to
Agricola. But by the last week I no longer marked off the days,
for I had begun to enjoy myself, engrossed as I was in the
hundred activities I had devised. I caught lizards, using grass
stalks looped at the end, attempted to adapt a wooden box to
float on the trench between Irving Street and Vlissingen Road
in order to voyage down it past the house where Wu-Li-Wong
the Chinese magician lived. I studied at length the drawings
made by Winifred that were exhibited on a partition separating the bedroom and gallery, did violence to the piano and
pretended to read the *Daily Argosy*, the newspaper to which
my uncle subscribed and which he exchanged at sundown for
the next-door neighbour's *Daily Chronicle*.
    Back home in Agricola I missed Queenstown as keenly as I
had once missed my mother's home. In Agricola there was no
ice cart, with its decrepit donkey and decrepit ice vendor, no
cinema flanked by hoardings, no bollarded pedestrian bridge
linking two streets across a canal, no passing cars, no
magicians next door, nor lovers conversing under a street lamp
– Agricola side streets were unlit – with secret, barely audible
words, nor trips to a bakery on Horace's borrowed bicycle.
Agricola was drab.
    One feature of my holidays in my cousins' house held a
peculiar fascination for me: beyond Vlissingen Road was a

poor village called Newton in which – I learned later – were thatched cottages. Although its proper name was Newtown Kitty, it was laid out long after Kitty proper, on land once cultivated with sugar cane. I have not the slightest idea why my attention was riveted on the entrance to this village whenever I sat on the porch at night. No motor vehicle ever went in or came out of this derelict suburb, and the people who did so bore the inescapable marks of their poverty. Ill-clad, furtive-looking, they gazed right and left before venturing onto Vlissingen Road, and seemed to me to be inhabitants of a world all the more remarkable because it was masked by century-old trees with the odd house peeping out from among them. The most substantial building guarding the entrance to Newtown was the Rialto cinema, in front of which the buses whose route took them round Georgetown halted. In those days no Georgetown cinema showed films from India, today the Rialto's exclusive fare. Then, the hoardings featured for the most part cowboys with rearing horses and pistols held ready. I made several imaginary journeys into Newtown, and whenever I saw a well-dressed stranger penetrating the line of trees and disappearing into this extraordinary world I would go along too, willing my spirit to leave my body and follow the bold traveller.

CHAPTER 2

Agricola

We settled in Agricola two years after my father's death. At first our migration from Georgetown took us to Bagotstown, a few miles farther up the West Bank, Demerara, than Agricola. But my mother bought a house in the latter village with money from my father's life insurance policy and we took up residence in Second Street, a road cutting across the main village street, whose gutters emptied into the main drainage canal to the south of Agricola. In and around the village could be found every type of drainage device, a duck pond behind our house, the two-foot-wide gutters in front of it, the eighteen-foot-wide main drainage canal, the main and sideline irrigation canals in the backlands, designed, with earth dams, to control swamp waters and irrigate sugar-cane fields and vegetable plots; and finally the Demerara River, at the mouth of which lay the city of Georgetown.

The coastal region is below sea level. The sea is kept at bay by a wall, while the extensive swamps to the south are controlled by a network of canals with sluice gates which open when the river is low enough. These kokers have become part of our lore, accommodating tales of mythical figures like Fairmaid, one of the Water People who lure men to their destruction beneath the water. There are unexplained drownings near them and tales of phantom koker men, controllers of canal levels. An outstanding Guyanese artist at one time painted hardly anything else but kokers, reflecting in his canvases our unconscious obsession with these boundaries between canal and canal, between canal and sea. They are comparable to Japanese spirit gates and lich (corpse) gates at the entrances of old English churchyards.

During periodic floods resulting from excessively heavy rains which exposed the inadequate drainage system, shrimps found their way into the street gutters from the main drainage canal. And on these occasions all the village children would go out with baskets to share in the unwonted harvest. I remember well taking up a position under the neighbour's drooping cherry tree and shrieking in disbelief at the sight of my pink catch.

But, large as the village was, my two sisters and I were confined to our yard – a fate suffered by all *decent* children – and only left it to attend the village school on the main street or to visit one of our innumerable 'aunts', none even distantly related, all of whom, except Aunt Ethel, lived on the broad road that led to Georgetown. There was an aunt opposite the perpetually flowing artesian well, another whose house stood next to an ancient silk-cotton tree and a more sinister aunt who lived in a cottage with three calabash trees, each growing beside a paling fence dividing her yard from a neighbour's. According to M., younger of the two servants who looked after the house while my mother was at work, the calabash tree was the haunt of spirits that protected the yard. My aunt would never be troubled by her neighbours, source of much distress 'in this world'. This latter aunt was as unprepossessing as her calabash trees; and my mother could never give us a satisfactory answer when we enquired why we were obliged to visit this calabash relation, whose windows were always closed and whose bad-tempered dog, which had never become accustomed to us, frothed at the mouth whenever we shook the gate. Although it was chained during the day we never dared to enter the yard until our aunt came downstairs, for fear of being mauled if it managed to break loose.

On one of these visits we interrupted a quarrel between our calabash aunt and her husband, a man we never once saw. We heard her shout out to him, 'Go to hell!' to which the answer came in a detached, almost disembodied voice, 'Not now, dear.' My elder sister, Avis, laughed. Now, any other lady of our acquaintance would have reminded her that she was only six years old and not yet entitled to display any emotion which might offend an adult. Our aunt said nothing and behaved as if she had noticed nothing. But when she brought in lemonade and cake on a tray there were only two glasses and two saucers. Sophie, the older servant who always took us out, made my younger sister divide her drink and cake into two and share them with Avis. At the time it did not seem strange to me that I was not made to give up anything, for I had become accustomed to being spoiled. Our aunt ignored Sophie pointedly. In future we only went to her house in the company of my mother.

The other two aunts, the artesian well and the silk-cotton tree, were both affable ladies who dispensed the obligatory lemonade and cake, one with admonitions as to our deport-ment, the other with requests that we join her in singing hymns composed specially for children.

Aunt Ethel, one of my mother's closest friends, lived in a street on the other side of the Public Road. She and her family moved to New Amsterdam about two years after our arrival in Agricola, when I was about five years old.

In that uneventful period, when life was measured out in visits, in the daily routine of school and in wickedly loitering on the way home with village children, visits to these latter aunts were uncommonly agreeable events, during which we could watch the passage of trams on the way to Peter's Hall, up the Public Road and down towards Georgetown. I was told this by Sophie, for I have no definite recollection of these trams, the line having been closed in 1930 before my fourth birthday. I say 'definite' because I recall waiting for a tram, and my request to urinate being brutally denied – by whom? – on the pretext that it was due any minute.

Agricola must have been the most tranquil village in the country, for, apart from my calabash aunt's outburst against her husband, I never once heard a raised voice, except that of a child being flogged for some misdeed. Once, when a neigh-bour living opposite saw me hacking away at a pillar of my mother's house with an axe she called out to her husband to punish me. I was summoned over and flogged with an old cord from a pedal sewing machine, and it never even occurred to me to protest that we were not related or that I would complain to my mother when she came home. I had done wrong – although I had no idea that I was doing wrong at the time – and an interested neighbour was punishing me for it. Morality, like funerals and weddings, was a public affair.

Family servants were an indication, less of an ability to afford them, than of widespread poverty which depressed the cost of labour. My mother was earning very little as the head teacher of a small village school, yet she could afford to keep two servants, both of whom lived in. But then she paid neither of them, for they were the daughters of very poor families. Sophie, the elder, behaved as though we were her children, and was allowed to take us anywhere. M. could not take us out unless Sophie accompanied her.

Once, we children were taken by Sophie to a visiting fair held in the grounds of the primary school I attended. I must have been seven years old and my sister Avis nine. Lynette, my younger sister by a year and a half, received no money to spend at the fair. Both Avis and I were given one cent each and had some difficulty choosing what to spend it on. Since the cent was the smallest coin only one purchase could be made with it, and after a lengthy deliberation I decided to go for a ride on the roundabout of wooden horses. I waited, screwing up my courage to board the monster. M. flirted with two young men while Sophie shepherded my sisters round the fair, leaving me with friends from school, most of whom had come with no money. They were biding an opportunity to leap on an empty horse before the merry-go-round gathered enough speed to make the enterprise dangerous, but when it was already spinning too fast to be dragged off by a vigilant attendant. Finally I parted with the precious coin and waited, my heart pounding at the thought of going round at a speed I might find unendurable. Next to me stood Joel, one of the few boys with money and the most intrepid of my friends. I clambered on to the painted pine-wood horse behind Joel's mount, no doubt in the belief that I would be protected in this position behind a school mate a full year older than myself. I imitated his posture when the roundabout shuddered and began to turn, trunk bent diagonally to my mount and head up. Soon the desperate speed of the horses banished all thought and I was no longer aware of Joel ahead of me until I saw a stream of vomit issuing from his mouth like a banner in the half-darkness. His head turned sideways, he seemed to be clinging urgently to the wooden neck. And at that moment I was overcome by an exhilaration so all-consuming I began to shout and drive my horse forward with an imaginary whip. At the perceptible slowing of the monster I could have wept with disappointment and cursed the limitations of my poverty.

Joel, one of the last to dismount, left the grounds on the side where adults had congregated; but at the sound of the bell he appeared once more in the line of those waiting to pay their money for a ride on a painted horse. As it turned out his pocket was full of copper coins and he soon became the centre of attention for the children. Unable to resist the malevolent horses with gaping mouths he rode with each new round, vomiting without fail, until the attendant, worried by his persistence, forbade him to approach the roundabout again.

Joel became the hero of his class, and from then on his teacher, who had always turned a blind eye to his truancy, showed him an even greater indulgence. The hero, who was said to have some mysterious hold over the taciturn disciplinarian, no longer saw fit to bring him mangoes and other fruit from his yard.

While still in the first two classes – called the Little ABC and the Big ABC – I enjoyed lessons and did not let an opportunity pass to raise my hand when a question was asked. Unaccountably, my enthusiasm vanished in the First Standard. Was it my difficulty in mastering division that caused me to lose interest or could it have been that I felt intimidated by a male teacher, a gentleman whose forbidding appearance made the use of a cane unnecessary? This lack of interest, almost abnormal in its persistence and completeness, was to dog me until I left secondary school. All the remonstrations, the threats, the encouragement from relations and acquaintances could not shake me out of my intellectual lethargy, and I went through school in a haze, from which I viewed the industrious world around me.

When I was eight and in the Second Standard my mother sent me to learn long division from a man who lived on the edge of Agricola. The story ran that he lived alone because his lady friend broke off their engagement and he vowed never to marry anyone else. He had won seven thousand dollars in a sweepstake and, without consulting her, spent most of the money on things he did not need. His first acquisitions were an ancient pistol and an attractive oil lamp that, on account of its insufficient light, had gone out of fashion. For a pile of newspapers dating from the time before slavery was abolished, he paid a small fortune. Determined to spend all he had won, he bought a silver cigarette case together with a set of golf balls made of balata. Then, still unable to exhaust his fortune, he presented his beloved with an expensive diamond ring before confessing how much he had won and how he had spent most of the money. The young woman's mother, who deemed it a blessing that her daughter found out his character before they got married, declared him a wastrel and advised her to break off the engagement. She made her keep the ring as a reminder of a narrow escape.

The arithmetic teacher did not fit the stories told about him. But then what should he have looked like? As a child, to me, grown-ups invariably looked the part they played. Teachers were large and imposing, ministers of the church remote, shopkeepers perspired profusely, while drunkards were gaunt and inarticulate. The arithmetic teacher and my calabash aunt were not true to type.

Although I did not manage to learn long division with him he never once appeared distressed, nor did he bother to dwell on my obtuseness. He would give me a single sum to do, leave me for about an hour and then come to correct it, before launching into an inconsequential tale of his past life. Impressed by his indifference to my lack of aptitude, I wanted to ask him if my mother was paying him. I knew she lost no opportunity to capitalize on her widowhood and wondered whether he had been persuaded to help, with the words that had become so familiar to us children, 'You must help me: I'm a widow.'

If I were capable of being influenced by a stranger at that age I would have been influenced by that man; by his detachment, like a challenge thrown down to a society of people whose struggle to survive gave off an emotional intensity which, even as a child, I felt to be discomfiting.

My poor understanding of long division set the pattern for my future performance at school. And, that pattern established, I began to live up to what teachers expected of me, especially at secondary school. Once, when I knew the answer put to me by a young English teacher – English was the subject that attracted all the unqualified teachers – I gave an incorrect one, impelled by some irresistible urge not to disappoint. Curiously, I had, and preserved, an unfailing conviction in my intelligence, fortified no doubt by my mother's equal certainty that I was endowed with unusual, if as yet obscure, talents. Her belief in me was not shaken by the attentions of a sceptical and malicious friend who, after submitting me to an oral test, pronounced me 'below average'.

Like all villages Agricola possessed a secret side, a hidden reality. Just as the genteel middle class with its afternoon *collations* of tea and cake were a mystery to the working class, so the domestic life of servants, weeders of trenches, cane cutters, revenue runners, messengers, market traders, hucksters, umbrella menders, iron-pot solderers, rum-shop counter hands and all members of the working class was a *fact* so hidden from the view of their exploiters it possessed the power to attract and repel. What was concealed was both fascinating and frightening.

In the case of Agricola there were two distinct working-class groups, the East Indian and creole, each with its own religious and secular practices. At that time I knew little about the East Indians and had to wait until I worked on the West Bank Demerara before I discovered the powerful undertow behind their passive conduct and outward display of prayer flags and temple architecture.

But if Agricola appeared to be tolerably well off, this was because school teachers, village council employees, policemen, dressmakers and others with stable jobs lived on or near the Public Road. The deeper one went into the village the smaller the houses became. One cottage built aback in 1932 cost twenty-five dollars, which could not now buy a pair of shoes for a small child.

From these nether regions, at certain times of the year, came the sound of drums with a forbidden beat, which silenced us children and caused my mother to glance eastwards, where the village ended in subsistence plots and continued into cane fields. Later I discovered that she feared the people of Mocha, the village in which she taught, five miles east of Agricola and two miles from the Public Road.

This dread of backland villages goes back to the time of slavery, when runaway slaves established villages in the interior, where the king's writ did not run. The only evidence of their presence would be the drumbeat that arrived on the wind at the dead of night, when their inhabitants lost their fear of marauding soldiers, who were frequently sent to destroy their crops and attack their villages.

My mother never spoke of these things and my sisters and I, attuned to every movement she made and to the slightest change in inflection of her voice, could only guess at the anxiety that troubled her.

She began to speak to me about serious matters when I was fifteen years old and firmly established as the favourite among her children. Then I realized how much she knew, not only

about her own class, but also about the class from which our
living-in servant girls came. Besides, she gave me, as it were, a
key to a whole cabinet of secrets touching on her courting
days, the misdemeanours of my father – who, while I was a
child, had been held up to me as a paragon among men – her
strict upbringing by a mother of whom she hardly ever spoke
and a father whom she adored and who belonged to that
savage breed of middle-class men who caned their girl
children as assiduously as their sons. From my mother I
learned how, amongst the people living aback, mothers were
responsible for the discipline of their offspring, that fathers ate
alone, being served by their wives who dined with their
children only after their husbands got up from table. In short, I
discovered the gulf between classes, as wide and often as
profound as that between cultures.

But as a child I knew none of these things, from which I was
protected, not only by my mother's reticence, but also by my
inability to interpret impressions and even incidents which,
occurring in isolation, were promptly forgotten.

Two families in Agricola became life-long friends of my
mother, the Harpers and the Carews. Mr Harper was headmaster of a school on the Public Road. It was common
knowledge among children of my primary school that in
Mr Harper's school slates were still used in Fourth Standard.
Whenever the Harpers' name came up, years afterwards, my
mother always repeated how Mr Harper's wife often saved
our family from going hungry with gifts of vegetables.

Mrs Carew – Aunt Ethel we children called her, using the
same fond epithet employed in addressing Mrs Harper – was
an enterprising lady. She summarized those qualities that
distinguish the finest of our women, who rarely appear in
those silly manuals that purport to single out 'the most
famous' Guyanese. Long after retiring from her post as head
teacher she set up a hostel for young aboriginal Indians in
Georgetown, where they could live at no cost for accommodation.

Teacher family stuck to teacher family. Although in none of

my mother's conversations with Mrs Harper do I recall any discussion about teaching, it is unlikely that the families were brought together by anything other than a shared profession.

My views of my mother's relations with people were conditioned by these early experiences; and later, in the face of evidence that belied this easy, affectionate intercourse, I stubbornly clung to the vision of a saintly mother occasionally misunderstood by a malevolent person – almost invariably another woman. Nevertheless, her distaste for Mocha village provided a clue to a distaste many people shared for her, I discovered in years to come. Generally regarded as a snob, her prejudices caused dismay among her acquaintances and neighbours. A cousin related to me only recently that whenever my mother visited hers – her mother was my mother's first cousin and daughter of Aloysius de Weever – she invariably left her in tears. I can only guess at their conversation. Yet that self-same first cousin of my mother's never let a Christmas go by without sending her son to Agricola with a basket full of toys for my sisters and myself. It was precisely this feeling of solidarity my mother managed to inspire in some that I cannot reconcile with the judgment of her by many others.

A few of the East Indians living in Agricola and the adjoining villages were in business, shopkeeping in the main. If their wealth gave the impression of a prosperous Indian community, the reality was entirely different, for the overwhelming majority of them worked in the sugar industry as seasonal labourers. Creoles avoided cane-field work as degrading, not only because it paid derisory wages, but also because it reminded them of slavery, abolished a hundred years before. (Anything connected with slavery was despised and avoided, even the breadfruit, a highly nutritious food.) East Indians, on the other hand, starting with the disadvantage of speaking poor English or none at all, took whatever work they could find. However, a powerful parental authority which allowed them to marshal the assistance of their children gave them an enormous competitive advantage over creoles in business. No comparison between the creole and East Indian communities provided more eloquent evidence of this than two nearby shops owned by a representative of each. The East Indian shop, a thriving, well-patronized establishment, was served by two or three members of the same family, while the creole shop, attended to by a single person, appeared to display an unwritten sign, 'You come in or stay out, it's all the same to me.' The creole owner's independence cost him dearly.

I am certain that the history of the two communities before they came to Guyana had something to do with their relative attitudes to buying and selling. The subsistence peasant economies of West Africa in the eighteenth and nineteenth centuries did not, as a general rule, push its inhabitants to the brink of survival. Famines were almost unknown in Nigeria, Ghana (then the Gold Coast) and Western Congo (now a part of Zaire), where so many slaves originated. So when creoles earned money they did not see it as an opportunity to create greater wealth by investment.

East Indians' appreciation of the potential value of money is enshrined in creole stories. Even as a child I heard that there was no point in giving money to an East Indian beggar, because he or she was certain to have a horde of silver coins stored away in an iron box, an exhortation that seemed to be supported by the excessive publicity given to the death of an old East Indian beggar who had left an estate worth hundreds of dollars.

Another perceived difference between the two communities was their relative attitude to professional work. Popular creole prejudice has it that the creole is gifted, while the East Indian will succeed through application. Two barristers are cited as the finest ever known to practise at the Criminal Bar in Guyana, one a creole, the other an East Indian. The creole, defending an East Indian man accused of having murdered his wife, was faced with an apparently impossible task. The prosecution case rested mainly on a confession alleged to have been made to the police by the accused, who had said, 'Me kill am!' (I killed her!) The defending barrister, in his closing speech, pointed out that there were no witnesses to the deed, that the accused himself had raised the alarm, and that only a week before he had bought the dead woman an expensive necklace. He went on to make a sensational claim: the principal piece of evidence was actually in the accused's favour. Although the words were accurately conveyed by the police they had been spoken in a different tone of voice. His client had not said 'Me kill am!' but 'Me kill am?' The words amounted to an expression of outrage. The accused was acquitted.

The equally famous East Indian barrister was a model of hard work. If, for instance, a case demanded a knowledge of ballistics, he left no stone unturned to acquire that knowledge. Having done so he would go to great lengths to set up experiments in pursuit of evidence to support his interpretation of the facts.

Such testimonies of character differences are of little value, since they tend to be chosen with the intention of proving something a community sees as flattering to itself. Yet once the desired prejudice takes root it becomes a conviction, to be passed on from generation to generation.

In those days Mohammedans of Agricola and the neighbouring villages celebrated the festival of Hussein and Hassan by carrying the tajah, a tall, glittering structure, along the Public Road to a destination unknown to us children. People from the East Indian as well as the creole community co-operated in its construction and followed it to a secret place where it was reputed to be destroyed by fire. The festival was banned in the late thirties, just as the creole masks worn at Christmas had been. The colonial regime availed itself of the flimsiest of excuses to thwart any powerful cultural expression. At the time of slavery no excuse was needed: drum-playing was suppressed in the earliest days simply because it served to reinforce solidarity between disparate groups (Fanti, Ashanti, Congo and others).

The Muslims, the most enigmatic Guyanese community apart from the aboriginal Indians, did not tolerate any attempt at conversion to Christianity. While missionaries have had much success with the Hindu population, who make up about sixty-five per cent of all East Indians, the Muslims assigned the evangelists to hell with such firmness that the latter learned to avoid the Muslim heathen and concentrated their attentions on the more amenable creoles and Hindus. To this day, while the Hindu and creole populations have moved closer together, sharing, for instance, the same interest in sport, the Muslims have never been deflected from their single-minded pursuit of an identity free of all outside influences. Recognizably Guyanese by their language and accent and by their preoccupation with Guyana as the country in which their consciousness has been formed and fostered, they compromise their principles only to the extent that they believe such compromise essential to their survival.

The Muslims living in Agricola showed themselves in any numbers only on the occasion of the festival of Hussein and Hassan and at Ramadan. And even on those occasions only the men appeared, in striking contrast to the Hindus, whose women went out to work in the rice and cane fields, often scantily dressed. Nonetheless creoles continued to refer to Muslims and Hindus indifferently as Indians.

Everything before Agricola belongs to the realm of impressions, half-remembered people and objects, memories like photographs taken in ill-lit rooms where shadows challenge the recognition of familiar things. But from the time of Agricola every recollection is well defined: an umbrella mender – a skeletal giant bearing the skeletal remains of his stock-in-trade – a peripatetic fishmonger crying his wares of banga-mary, twin children being doused with a calabash of water by a parent who would not allow them to run about and get dirty before they were clean, a hovering chicken-hawk spreading terror among hens in the yard, the man who came

back from abroad every three years to die, the sky, discovered
at six or seven, adding to a horde of fantasies, M. sprawled
naked on my mother's great bed when only we children were
at home. Evidently the years between five and eight ushered in
the age of discovery, the beginning of life as revealed by
memory.

It is surprising that memory, like a camera, is capable of
using film of diverse sensitivities and that it provides a certain
period of childhood with its most impressionable images. It is
equally surprising that my mother, whose return home I
awaited every afternoon at the window or on the front
staircase, does not appear in any of the most vividly recollec-
ted incidents of that time.

Once, on leaving school at the end of the afternoon session,
my attention was drawn to a knot of people by the pond, only
a few yards away. As curious as the other children ahead of
me, I went and joined the group. In the middle of a circle of
onlookers lay, curled like a wound-up spring, a large
comoodie* about fifteen feet long. Some older children kept
pushing one another towards the apparently sleeping snake,
while others did not wait to be pushed, but jumped over it,
accompanying their leap with a whoop for the benefit of the
girls.

The circle round the snake became smaller and smaller and
I, at six one of the youngest present, now had a good view,
needing only to bend down to touch the reptile's diamond-
shaped head. Suddenly I felt myself dragged backwards and
before I knew what was happening I was slapped repeatedly in
the face. Sophie had arrived late to fetch me from school, and
imagining what would have befallen her if I had been hurt, lost
her temper. I only did what the others were doing, I protested,
and received a stinging blow from the exasperated Sophie
who, on stopping to explain to a neighbour why she had lost
her temper, confessed that she was 'in a state' because I might

*anaconda

have been attacked by the snake. The lady told her that a number of pigs had disappeared over the last year and that a stranger who had settled in the village had come under police surveillance. It was evident that the comoodie had devoured them; perhaps they would leave the good-looking young man in peace now.

Sophie ordered me to tell my mother nothing about the incident. If I did not obey she would leave me at home when she took Avis and Lynette to the Botanic Gardens in town.

CHAPTER 3

A Ball of Fire

My mother's father and uncle – the two de Weevers – had a brother about whom no one ever spoke. (I found out later that every family worth its salt had a brother or sister, the mention of whose name was forbidden in the house.) I first heard of him the afternoon we were told that he had died in Panama and that we were going to Georgetown to share a house with his wife, a Panamanian lady who had come to settle in the land of her husband's birth for sentimental reasons. This fateful move to the corner of Camp and Regent Streets, the centre of Georgetown, was attended with all the excitement small children often invest in an experience trying for adults. Not only were we moving house, we were going to town, where the Botanic Gardens were, and the wall dividing the sea from the land, and where children did not tremble at the sight of a policeman. My sisters and I had not forgotten that we were born in Georgetown. It had simply been relegated to a deeper layer of memory with that swiftness peculiar to childhood. Avis was then ten years old, I eight and Lynette six and a half. Neither Avis nor I saw Lynette as a person, but rather an appendage of my mother's, just as my eldest brother Sonny did not see me as a person at that time, only granting me official recognition when I reached the age of thirteen and could stand up to his leg breaks. However, he did not take part in the move as he was living at my grandfather's.

The tramway system – owned by an American company, as many tramways in South America were – had closed, and our trip to Georgetown, which would normally have been made by that most convenient means of transport, was made by carriage. To the accompaniment of the sound of a trotting horse we took in all the familiar landmarks, the Paynes' sprawling house at McDoom, the calabash aunt's cottage, the century-old silk-cotton tree marking the boundary between McDoom and Houston, the Hindu temple, the artesian well with its perpetually flowing water, until we came to Ruimveldt, the large sugar estate at the approaches to Georgetown. Here we fell silent, suitably awestruck by the realization that we were entering a town with ships in port and along whose asphalted highways hundreds of motor cars passed and where all roads were public roads.

Sophie was not with us, having been sent on to await our furniture and to have things ready when we arrived at Aunt Anna's. Curiously, I cannot recall seeing her on our arrival. In fact, there is no recollection of that arrival or any following the several moves the family was to make before I was twelve years old. Most of the departures I remember with greater or lesser intensity, but the arrivals are shrouded in mystery.

Aunt Anna was a rotund lady in her middle forties, 'a ball of fire', as she described herself, 'a virago', as my mother saw her, and a 'succulent orange', as her dead husband called her on a photograph she kept by her bedside table. Avis and I liked her because she gave us money to pluck out her grey hairs while she pretended to be asleep. We earned one cent for every offending hair, but I usually made twice as much as Avis because I broke the grey hairs in two. Aunt Anna, fleshy, with jet-black hair – I imagined all Panamanian ladies to be exactly like her – was excessively vain. She spent hours making up in front of her dressing table, applying layer upon layer of different powders before daubing pink rouge on the well-laid foundation. And finally, when her facial preparations were complete and her last garment was in place, she would examine herself in the mirror with such narcissistic devotion I came to the conclusion that it was infinitely preferable to be male than female.

Aunt Anna had a keen business sense. Whilst creole middle-class women dreamt of personal independence through teaching, midwifery or dressmaking, Aunt Anna was full of money-making ideas which included none of these things. She had no intention of succeeding by the sweat of her brow. She settled on the production of pomade, a sweet-scented, green concoction with the appearance of tinted petroleum jelly and the consistency of candle grease. Her first outlet, the drugstore over which we lived, was run by two lanky dispensers – identical in appearance and sparing with words – who had fallen under Aunt Anna's spell. 'Anna's pomade' was an instant success and soon Aunt Anna took on two boy employees who encumbered the kitchen on Saturdays and Sundays to the annoyance of Sophie, accustomed to being mistress in her domain.

I have no idea what originally caused enmity between my mother and our Panamanian aunt. Knowing my mother, a connection with business, however tenuous, was enough to rob anyone of the credentials to respectability. But for a woman to engage in business in the house my mother occupied must have been a trial of the utmost severity. Whatever might have been said or done there began for my mother a period of unrelenting persecution. Whenever she had a visitor Aunt Anna would unscrew all the electric bulbs in the house, so that conversation had to take place in the dark. She would then walk up and down the area where my mother and the guest were, muttering to herself until, evidently angry at being ignored, she would sit down noisily at a window. At other times Aunt Anna would lock the front door at the foot of the covered staircase, so that my mother, on arriving home from work, would have to come up by the back stairs.

Aunt Anna, surprised that Avis and I refused to continue with our Saturday job of pulling out her grey hairs, raised the price from one to two cents. But our mother's suffering, all too plain to us, obliged us to persist in our refusal, and I used to go to bed with thoughts of my aunt's imminent death.

We had moved from Agricola mainly on account of our frequent debilitating bouts of malaria. At best an attack left us huddled beneath the sheet and blanket, our teeth chattering from the feeling of being held in an icy embrace. At worst we fell prey to hallucinations in which monsters became our companions of the night. 'We're moving to town,' my mother had said. 'There's no stagnant water where Aunt Anna lives.' We had exchanged the attentions of the anopheles mosquito for the terrors of an embittered woman who had taken to lying in wait for my mother at dusk.

Nevertheless, there were weekends and holidays, times of respite, when Aunt Anna fell into a brooding, watchful silence, seemingly neutralized. It was not possible to waylay someone who did not go out.

Saturday nights in town resembled the annual tajah celebrations in Agricola. The crowds in the streets below were even larger. Young men and women walked the length of Camp and Regent Streets, along which nut-sellers and vendors of black pudding and souse sat on the pavement, having taken up prime positions as early as mid-afternoon. This picture of ritual strutting can convey nothing of the atmosphere, the noisy crowds, occasional fights, the rowdy women, as likely to challenge a man to a stand-up contest which might end in bloodshed as to taunt a young policeman who had not yet become accustomed to a tight-fitting uniform. My sisters and I watched the goings-on from the heights of our above-the-shop house, the chance encounters, the notorious ruffians who were known to everyone, like Bruck-Foot Johnny and Tiny Balls, men reputed to fear no one.

On the corner diagonally opposite our house stood a rum shop with swing doors, the kind of establishment that would become familiar to me in the Western films I saw in later years. Nothing pleased us more than to see a drunkard emerge from this den, momentarily stopping to stare up the road or trying vainly to light a cigarette with a match which missed the mark by a foot or more. One man in particular never failed to perform this ritual in front of the swing doors. One evening, after several fruitless attempts at lighting up, someone came out of the rum shop, accidentally striking the man's arm with the flying door. Recovering from the mishap the drunkard looked down and saw that his cigarette was already lit. The impact of the door had impelled his hand straight towards the unlit cigarette.

The wasted wrecks who frequented Georgetown rum shops contributed to my impression of the capital as being special, a repository of the eccentric and exciting, where policemen patrolled the streets even after townspeople had gone to bed. One night, when my mother and I were brought home late by my grandfather, she opened the front door while a few feet away a constable was trying the padlocked shutters of the drugstore over which we lived. Apart from the constable the only living creature about was a stray dog which got up and moved away as we approached. The street lamps, the shuttered shops, the retreating dog, combined to leave an indelible picture on my mind.

Below the house, under the back stairs, was a tiny barber-shop in which a single barber worked, while adjoining the house on the Regent Street side lived the Brutons, a family with numerous children, the youngest of whom, Doreen, was my age. She and I attended the same secondary school much later. I often went to their house, climbing through a window and walking along the wing-like structure that served as an awning over the pavement below. I must have complained of being hungry one afternoon, and received a makeshift meal of rice and fish; and for some strange reason the sensation of having a meal outside my home gave me the peculiar pleasure of a forbidden indulgence. I believe that the act of consuming that meal persuaded me that I had found another family to whom I could turn should anything befall my mother. The promptness of the offering and the agree-able atmosphere in that unpretentious household, only a window away, sum up the Guyana of the middle thirties, a country bled white of its resources by an imperial power, yet far from demoralized.

Whenever Mr Bruton met me he took to cracking my knuckles; even after I became a young man and he, visibly older, had begun walking with a slight stoop.

In the yard next to ours on the Regent Street side lived the Mings, a half-Chinese family. Their father manufactured and sold confectionery, and in our back yard there was a permanent saccharine smell of boiled sweets. His children were all weightlifters, even the girls. At weekends their friends congregated around the lifting board, a low platform about six feet square, on which the weights occasionally fell with a thud that brought my sisters and me out onto the back porch, until we became accustomed to the sound. We liked watching the muscular teenage girls saunter up to the platform with the same assurance as the boys, and hoist the weights above their heads.

There were no houses on the Camp Street side, as I recall, only business premises without a superstructure for living accommodation.

My sister Avis and I were obliged to change schools as a result of the move. We were both sent to St Barnabas's on Upper Regent Street, between Orange Walk and Cummings Street. As is the case throughout the country the church stood next to the school, in a juxtaposition that appears natural to all Guyanese. In Britain, after the introduction of free primary school education, many working-class parents refused to send their children to the free schools, on the grounds that religious instruction featured too prominently in the curriculum. They continued to patronize the private schools, preferring to pay a few pence every week to some unqualified householder for instructing their offspring in the rudiments of reading, writing and ciphering. It was only after an Act of Parliament confined the power of granting valid school leaving certificates to the free schools that 'uncooperative' parents gave in. But in

Guyana, where church and school were like teeth and gums, the authorities saw no need for the refinement of duplicity.

At that time St Barnabas's church was in a dilapidated condition. Fifty-four years later it was still in a dilapidated condition, like an old woman who, having achieved a respectable age, is then rewarded with the secret of immortality. The brightest boy in the second standard confided in me that the priest of St Barnabas's had ordered a coffin made for himself years before, which lay in the church loft. Three of us were so intrigued by the information that we came back to school early one lunch time and went up the rickety stairs leading to the loft. One boy whispered urgently, 'Look it!' And we all gazed in terror at something which had not the slightest resemblance to a coffin, but we dared not climb up to the loft again after that, for fear that we might not escape the next time from what we saw the first.

Our capacity for dread was borne out in another incident. On the façade of a grocer's shop in Cummings Street, just round the corner from the school, an embossed cross was nailed above the entrance. Having learned that it was an obeah cross my best friend and I stood back from the shop at a safe distance, wondering how the customers who came and went without a glance at the potent symbol dared brush past it. Adults evidently possessed some power to weaken the effect of the dangerous metal cross. We had seen no child enter or leave and drew the necessary conclusion. Time and again during childhood I had occasion to yield to the fascination of an object.

If Agricola was full of secrets, Georgetown turned itself inside out for all to see. Even quarrels were often public, especially those between neighbours.

'You got a face lak a hawse!'

'It tek a hawse fo' know a hawse!'

'Me husban' don' got to beg the Chinese man fo' credit. Ah say *beg*! You in' shame?'

'Wha' I goin' shame fo'? I in' t'ief from nobody. No' like some people I could name.'

'You call me Alfred a t'ief?'

'Who the cap fit mus' draw the string.'

'Look story! She brother is a t'ief. She sister is a t'ief. She fader does t'ief from Sproston's Wharf. Ah in' surprise you t'ink me Alfred does t'ief, 'cause everybody round you got they han' in somebody else' pocket.'

Almost all the quarrels were between women; ritual stand-up affairs in which each participant allowed the other to have her say. Only occasionally did they end in fights and any attempt to involve their menfolk rarely succeeded. Serving some secret purpose that was evident to no one, such quarrels provided amusement for neighbours and passers-by, whose interest was never resented by the protagonists. The history of drama in Guyana cannot ignore the public quarrel, its rules, props, subject matter, length and setting, and above all its spontaneity. Although the experts in the craft were women I once heard a public quarrel between a woman and a man, an anaemic affair that suffered from the man's inability to stimulate his opponent to the improvised abuse audiences of the otherwise classic encounters found so compelling.

In a domestic quarrel no one expected that the occasion would be enjoyed by third parties, but there were times when circumstances dictated otherwise. I recall how, one night, a youth of about twenty living a few houses down the road came home a few minutes late. His grandmother remained on the stairs waiting to bar his way, stating that it was ten minutes past ten, when he should have returned by ten. He would not sleep in the house that night. While the youth protested that he had been held back his mother came to the window to find out the cause of the altercation; but, discovering her son's plight, she burst out laughing and did nothing to make things easier for him. This acknowledgment of the grandmother's status gave to the scene an extra comic dimension. The youth's embarrassment grew as he realized how many people were enjoying the scene from their windows. He pleaded with his grandmother to let him get by, but she remained unmoved, so that in the end he had to go away.

Many quarrels were the prelude to a flogging, the victim usually being a wife or mistress or a child. A few men flogged their women regularly, imbued with a kind of religious fervour. It was the women who usually beat their children, with the belt in town, and often a rod from a gooseberry tree in the country. Sometimes, if the child slipped away, the mother would wait patiently for its return, when she would continue where she left off until her offspring had received the intended ration. The most docile, inoffensive women were frequently practised floggers.

An acquaintance described to me how his father would set about beating him after an obligatory introductory lecture: 'Son, this is going to hurt me more than it hurts you.' With these words the leather would descend on his backside. And, as the son related, he could never understand how such blows, which shook him to the bone, could be less painful than his father's distaste for punishing him.

I could view tales like that with detachment because, far from knowing how it was to be flogged by a parent, I had got into the habit of practising a kind of blackmail on my over-indulgent mother. Once I realized that she became anxious if I left home without breakfast (called *tea* in those days) I threatened to do so if she hinted at the slightest punishment for misbehaviour or failure to work at school.

Georgetown meant not only excitement, but a freedom I had never enjoyed until then. It is not easy to discover the reasons for this. Georgetown children were, of course, far more independent than those in Agricola; and I probably followed their example, a process facilitated by the absence of a male disciplinarian in the home. On the face of it the same rules applied: you did not play on Sundays, you obeyed your parents, teachers and elders; you went to school unless you were desperately ill. In Agricola I could recall only one anarchic character: the boy who rode the wooden horses endlessly. Georgetown bred many such people, suggesting that there is a deep need for extravagant behaviour in a city. Yet, as I learned years later, as a grown man, it is precisely in the cities of Europe and the United States that a highly sanitized behaviour is cultivated; and this, together with the lack of spatial tolerance – which allows you, for instance, to remain in a cake shop for hours without making a single purchase – was to have a deadening effect on many Guyanese destined to settle in one of these countries.

The heady atmosphere of the capital city influenced me to such an extent that I dared to do what I would not have dreamt of doing in Agricola. I learned to ride on my mother's old bicycle, making my first attempts in the concrete yard behind the pharmacy and finally graduating to Regent Street and its tributaries, with their hectic traffic, apparently incapable of maintaining its perpetual motion without a frenetic honking of horns and clanging of cycle bells. By the time my mother discovered the abuse of what was, in fact, her most prized possession, I already knew to ride well. She forbade me to touch the cycle, and for weeks afterwards kept telling visitors that she could not understand how I had learned to ride in secret. Only a miracle had saved me from the buses that raced along the highway in competition for passengers. And suppose one of the innumerable louts hanging around at street corners and in shop fronts had taken the bike from me and smashed it beyond repair! She would not have been able to go to work and we would all have starved. I had to endure innumerable lectures from friends and acquaintances of the family on my irresponsible conduct and was often made to promise that I would not put our livelihood in jeopardy again. After that I resolved not to touch the cycle, not because I understood that I had brought the family to the brink of that abyss so commonly evoked in conversation, *destitution*, but because of the hornets' nest I had raised. Whenever I recalled these lectures I used to imagine myself standing in the midst of people pointing at me with alarmed expressions and talking incessantly, all repeating variants of the same exclamation: 'You brought your family to the brink of destitution! You wicked, wicked boy!' It was enough to put me off cycles for the rest of my life.

Destitution, the nightmare of middle-class expectations, sometimes came with an incapacitating accident or a grave illness, or most often with redundancy. A family displaying all the trappings of *respectability*, a two-storey house, servants and a well-stocked table, might suddenly find itself without a breadwinner. In those days, when a home with six children was a commonplace, such an occurrence could be disastrous. Thus people avoided the word *destitution* or spoke of it only in whispers, like those stories children recounted under their breath of monsters which roamed the bush.

In one case, when the father of a family lost his job, having been retired prematurely from the civil service, their servants were dismissed and their four secondary school children had to be withdrawn from classes. The mother, who had studied music as a girl, began to give piano lessons, and the little she earned was enough to buy food for the family. The father took to doing book-keeping for various rum shops, earning even less than his wife. They had come down in the world, so much so that they gave up the rounds of Sunday visiting and carriage rides to the Botanic Gardens where crowds gathered for the militia band concerts. The father continued to frequent the homes of friends, but could no longer afford to entertain. Everyone admired him for his fortitude and cited him as an example of dignity. Late one night two fishermen about to take out their boat found him dead on the foreshore, wearing his serge suit and patent-leather shoes, dressed, as it were, for an important function.

Even at the age of eight I was astonished that a man surrounded by evidence of the most abject poverty, families without the wherewithal to light their homes at night, people who consumed nothing but rice as their main meal, East Indian beggars occupying stretches of pavements at night; that a man who owned his house and a piano and possessed skills that allowed him in tandem with his wife to eke out a living, should take his own life.

Experience of middle-class family life taught me that coming down in the world was a kind of death. There was nothing sadder than the remnants of affluence in homes marred by such tragedies. If the piano had to be sold and the single shirt laundered with care, photographs of the well-clad family remained displayed on walls as mementoes of better times, and the scent of vanilla still came from a kitchen where offal was prepared once a week instead of the veal and mutton of a once-daily fare.

This kind of story, told over and over, should have instilled in me the need to work hard at school. I must have been cursed with a special kind of insensibility, because the 'bone idle' which appeared consistently on my annual reports was to adorn them to the end of my school days. Never a good pupil, I simply did not possess the ambition to be one and did just enough to pass my secondary school examinations – those that counted. I would do just enough to stave off destitution.

My mother had brought us one step nearer to destitution in the move to Georgetown from Agricola, where we had owned a house with a back yard full of fruit trees, one of which was always in season. But I cannot help feeling that she had missed Georgetown and had seized the opportunity to come back to our collective birthplace where her first cousin and closest friend Mrs Dolphin lived. There, too, was the home of her father, P. M. de Weever, whom she idolized and with whom she never lost a chance of staying during the school holidays. She did not care for her stepmother, but she went all the same with Lynette on her arm, while Avis and I had to be content with Sophie's company, and latterly with that of our florid Aunt Anna. She went off to that house in Queenstown with its two verandahs and constant comings and goings, while we pined after her and I, in spite of my resolution to the contrary, took my revenge by riding her bicycle, put away for the time, its wheels smeared with petroleum jelly against the humidity of August days.

Childhood longings leave an unmistakable residue, like the volcanic ash of ancient eruptions. I idolized my mother, just as she did my grandfather; but I did not forgive her these desertions until late in adult life.

CHAPTER 4

The House in Forshaw Street

Forshaw Street runs east-west on the grid pattern that is Georgetown. The house in which my grandfather lived stood next to a cottage at the corner of Forshaw and New Garden Streets. Queenstown is an elegant, tranquil part of Georgetown. Like Kingston in the northwest part of the city, it was laid out as a residential quarter, hence the absence of shops. Many mansions in Queenstown had flourishing gardens, always in the front yard; and some of them displayed small signboards nailed to the white-painted paling fence advertising flowers for sale. More often the flowers were sold to be made up into wreaths for a death. It seemed strange to me that Hindus used wreaths at weddings while creoles filled their hearses with them.

Flowers, green-painted roofs and an air of abiding peace summed up Queenstown. The very names of the streets were evocative: New Garden, Almond, Peter Rose, Laluni, Crown, Oronoque. Everything I saw there, then and in later years, seemed remarkable: the municipal employee with a can on his back, from which he sprayed the concrete gutters running down the middle of alleyways with a film of oil; a postbox overflowing with letters on Christmas Eve; and above all the absence of stray dogs, those symbols of decay which haunt the back doors of restaurants, some dragging pendulous teats along the ground.

Now that we were living less than two miles away from my grandfather's house I went there more often than the once a year visit at Christmas time. I always looked forward to meeting my elder brother Sonny, who lived with my grandparents between the ages of seven and fourteen, apparently because my mother was too poor to raise four children. I remember how he and Hilton, youngest of my mother's half-siblings and about the same age, were inseparable and used to stand at the gate playing a game of 'spotting the bus'. The one who shouted, 'That's mine!' first when a bus came into view earned a point. I saw this game as the exclusive property of 'big boys' and looked forward to the day when I could play it. Now, at the age of thirteen, they had taken to mechanical games. In their bedroom they used to project images onto a makeshift screen (the bed sheet) through a hole made in the side of a shoebox. I was as impressed by this as I had been by the spot-the-bus game. Anything the two older boys did could only be exciting, to my impressionable mind.

But I saw little of them, for they went off on their jaunts without taking me along. Sonny, especially, saw me as intensely irritating, an embarrassment even, and shrugged off my attempts to take part in their activities. The five-year difference was a gulf I would have liked to bridge; but it was hopelessly large and I could only look on as they paraded their maturity before my astonished admiration.

There is little I can say about my step-grandmother. I recall her barely as a presence and wonder whether I did not participate in my mother's disapproval of her. As for Aunt Edna, it is interesting that the only clear memory of her is connected with the piano recital at someone else's home. She neglected me and perhaps that was reason enough to forget her.

My grandfather always seemed to be attended by people, music pupils or friends or other visitors. His reputation rested on his work as teacher, songwriter, producer of plays and music teacher. Some of the people who came to see him were unusual, to say the least; and one of them, the Much Dreaming Woman, always seemed to be telling jokes or relating her dreams, strange night experiences full of mythological figures: 'He was half man and half bird and I did tell him to go away and he just stood there and I fling a snake round my waist at him . . .' 'And the old man tell me everything would be all right. Look! And he put the sack he had on his back down on the ground and opened it. And when I looked inside there was a dead child . . .' She was calm, well balanced and laughed a lot. A few minutes after she arrived the circle of women round her would be in fits of laughter and I got the impression that everyone looked forward to her visits. In those days few homes boasted a telephone and no one announced a visit. The Much Dreaming Woman dropped in any day, but always in the evening. I never once saw her in broad daylight. She evidently belonged to that ilk my mother described as Night People, who made excuses when invited to call during the day, to attend a wedding or christening or on some special occasion. Another invariable detail connected with her visits was the fact that Beryl would always make her a cup of steaming chocolate, to which she must have been addicted, for she never failed to hold the cup lovingly, as alcoholics would fondle a schnapps glass full of rum.

I learned later that the Much Dreaming Woman did not have a good reputation and was in fact detested by a few women, who regarded her as a sponger with a propensity for haunting places where free food was available, functions at which no one checked the guests' invitations. I believe, too, that her good humour worried those whose acquaintance she made. How could a poor woman with no evident means of support be so optimistic? She never complained, as though she had made a resolution to banish any thought of distress. Her laughter possessed the quality of bright moonlight, eerie and disturbing, and her dreams were full of snakes and ants, symbols of an underground world.

I saw the Much Dreaming Woman occasionally when I became a young man, and was surprised that, unlike others of her generation, she had hardly aged. She always waved to me, without that condescending restraint of middle-aged people towards the young. I often wondered why, so welcome in the de Weever home, she was disliked elsewhere. Perhaps as hosts of a hospitable house my grandfather's family accepted her as she was. Perhaps there existed some secret attachment between them and the Much Dreaming Woman. Guyanese society was full of secrets and secret places, back yards where mistresses were kept, enclosed staircases above which flourished brothels in which voices were never raised, illegitimate births that haunted people for a lifetime, thefts that established a dynasty of respectable ownership, twins of startlingly contrasting colours, turrets in the roofs of mansions constructed as look-outs for ships from across the ocean, but used as prisons for stricken relations.

According to biologists the giant insect of fantasy tales would, in reality, disintegrate, since insects have no spines. The Much Dreaming Woman, like a giant insect that did not disintegrate, defied the rules and was seen as a threat to some of her acquaintances. But if there was some unexplained affinity between herself and my aunts it is worth mentioning that, like the servants, she never used the front door, arbitrarily relegating herself to an inferior status.

If the Much Dreaming Woman was the most unusual person to frequent the house in Forshaw Street, there were many other visitors, striking in appearance and behaviour to a boy of eight. One man, who would do small repairs about the house, I watched with particular interest when he dismantled the green Venetian blinds. Seeing the thin, pliable wooden laths laid on the floor of the drawing room, I felt certain that they could never be put together again. I used to hang about while he worked without taking any interest in what went on in the house. But once he had aligned the buff-coloured cords on the floor he had no difficulty in running them through the holes in the laths and reconstituting a whole out of its several parts.

The Venetian blind mender, as taciturn as the Much Dreaming Woman was voluble, was not discourteous. He simply lacked courtesy in his make-up, and exemplified the Guyanese adage that 'too much *please* and *thank you* make

eye-pass★.' Many working-class males saw courtesy as a
weakness in a man; it was either a sign of effeminacy or of
hypocrisy.

Hangers-on were of great importance to certain households, but in others they were shadowy figures who came and
went, leaving hardly a trace. I knew an old revenue runner
who actually received a private pension from a man whose
chauffeur he had been while he worked at the Commissary
Office at Pouderoyen. He took the ferry at Vreed-en-Hoop,
where he lived, and came to town specially to receive the
monthly allowance. Not once was he disappointed, he told
me, although his benefactor owed him nothing.

But there were stories of ruthless exploitation of hangers-on
and servants who, at the beck and call of their employers or
benefactors, received little by way of payment for their
services. A society in which the unemployed made up more
than thirty per cent of the working population, where social
services were conspicuously slight, threw up characteristic
relationships of dependency. In such a world flourished
hangers-on, extravagant behaviour, particular freedoms and
exploitations of the most unwholesome kind. Such a world
was looked back upon with the same nostalgia as that evoked
by a period of wealth and expansion. People of my generation
speak of the thirties as the good old days, when public
telephone booths remained intact and grocers dispensed 'a
pinch of salt' free. And they are right, to the extent that the
evidence they put forward stands on its own. They forget,
however, that the misery of material deprivation was rife. If
memory is a conquest of time it also employs a selectivity
which makes nonsense of the claims for the good old days.

Much of what I know about my grandfather, Peter Moses, I
learnt from my mother. At home he was not the creative giant
she had depicted, but rather an unostentatious, kindly man,
and like her, a good listener. Like her, too, he used simple

★lack of respect

language, never caring for display. This most uncreole-like reserve in the use of words he is supposed to have shared with his brother, Aloysius, whom I did not know. (He died when I was about two years old.) Like Aloysius, Peter Moses was blessed with perfect pitch and used to entertain his friends by calling any note they played on the piano, without the benefit of a named first note. He insisted that if this unusual gift could not be taught it could at least be induced. Expectant mothers could bestow this talent upon an unborn child by listening to a great deal of music. Since the foetus developed a sense of hearing at an early stage the child was bound to have a musical bent and had a good chance of acquiring perfect pitch. My great-uncle Aloysius, according to my mother, called it *l'oreille absolue*. His own mother was a passionate singer and he had no doubt that the songs he heard while in the womb explained his life-long love of music.

I believe I learned more in those visits to my grandfather's house during that year than I did in any other period of my life, except in 1943 and 1944 when I worked for the better part of two years in the Pouderoyen Commissary Office. I speak of learning about people's behaviour, acquiring the raw material I could turn to account in the fiction I would one day write. If in Forshaw Street I did my apprenticeship in the ways of the creole world, in Pouderoyen I became initiated into East Indian society.

Forshaw Street draws its romance from the lore about my grandfather, its connection with my brother, aunts and uncles; from its proximity to gardens full of dahlias and roses, the buses intruding into an exclusive quarter, from its visitors and music students. But it was in Forshaw Street that I first fell in love, with a girl who played for hours on end with her dolls under the house next door. She played alone, usually, until joined by her sister who, being the drudge of the family, was more often than not in the kitchen or out on some errand. The drudge, in most cases the eldest daughter, provided evidence of poverty in a creole family. Among East Indians, even the wealthy family frequently had its drudge. The girl who played with her dolls was an East Indian. I only fell in love with her one afternoon when she looked at me, for until then she always seemed to be unaware of my existence. The moment she stared at me as if she had seen me for the first time I was smitten. I must have responded with an appropriate gesture because she raised one of her dolls for me to admire, an ugly, bedraggled, pink confection. I admired it duly and then pointed to another. She lifted in turn each one of the mute menagerie above her head and I did what she expected of me, when in truth I wanted to offer her one of my cigarette star pictures in exchange for a kiss.

Every day after that I came out on the verandah overlooking her yard, when all the women were lying down after the midday meal and everything was deathly still. The ritual inspection of her 'children' would begin and I would shake my head in approval. If she was to love me I must love her dolls, she seemed to be saying. I was prepared to admire her whole family, provided it meant progress towards my intention. One rainy afternoon I came out onto the verandah, and before she could lift up the first of her dolls, I showed her a star picture and gestured that she could have it if she gave me a kiss.

'What?' she asked, uttering the first word that ever passed between us.

'A star picture . . . a k–i–s–s–!'

She stood with her mouth open for a while then, with a sudden about-turn, fled up her back stairs.

I waited for the storm to break, imagining every calamity from a parental intervention or the disappearance of the girl to a visit from the police. All afternoon I waited, angry with myself for having brought disgrace to my grandfather's house. This was not an area with rum shops, where crowds gathered on Saturday nights and young men courted their young women under the awnings at two o'clock in the morning. Nor was it Agricola! I sat alone in a corner of the gallery, not daring to imagine the details and extent of my disgrace.

When I woke up the rain was pounding on the roof and for a while I had no idea where I was. Suddenly recalling what had happened before I fell asleep I got up and opened the door to the verandah on which the rain was pouring down. I went out and looked over the edge, but neither the girl nor her dolls were under the house.

Not until the following afternoon could I be certain that my rash proposition had brought no serious consequences in its train. Looking out cautiously over the verandah I saw the object of my indiscreet advances walking up and down, a stick in her hand, while she harangued her grimy dolls, the way parents did when their children misbehaved.

This affair is irrationally connected in my mind with a torrential downpour and a verandah enveloped in something impenetrable, trance-like outside myself, but yet within me, a kind of perpetual storm that goes away but does not stop, akin to the phases of the moon, tides that ebb and rage in turn, working minutely on my aunts and uncles, on my mother, my dead father, my grandparents and the shadows of dead ancestors, on my brother with his other-worldly smile and on the inconstant flux of memory.

The house in Forshaw Street with two verandahs had changed me in a way that is not clear; for what remains, above all, is its powerful fascination. Even today, whenever I return to Guyana I walk past the lot where it used to be. I know it is no longer there, yet, borrowing the prerogative of dreams, expect to see it materialize. Only the house at the corner of New Garden and Forshaw Streets has survived. A once elegant cottage, it stands abandoned, with a tree piercing its floorboards and surrounded by a yard overgrown with weeds. And for me that house represents an era, childhood, the secrets of old, sepia snapshots, an elegant quarter of white palings and painted gardens.

CHAPTER 5

The Move

When we had been living about ten months at Camp and Regent Streets Aunt Anna's persecution of my mother reached its height. The family spent whole evenings until bedtime in the bedroom, where we read by the light of a kerosene lamp. Any attempt to sit in the drawing room put Aunt Anna in a rage and she would chase us back into the bedroom.

It was the Christmas season. On the way to and from school the tinny sound of a gramophone emerged from a back yard or a shop. The stretch of road from our house over the pharmacy to the school I attended was the most mysterious part of Regent Street, starting with commercial enterprises, cake shops, a cloth store, tailors' shops, barbershops, a shoe-maker's shop, and tailing off into the residential quarter from Cummings Street onwards. At the corner of Cummings and Regent Streets a house over a cake shop bore a plaque with the Latin inscription, *Damus petimusque vicissim* – We give and seek in return. By a mental process that escapes me I associated the plaque with Aunt Anna. Perhaps the fact that she came from abroad and the plaque was in a strange language suggested the coupling. Perhaps I had been told that the language of the inscription was dead and I wished unconsciously for Aunt Anna's death. But the unusual inscription, seemingly unaffected by the weather, aroused such hostile feelings in me I deliberately kept my head low as I went by the house on which it appeared. Although I did not consciously dwell on the subject of Aunt Anna, my mother's terror in her presence and our confinement to one room had affected me deeply.

I had no idea that my grandfather was looking for a place to which we could move. In Agricola, my mother occasionally had long conversations with me and allowed me a certain degree of freedom, like going to church services on my own. But since we came back to Georgetown she had become withdrawn and only spoke in the old way to my grandfather and my godmother when they came visiting. One night when Aunt Anna was raving, threatening to batter down the bedroom door, which my mother had locked, there came a knock out front. My mother unlocked the bedroom door and made for the stairs, followed by Aunt Anna. I leapt after them, determined to restrain her in the event of an attempted attack on my mother. But the scene took such an unusual turn I could only stand and watch from the top of the stairs. I saw my grandfather in the doorway at the foot of the enclosed staircase, looking up at Aunt Anna. She remained stock-still ahead of me, her posture in astonishing contrast to the frenzied manner in which she had been pursuing my mother only a moment before. My mother, also transformed by her father's arrival, walked boldly back up the stairs followed by the old man, who spoke not a word, taking full advantage of the authority invested in him by the two women. I looked on, amazed at his power to bring calm to a household in turmoil. A small man with greying hair – pepper and salt – his usual warm and affectionate expression had been replaced by a forbidding mask.

He watched us children go to bed and then went out into the drawing room to talk with my mother. I have no idea whether Aunt Anna had gone to her bedroom or taken a chair in the drawing room or gallery, but I am certain she was listening attentively. One could eavesdrop without difficulty, since there was a gap between the roof and partitions to facilitate the circulation of air. But my mother and her father must have been speaking in exceptionally soft voices, for not a word could be heard.

When my grandfather was taking leave of my mother, just outside the bedroom, I caught her parting words: 'I suppose he never gives us more than we can bear.' And my grandfather replied, 'I'm beginning to think he's a sadist.' I am sure they were talking about God, invoked in moments of despair.

My view of my mother was transformed. Until then she had seemed to have magical powers, had seemed capable of performing any feat. Cooked food appeared miraculously on our table, rice and vegetables we did not grow; shoes and clothes were replaced when they wore out. She even seemed to control the people around us, the servants in the house and her teachers at school, giving orders they obeyed unquestioningly. Even Aunt Anna's domination had done nothing to call my conviction of her unique powers into question. If my mother had seemed a benign magician Aunt Anna was the devil, who controlled another source of power. But the sight of my grandfather obliging Aunt Anna to yield without so much as a word or gesture demonstrated that my mother's powers were less than magical. Yet I was stubbornly to persist in describing her as extraordinary, unconsciously perpetuating some profound need to cling to a personal myth.

Masquerade bands roamed the streets of Georgetown, trailing behind them a crowd composed mostly of small boys. The dancers – all men – strode arrogantly in the midst of their admirers between performances, looking neither to right nor left. My sisters and I stood at the window, on the look-out for Mother Sally, the transvestite stilt-dancer reputed to transfix children with his penetrating gaze. But Mother Sally did not pass by that day and we had to be content with the little dancers in scarlet tunics who, accompanied by fife and drum, spun and leapt, their steps and gestures perfected during endless practising sessions in the halls and back yards of Charlestown in the southwestern section of Georgetown. While my sisters admired the red-coated performers I could not take my eyes off a boy dancer with rubbery legs, an acolyte in the wake of seasoned men. I did not doubt I had found my calling. Inferior in no way to his elders, he lacked only the arrogance and skill in suggesting a hidden power when he walked under our windows. He seemed to be possessed by a hundred demons, some lodged in his head, some in his neck and most of the others in his legs, the repositories of an unquenchable energy. Swaying and feinting, he came into his own when the fife fell silent and the drumming ceased, and the mature dancers stood with their gaze on our windows in an unspoken demand that our household throw down a silver coin. My sisters, frightened by the upturned faces, withdrew from their vantage point, while I followed the unaccompanied performance of the demonic boy. I can no longer recall who threw the men a coin, but they went away eventually, leaving in their wake the mystery of their ritual and memories of a papier-mâché bull, men in scarlet and a boy dancer who had infected me with my first ambition.

Christmas Day came, bringing with it that peculiar sadness I have never fathomed. The season was associated with York ham, apples, almond nuts, walnuts, prunes, wrapped toffees, all imported and originally designed to cater for the palates of British expatriates. These exotic eatables had seduced our tastes and become the Christmas fare for families who could afford them.

The principal Christmas drink, called fly, was made from imported Irish potatoes. The perversity of the name conveys only too well the perversity of the practice, when one considers the variety of available local fruits. But in the thirties few people seemed to mind. A cousin of mine described the colonial period as a time of torpor, which desensitized our reactions. I was to discover that there were, indeed, many people who resented the domination and managed to resist the effects of a sustained attack on our cultural identity.

We children were taken to Forshaw Street, where we received our Christmas toys. And for the first time I went to my godmother's house in South Road. In fact this visit was the first I made in town on my own and it marked the beginning of what, I discovered later, was an unusual independence, at least for a member of a family with our pretensions.

And with Christmas came a lull in hostilities between my
mother and Aunt Anna. The time was marked by visits to our
house and trips by us to look up scores of relatives, both
notional and of the blood. As usual the ladies remarked on my
resemblance to my dead father, often embracing me to prove
their point. One aunt kissed me so firmly on the mouth I was
overcome by a new sensation that descended from my stomach
to my knees and almost prompted me to say that I would come
visiting before next Christmas; but the presence of my mother
and sisters held me back and I could only look at her, wearing
that dumb expression youngsters reserve for grown women
who have, by some deliberate or inadvertent act, awakened the
slumbering beast within them.

Whenever we came home from Grandfather's we rode in
someone's car. But from other houses we took a carriage. My
younger sister Lynette invariably slept during these night
journeys, while Avis and I looked out into the darkness to see
the houses and shops speeding by and the telephone wires
falling and rising between their poles. And as the horse slowed
down for a turn into Regent Street I would bend forward to try
to catch a glimpse of one of the enclosed staircases, whose
doors were flush with the pavement.

'You'll fall out,' my mother constantly warned. 'And what
are you looking at anyway?'

I never answered, for I felt there was something unwholesome about my interest in those hidden stairs, like my passion
for the scent of vanilla. I *knew* that behind the red and blue
façades lurked another world, austere illustrations of charcoal
sellers carrying baskets on their heads and children being
instructed in the mysteries of an obeah cross. Obsessed with
prohibitions, I believed that all I was forbidden to do or see was
permitted behind those closed doors. Georgetown, the fanciful
world embellished by my mother, Sophie and M. while we still
lived in Agricola, now spread all around us, engulfing me in the
romance of its centre, where no trees grew and its asphalted
roads, highways for a noisy traffic by day, slumbered under its
electric bulbs and flickering carbide lamps by night.

*

I have no recollection of Aunt Anna from the time she was silenced by Grandfather and the moment we went away, but soon after my ninth birthday, my mother announced that we were moving to Charlestown, a part of the town we did not know. The day came upon us suddenly. The afternoon after the announcement we were taken to the house by Sophie, where we met my mother and grandfather, who had chosen the cottage from among the many with a 'To let' sign. Small and nondescript, it stood at Lot Six Drysdale Street, between two larger cottages. Behind it were two other houses, both owned by our landlord, one Mr Cendrecourt, a relation of the founder of the Cendrecourt Drugstore about one hundred and fifty yards up the road, at the corner of Ketley and Broad Streets.

The first thing we heard about Drysdale Street was that it flooded in the wet season, thus closing it to the traffic of cycles and cars.

Drysdale Street, running east–west, was no more than two to three hundred yards long. At one end it ran into Charles Street, expiring where two mansions faced each other. At that time Mr Brazõa, a man of Portuguese extraction, lived in the one on the south side of the street. This imposing house was distinguished by an aviary of glittering birds which looked out on Drysdale Street.

At the corner of Drysdale and Ketley Streets stood an enormous house owned by one Mr Peters, a lawyer and minister of the church. The grounds in which the house stood, with church and attendant school, stretched all the way from Ketley Street to High Street, a distance of more than one hundred yards, and seemed as extraordinary as Mr Brazõa's. While the yard with an aviary was overgrown with fruit trees and expressed itself through its encompassed birds, Mr Peters's gave the impression of a great emptiness relieved by a towering plum tree and an old Dutch grave with a sandstone cross. The school, a dilapidated two-storey building overlooking Drysdale Street, had long ceased to function as a school and was hired out as a dance hall on Friday and Saturday

nights. The story ran that one of its former head teachers had
been convicted of practising obeah, and on being released
from prison emigrated to the United Kingdom, where he
became an actor. He later took the leading role in a film called
Man of Two Worlds, an embarrassing affair of the kind British
and American film makers produce when they venture to
portray dark-skinned people.

Our next-door neighbours – on the eastern side – were a
family of children and their postmaster father. The children's
mother was dead, so that the eldest son and the elder of two
daughters had the responsibility of running the household
when their father was out at work. An unusually soft-spoken
man, Mr Moore would remarry within a year of our moving,
and his new wife, a plump Barbadian lady with a sunny
nature, settle readily into their harmonious household.

I fell in love with each of the Moore girls in turn before
transferring my affections to the two eldest sisters of the large
Portuguese family who lived in one of the houses behind our
own. Even then I could not understand why my capacity for
romantic affection could not entertain more than one
object at a time. One attachment inevitably drove out the
other as though, possessing an independent life, it availed itself
of some right to expel the occupant of a position to which it
aspired.

Immediately behind our house was a very small cottage
occupied by two Portuguese young men and their mother. I
remember nothing about them except that once they went off
hunting and came back with a deer, the meat of which they cut
up and distributed to the neighbours.

We were told that a Mr Small once occupied our new home
and had been obliged to move because he kept falling through
the floorboards. I would not normally have credited such a
story, even at the age of nine. But I knew this Mr Small by
sight and had often seen him getting into a horse-drawn cab in
D'Urban Street on his way home from church. He was the
largest man I had ever seen. For him, walking was out of the
question, as was travelling by a motor car, since none existed

with doors wide enough to accommodate his frame. People passing by would watch Mr Small board his cab for a very good reason: the vehicle leaned so alarmingly when he put his leg on the step that even the horse would turn its head to watch. Each time I witnessed the spectacle of Mr Small climbing into his cab I felt certain that it was the last; if the vehicle had defied the laws of equilibrium until then, it could not go on doing so for ever. Equally amusing was the cabman's complete indifference to the drama being played out behind his back.

At first I found Drysdale Street disappointing after Regent and Camp Streets, the hub of city life. No crowds ever gathered there on Saturday nights, and the Christmas masquerades, no doubt working up to the frenzy that would take them on to the broad thoroughfares, danced in desultory fashion. There were no houses above shops along whose awnings you could walk, nor covered staircases that climbed to a forbidden world, nor recesses where ageing tailors plied silent needles, nor channa sellers with carbide lamps, nor the plangent laughter of hangers-on who spent half their lives in a favourite shop. That was the centre, and this, the perimeter, in which silence and discretion reigned. Mr Moore symbolized the quarter, where even the working people's dance hall in Mr Peters's yard attracted no attention from the police on nights when the latest hits could be heard as far away as Charles Street.

Our new house was of the simplest cottage construction, with concrete pillars rising about ten feet above the ground, a small porch and front and back staircases. There was, naturally, a right of way in favour of the tenants of the houses behind our own, so that at any hour of the day or night we might hear noises coming from our bottom house.

It was while playing under our house that I first met Frankie D., eldest son of the Portuguese family with many children. Without so much as a quarrel he challenged me to a fight, claiming that I barred his way to the gate. Before I could even make up my mind what to do he had struck me and when I stumbled to the ground he leapt on me. I heard a voice call out, 'Turn him over! Turn him over!' Taking the voice's advice, I turned my neighbour over almost mechanically. 'Now hit him!' I cuffed Frankie, a thumping blow full in his face. 'A'right! Stop!' he pleaded. I immediately got up, pushed out my chest and strutted threateningly, when Frankie got up in turn, backed away towards the gate and hurried off on reaching the bridge.

I looked for the voice that had instructed me during the affray and saw a head peering through the paling fence that divided our yard from Mr Moore's. It belonged to Archie, the eldest son of the family. He told me that Frankie, a notorious bully, would pick a fight with me again, since he was bigger than I. But again he might not, since I had stood up to him. He also said that Frankie's second sister, Eileen, had witnessed the set-to and that was probably the reason why he had given up so readily. I looked in the direction of the D.s' yard and saw Eileen standing at their gate, her hands on her head, and staring unashamedly at us.

For the two years we lived in the house next to Archie's he and I were to be friends. As quiet as his father, but less austere, he smiled readily and always gave me good advice. A monitor at the new primary school I attended, he was responsible for marshalling the younger children at the end of recreation and overseeing their orderly return to the classrooms. A year later he became a pupil teacher and impressed me, Frankie and the other children in the district with his status as an earner, an expression used by Sophie. In those days there were men who had never worked, and who depended on their women and relations for food and cast-off clothes. Archie, no more than thirteen or fourteen when I first met him, knew how to manage a household. I, protected and cosseted, did no work in the house and could not even repair a punctured inner tube.

When we moved house, two years later, I lost contact with the Moores. I met Archie's father forty-four years later and found a warm, communicative man, enjoying the last years of his decline in retirement. He and his wife, after residing in Berbice and the Essequibo, had come back to settle in Georgetown in a cottage a short distance away from their former Drysdale Street home. Archie had by then married my younger sister, Lynette, having been married once before and fathered many children. His first wife, whom I never met, had died some time before.

I became intrigued by the contrast between the Mr Moore of my childhood and the retired postmaster, between the dour, distant persona of the middle-aged family man and the affable gentleman in retirement. Had he been playing a role expected of him, one which characterized the public face of so many Guyanese married men of the period?

The most unusual family in the yard was undoubtedly the D.s. Like all Portuguese they were Catholic, and like all Portuguese – so it seemed – a grandparent lived with them. In this case it was the mother's father, a discreet, grey-haired man who inhabited a makeshift room under the house, which he defended against the seven children with uncompromising vigour. He spoke Portuguese, according to the children, though I had only heard him speak English. Unlike so many of the older Portuguese he did not drop his aitches; but for all that he used quaint, evocative words, like *potah–potah* for puddle, and seemed to belong to a hermetical world neither Guyanese nor foreign.

Mr D. was a master carpenter. His workmen knew him as a master who kept their wages in arrears for weeks on end. His favourite child, the eldest daughter, was eleven and the drudge of the family. She dreaded Saturday nights, when her father invariably came home drunk. Even before he sat down to eat he would summon Baby and demand how hard she had worked that day – an absurd question, since she toiled from morning till night. Whatever she answered and however much she insisted her mother and sisters would confirm that she had not been idle, he would, in the end, undo his belt and begin thrashing her until she was cowering at his feet.

Yet it was for Baby that he bought a grand piano, even though she could not play a note and had little prospect of finding enough time to learn. Mr D.'s ambivalent behaviour towards his daughter did not seem unusual at the time, perhaps because so much that went on around me was ambivalent. My mother professed to be very fond of Sophie, yet sent her back to Mocha when she became pregnant. Aunt Anna persecuted Mother, but indulged her children. The headmaster of the new school I attended – a cousin by marriage – ignored me at school but made much of me when I visited his house. The idea that contradictions were absurd and should be expunged from the conduct of *others* came much later.

Reflecting now on those long past years, it has occurred to me that the bad parent found in all cultures inflicts deep, lasting wounds on some children, more particularly among the middle class, where parent fixations are often the rule.

Baby, in an uncharacteristic gesture of revolt, left her home to live with a man at the age of twenty. On hearing the news I wondered how the father took the blow and which of the three other girls stepped into her shoes as the house drudge. I had no idea, since by then they had moved to La Penitence, a district on the edge of town.

The Portuguese minority, descendants of immigrants from Madeira, occupied a curious position in Guyanese society. The educated ones enjoyed high status, while the uneducated were despised in spite of their light skin. Prejudices of this kind, though not created by the creole middle class, were fostered by its members, themselves the victims of the myths of an arrogant, if insecure expatriate class. Portuguese were ignorant, East Indians were weak, Chinese could not hold their liquor and aboriginal Indian women had a partiality for teenaged boys – a predilection to which many women from other cultures would confess in an unguarded moment.

The D.s' household was interesting in many other respects. It was there that I first ate bol-de-miel, a rich honey cake; and it was there that I first saw young rice in waterlogged plant pots, cultivated as a harbinger of the coming Christmas. Christmas, the winter solstice, the death that bore seeds of renewal, became symbolized by these tiny flower pots aligned on a mahogany piano.

When Mrs D. was expecting her eighth child I went over one stormy night to keep the children company. Because of the impending birth, Baby, Eileen and I began talking about infants. I explained that the child who would be born already lived in their mother's belly, a piece of information that did not impress Eileen. The next night when I went visiting once more, on the father's invitation this time, I followed him into the kitchen, where he lectured me, saying his home would be forbidden to me from then on if I undertook to instruct his children on the origin of babies. I promised readily, for his daughters' company and for the proximity of the house at the back of the yard which, despite its strictures and my mother's disapproval of the association with this odd, non-Protestant family, possessed a quality I found intensely liberating.

My instincts had not failed me. One afternoon I was playing draughts with Frankie while Baby was washing clothes in a tub and chatting with Eileen. Baby left her tub, came over to us and kissed me. Then, without explanation, as if she had done no more than address me, she went back to her washing and conversation with her younger sister. I pretended to be as unmoved as the others, but felt, from then on, a certain attachment for this hard-pressed girl, two years my senior.

CHAPTER 6

School of Vanity

The move to Drysdale Street appears to have been one of the
landmarks in my awareness of what went on around me. My
memories of the new environment are vivid and detailed: the
twelve-year-old girl living in the house on the right of ours
who spent much of her spare time playing on her own and
writing obscene rhymes; the bamboo clump in a back yard
further down the road where turkeys retired to lay their eggs;
cyclists taking care to keep to the middle of the flooded street
in order to avoid falling into concealed roadside gutters;
wandering minstrels with eloquent guitars, who sang for the
pleasure of singing and belonged to a tradition stretching
across the northern half of South America, that included the
Batacuda brotherhood of Brazil; street lamps clattering in a
high wind; remnants of kites encumbering electric wires;
diminutive yard dogs so ferocious that strangers and visitors
dared not venture beyond the gate, in spite of their owner's
assurance that they were securely chained; the face of urban
poverty so degrading even its contemplation seemed obscene;
municipal workers cleaning street gutters, and armed with
long poles to expel rubbish accumulated under the culverts;
balustraded crossings built at a time when scores of carriages
were plied for hire and cab drivers looked down on the
thoroughfare. (Chauffeurs now complained that they obstruc-
ted their vision.)

Had my sharpened focus been the result of contact with that
part of the city? Or was it the culmination of a process that
began in Aunt Anna's house and coincided with the attain-
ment of my ninth birthday? Nearly ten, I was no longer

content to allow things to happen to me. I wandered up the road to the main street in pursuit of new experiences. I rose early in the morning to gather ripe plums in the churchyard at the height of the dry season. And, above all, the torment to which I submitted my younger sister Lynette was now deliberate. An unconscious misconduct had matured into vindictiveness, with its particular purpose and fear of discovery. Remorse came much later, like a bird of prey that arrives furtively and nests on the inaccessible canopy of a nearby tree. I pinched Lynette, bullied her and struck her. Yet these unprovoked outbursts were matched, at other times, by feelings of such tenderness that I would imagine myself protecting her from a rampaging wild animal or righting some wrong she had endured. Those swings from wickedness to a desire for an ineffable goodness began afflicting me at that time and were not to leave me before the autumn of my life, before I realized that I was subject to a periodic table of moods capable of being anticipated and against which I could arm myself.

It was at this age that I began getting my hair cut at the American barbershop, owned by one Mr Stephens, a quiet man who promoted boxing matches on the side. He was reputed to earn far more from his entrepreneurial activities than from cutting his customers' hair. As in other barbershops many of the men who frequented Mr Stephens's establishment came to read the newspaper, to chat or even to take an afternoon nap on the customers' chairs.

The American barbershop was famous for its philosophical discussions. While the reading rooms and the public library were places of silence and retreats for studious middle-class men – women avoided them as they did the drinking places of their husbands and lovers – my barbershop was a public room, in which visitors could relate their dreams or debate the most abstruse ideas or be entertained by notorious liars. One man was in the habit of seeing the devil sitting on a coconut tree, at times in anthropomorphic form, at times in theriomorphic form, with a luminous tail which quivered while he gazed down at him. Another claimed he had never worked, but learned from a lady who unfailingly appeared in his dreams at month-end where he could find his wages. Always impeccably dressed and shod, he displayed an old-world courtesy which earned him the name of Polish. He was charged two or three years later with burglary and sentenced to seven years' hard labour.

Once I heard the 'Minister', a self-made priest, talk about Maya, the Hindu concept of the web of illusions which we all spin for ourselves and through which we continually view the world. If I did not grasp the significance of this idea at the time I never forgot it, nor the silence that accompanied its elucidation. The Minister was invariably listened to with respect, not least for his soft, mesmeric voice. He had left school at the age of nine, but at thirteen met an older man who possessed a library and many girl-children. The Minister conceived a passion for two of his benefactor's daughters and visited his home on the pretext of using the library. In the event he never associated with either of the girls; but the reading habit he developed while visiting did not desert him.

The story of the Minister as a young man was well known, yet his private life remained as secret and inviolate as that of any Catholic priest. In spite of his professed Christianity he frequently spoke about Hindu thought and the Vedas, a word which, like West Coast East Indians, he pronounced Veds. He was the first person to represent for me the principle of Perfection, something I came to recognize much later as a deep-seated source of spiritual energy within us, an archetype. I met men like him when I went to work on the West Bank; creoles, Christians by upbringing who became fascinated by the ideals of Hindu thought, like Karma and Maya. The Adlerian concept of projection is clearly inspired by Karma.

The Minister was also one of the most gifted teachers I knew, capable of reducing complex ideas to their simplest elements. Some months later, after I began to understand more of what he spoke about, I thought I discovered the first chink in his logical armour, when he declared that an opponent's claim of many causes lying at the root of a certain phenomenon was untenable. There was only a single cause; attendant causes could always be found. In the case of the opposite phenomenon attendant causes were also at hand. I found this proposition implausible at the time, and, for that, the Minister fell in my esteem.

The majority of people frequenting the American barber-shop were far simpler, more earthy than the Minister. Some of the women who looked over the low swing doors in search of a missing man friend were unbelievably coarse, and at the slightest provocation would unleash a series of curse words aimed at the male who dared cross them. One of these women, a notorious brawler, invaded the sacred male preserve and felled the friend she sought with a single hefty butt. The man came back the following day, his head swathed in a bandage. Unabashed that he had come off the worse in a physical encounter with a woman, he took his accustomed place in a corner and waited patiently for his turn to read the newspaper. An incautious acquaintance took it into his head to make a scathing remark about his part in the incident, to which the bandaged head replied, 'If you don' shut you' mouth I goin' get she to do fo' you too!'

On another occasion a young boxer lost his temper because Mr Stephens refused to give him an advance on a sum he expected to receive for a forthcoming fight. He began smashing the mirrors in front of the swivel chairs, and by the time he was restrained the shop was strewn with fragments of broken glass. Mr Stephens had not even had time to put down his cut-throat razor, so swiftly had matters come to a head, and he could only stand aside watching his two assistant barbers hold the young man down until the police came to take him away.

These incidents, unusual as they were, served to remind people that the calm of day-to-day life, the restraint that characterized people's jostling relationships, concealed stresses they would rather have ignored. It is interesting that such cases of violence involved people associated in ways that generated stress. Indeed, the Minister claimed that the three

main sources of exceptional tension were the family, the
workplace and neighbours. He also declared that it was
astonishing to find men and women living together after their
children had grown up. He believed that, theoretically, the
tension generated in the man–woman relationship precluded
such an arrangement. The function of sexual love was to keep
them together in the interest of the children. But the mystery
of togetherness when that function had been performed had
yet to be explained. Today these views appear less than
extraordinary, even banal; nevertheless, to broadcast them in a
parochial society like Georgetown's, at a time when a
profession of atheism attracted odium (it still does), was the
sign of a bold and original mind.

The Minister believed that the great stimulus to the
development of language among humans arose from the
mother–child relationship, not economic necessity. But his
most unusual pronouncement was that human society was
heading for a system that would strongly resemble the
beehive, when the word pleasure would disappear from our
vocabulary, a recent arrival anyway. Just as free will was a
vanishing concept in philosophy, so pleasure would recede
into the limbo of abandoned expectations. I believe that what
excited me most about the Minister's views was the implica-
tion that concepts, even feelings, were relative.

One of the barbershop's habitués told us that the Minister
did not like women. The fact is, whatever the motivation
behind his views, his matchless exposition of them took one's
breath away. By profession a tailor – he performed his
ministry by night – his true vocation lay in teaching. Two
years later, while at secondary school, I was disappointed at
the absence of vision among my teachers, some of whom were
excellent, purposeful men. There was not a single 'Minister'
among them. Of course, the classroom is not a barbershop.
Constrained by the exigencies of his or her subject and the
need to avoid accusations of subversiveness, the teacher is an
unlikely educator. The Minister would probably have lan-
guished as a teacher. He might even have agreed that education

in schools and universities takes away at least as much as it gives.

The extravagant characters I discovered during my Regent Street stay had been admired from afar, and I could enjoy the luxury of yielding to their fascination. Surrounded by them in the barbershop I was not a little afraid. Yet, within a few months, I not only grew accustomed to them, but looked forward to having my hair cut, spurred on perhaps by the bland surface reality of my own family life. In my ignorance I assumed that little happened in the circumscribed environment of my own yard and school, that my mother was happy, that her sister – the youngest of P. M. de Weever's first family – who smiled frequently, was even more content than her elder sibling, and that my brother who lived at my grandfather's and came home from time to time was fortunate in having two homes, when I only had one. I was too young to see below the surface of daily indulgences guaranteed by parent and family servants.

Apart from providing me with an introduction to the world at large, the barbershop on Lombard Street gave me my first lesson in vanity. Something in my demeanour attracted the attention of those self-educated intellectuals, men who returned to homes lit, more often than not, by a single kerosene lamp, where sleepers competed for space on the floorboards and everything was rationed. They exaggerated my merits as a budding intellectual; and if I listened to their arguments without any attempt at intervening, it was surely because I dared not risk my unearned reputation as a prodigy. I thrived on their silent adulation.

The school I now attended, called simply Government School, was unusual in being a non-denominational establishment. Unattached to any church it presented an incongruous spectacle. Each of the other schools in town and in the countryside had its companion, a well-maintained church beside or in front of it. Indeed, the officiating minister also functioned as the manager of the companion school, and was responsible for overseeing it and choosing its teachers. A head teacher took care to be 'in' with his manager, almost invariably a white expatriate.

Government School was an experiment and competition for its headship had been exceptionally keen. Mr Dolphin, my mother's first cousin's husband, its first head teacher, found me a place in the Scholarship Class for ten-year-olds, even though my mother was unable to pay the fees. Primary school education was free, but many schools ran an élite class, the members of which were chosen on account of their parents' ability to pay. Joining this privileged group gave me my first taste of patronage, a practice from which I benefited time and time again without even questioning its validity.

I have a detailed recollection of the day-to-day routine at my new school; its morning assemblies, after which sliding doors were drawn to isolate the classrooms; morning break when we played for our allotted span of time then filed back to our classes under the supervision of prefects and pupil teachers; the breakfast hour and a half – 'lunch' had not yet replaced the older word – during which pupils and teachers went home; and finally the shorter afternoon session of two and a half hours.

This ritual obedience of the rules provided an astonishing contrast to the conduct of schools in the bush attended by aboriginal Indians, when after morning break the number of children returning to class was often less than half. Many a teacher from town, unprepared for the degree of freedom to which the aboriginal Indians were accustomed, stood open-mouthed as they looked out of the window and saw the river covered with boats in which their pupils were paddling indolently as though the final bell had rung. We in town were more compliant. We filed in and out of school, respecting the rule that the boys' gate must only be used by boys and the girls' by girls. Teachers were objects of veneration, and their thin, supple canes the ultimate sanction.

Rebellious souls there were among the pupils, like Stanley

Devonish, a relative of the Scholarship Class teacher, who had promised his parents to keep an eye on him. Stanley Devonish often broke school rules and our teacher did not miss an opportunity to remind him that he had his interests at heart by administering six lashes with the cane on his backside.

But on the whole the discipline worked – at least at school – and its products were suitably cowed, to the extent of attributing to their teachers magical powers similar to their parents'. Our Scholarship Class teacher took to sitting with his back to the class when the level of noise displeased him. Suddenly he would say, 'So and So, come here! You were talking.' Mystified, the class would fall silent at once. How could he have known who talked when his back was turned? It took months to discover that our magician was able to see our reflections in a picture on the wall. But the spell was not thereby broken, for it depended not on any trick played on us, but rather on the power wielded by the teacher and on our willingness to participate in the mystique surrounding it. When I met this teacher a few years after leaving Government School I was surprised and disappointed to find a timid man, more nervous about engaging in conversation with a former pupil than I was about speaking to an old teacher.

A sinister lady teacher on the staff seemed to dislike me. It was said that she loved the head teacher to distraction. I never belonged to her class and yet I felt the effect of her baleful glances whenever I went by her in the playground. I do not believe she ever spoke to me, which, perhaps, contributed to my conviction of her hostility. Her habit of turning her head slowly and fixing me with her gaze so intimidated me I avoided her whenever I could. The country lore of Old Higue, the woman with the secret life of a witch, seemed to suit Miss B., and I imagined her taking off her skin at night, flying through the air to find an unprotected infant whose blood she could suck.

Had I been asked to justify my belief that Miss B. disliked me I could have put forward no tangible evidence whatsoever. Our judgments of people's reactions to our presence are hardly ever wrong and I never once doubted that this lady, a spinster in her thirties, had something against me or someone connected with me. Perhaps she disliked my Aunt Edna, Beryl's sister, who took one of the classes of younger children. But the latter had not spoken to me since I came to the school, so I rejected this possibility. Miss B. had singled me out for a reason known only to herself, a fact partly confirmed by my enquiries made to other pupils, who saw her as no more than an unsmiling mistress.

The reputation of the few women teachers on the staff of this show school was never in question. Not so that of the men. Mr Y. was courting, and this was as unsavoury as any behaviour an adult could engage in. Mr H. played cards until the early hours of the morning, according to a neighbour, and his wife never failed to quarrel with him when he returned home late. These bits of trivia were the sauce to the unpalatable staple diet of school with its unvarying routine and its scale of punishments for wrongs ranging from entering it by the wrong gate to smudging one's exercise book.

If I and most pupils I knew saw our school day as a boring preamble to the afternoon hours of play – the true aim of living – we saw little else of what went on around us: the fierce rebellions, the docility of girls seduced by a relative, the dedication of unwonted ambition. We came to school, listened to new gossip – the boys as avidly as the girls – were pleased at success without striving for it, anticipated morning recreation, and at home time fled with suspicious alacrity. It never occurred to our class teacher that we all harboured burning questions we dared not ask because of the gulf between bench and chair. I was as interested in the meaning of death as a schoolmate was in the purchasing power of dollar notes, mere pieces of brown paper. Had we been able to put such questions we would have learned much about the world as WE saw it, and consequently school might have seemed more relevant. I, for instance, would have found out that my preoccupation with death was matched by a national, if unconscious, obsession, due no doubt to our astonishingly high death rate. During the rainy season death hovered over the coastlands, using as its assiduous agent the anopheles mosquito, the malarial vector that sang by night. Yet, in a class of sixty or more, a gap in the school bench, unfilled for weeks on end, did not attract our attention unless the missing pupil was a friend.

Marked by the experience of death in faded images we all knew that a dead body lay with its feet pointing towards the east and that children attending a funeral were passed over the coffin three times. But death must have also left a mark on our features, for to outsiders we are known as a grave people.

I first learned about illegitimacy at school: the terrible secret, as the middle class saw it. Although spoken of as a working-class affliction, nothing could be further from the truth. It was common knowledge that middle-class men, doctors, lawyers, teachers, pharmacists, had mistresses, 'outside women'. Many a funeral was haunted by a stranger and her children, a group who stood apart, so obviously out of place that they were immediately recognized as the dead man's 'other' family. These long-suffering women, often cut off from their benefactors during the long months of a terminal illness, usually appeared, waited their turn to pass each of their children over the dead man and then left as discreetly as they had arrived. But occasionally one of them would proclaim her relationship to the deceased in loud, often offensive language and then set off for the burial ground in a car hired for the occasion.

Various churches condemned illegitimacy, advocating in their usual short-sighted manner a morality whose social consequences would have been disastrous for thousands of women. The Catholic Church and the sect churches were the exception, the former being more concerned with the number of souls it could claim and the latter because they alone were the true representatives of the working class, which benefited from the protection of middle-class men. Much later Catholic priests would affect to espouse the cause of peasants through-

out South and Central America, when the Catholic Church
began losing their allegiance. In the period from the sixteenth
to the early part of the twentieth centuries the priesthood
remained curiously silent about the depredations practised on
the ancestors of the self-same peasants by the ruling oligarch-
ies of the region.

'My mother and father not married,' a boy told me on the
way back to the classroom after recreation.

I delayed my response to the unexpected confidence, trying
all the while to understand why his parents had never married.
At secondary school my reaction to the discovery of divorce
was similar: at first, incomprehension that two people should
dissolve their marriage and then mystification at such an
unusual state.

'Why?' I asked naively.

He, wiser in the ways of our elders, met my question with
an offended silence. His attempt to elicit an expression of
sympathy had failed.

It took me many years to understand the devastating effects
of illegitimacy on those families aspiring to middle-class
status. While others boasted of fathers who did this or that,
they often harboured smouldering hatreds against a father
who spent a few hours with their mother two or three
evenings of the week. One Guyanese I met abroad in the
seventies would speak obsessively about his father. Sometimes I felt that he idolized him, while at other times he
betrayed his hostility in brief attacks on the old man's
integrity. On the day of his father's funeral he went to the
theatre to see a bawdy play, since when he spoke only once of
him again, explaining that the dead man had never married his
mother.

School was the institution of formal education; it also served
as a kind of exchange, where one was drip-fed with information about oneself and the world at large, in a slow, ineluctable
process that prepared one for adult life. Such was your class
position, such was your place in a group, such and such were
your abilities. Teachers were less responsible for this under-

ground instruction than they imagined; and even the kindly ones, those who looked at you with a benign expression or openly expressed their fondness in a show of favouritism, were not aware of the manner in which they were being used.

Whatever gave me pleasure or pain later – as far as the world at large was concerned – had already been experienced at school in an attenuated form, preparing me for events that would overwhelm me, directly or vicariously through my mother; like my grandfather's death and my brother's breakdown.

CHAPTER 7

End of an Epoch

Soon after our move to Drysdale Street my grandfather, P. M. de Weever, died. My mother was inconsolable. Her protector had gone. He had been the keeper of a mysterious power which had saved my mother from Aunt Anna's clutches; which had succeeded in installing her as head teacher of a village school after my father's death, even though many better qualified than she deserved to fill the post. He had been the hero of her childhood recollections and the source of innumerable stories destined to be passed on to his descendants.

One evening a young man came to our door, and after urgent whispering my mother declared that Grandfather was seriously ill. She sent for a cab to take her to the Queenstown house. We must do as Sophie told us and not forget to say our prayers.

By now Avis and Lynette accepted my position as mother's favourite, so that when she said I was going with her neither protested.

My mother stood at the window looking out on the street, protected by that silence that unsettled us all. That figure in a cotton dress seemed to belong there, framed by the painted square, ahead of which was darkness and behind, the appurtenances of domesticity.

When she signalled that the cab had arrived I had still not done up my shoelaces. Impatiently she helped, before dragging me down the stairs. In her agitation she refused to answer my question about Grandfather and throughout the journey to Queenstown stared stubbornly ahead. Had she shouted at me I would have been less anxious. Wild, obsessive images came to mind, as so often happened when I was unable to fathom her reticence . . . lightning dividing the sky, trees rising from the smoke of innumerable fires. My sisters and I had often been ill, but these events had been accepted with equanimity, it seemed to me. Even if Grandfather were dying, was that sufficient reason to rush out into the night? I once heard one of the barbershop intellectuals claim that death was a name for something which did not exist; life existed and what we called death was simply a lack of life. At the time I had not understood the remark, but its recollection served to fuel my irritation at my mother's conduct.

I resented her preoccupation with her powerful father; I resented the stories told about him; I resented his influence over her; and only because of her own attachment to him.

In the darkness the sound of the horse's hooves on the pitch road appeared to be coming from another world.

'I can smell flowers,' I said.

'Hush!'

The cab drove up Church Street, past the convent where she had gone to school as a young lady. Its high, white-painted wall defied the shadows, an opulent reminder that we were skirting the well-maintained northern part of the town.

'He wore braces,' I reflected. 'He wears braces and spells his name with a small d.' A small d, he always insisted. His favourite son, Clement, an uncle I never met, died in the bush in the arms of an aboriginal woman with whom he had lived for many years.

The stories about my mother's family came back to me, as though I had to know them by heart in order to gain entrance to the mourning house. For it became clear, from her behaviour, that my grandfather was going to die. No one could survive such a display of grief.

The line of carriages in New Garden Street and Forshaw Street betrayed the gravity of Grandfather's condition, for only weddings, funerals and terminal illnesses attracted so many people. My mother paid the cabman and told him not to wait. I followed her up the stairs and into the brightly lit drawing room of the Forshaw Street house. Aunt Beryl came over to greet us, then led Mother into the large bedroom where, presumably, a number of intimates had gathered, according to custom: relations, familiars of the house, close friends who never visited and others who claimed the right to watch him pass away. The Much Dreaming Woman was in the drawing room, uncharacteristically subdued amongst the others, all sitting on chairs ranged against the wall.

Looking back on that scene I am certain that, if breathing was rendered more difficult by the assembly of so many people in the bedroom, the terror of embarking on that final road must have been thereby considerably diminished for the dying man.

I took my place on an empty chair and waited, hardly aware of the whispered conversations, and imagined my mother looking down at the prone figure of the old man, disclosing nothing of her terrible grief, but engaged in an unspoken dialogue with him.

'Who will find me a place to live if I'm evicted? Where will I go for consolation when I'm sick with worry?' Carried away by the impetus of my fantasy I actually heard her speaking to him while those around her looked on.

I saw Aunt Beryl come out of the bedroom. She sat down at the piano – possibly at Grandfather's request – and began to play. I remember no one else in that drawing room except Beryl and the Much Dreaming Woman who, on hearing the first chords, said loudly, so that all could hear, 'So much dying! So much dying!'

Aunt Beryl played softly, and to such effect that some of the women began crying noiselessly. And in a moment I became infected by this collective display of grief and by the hymn which I knew from the Methodist services we attended on Sundays in the large, tumbledown church at the corner of D'Urban and High Streets: 'The Church's one foundation, Is Jesus Christ Our Lord.'

For a while I forgot my mother in the adjoining room and became part of the group mourning in anticipation. The whispered conversations had been replaced by a low humming, in which I joined, as inevitably as one joins in laughter, even when ignorant of its source.

Aunt Beryl, who was to spend more than half of her life in a mental hospital on the outskirts of New Amsterdam, presided at this funereal scene with that dignity I had admired in her even as a small child of three. Edna, her surly elder sister who refused to acknowledge my existence at the school I attended, was nowhere to be seen. Nor were Hilton and Guy, her brothers; nor was Grandmother.

Grandfather died the following night at eleven o'clock, and the funeral took place the next afternoon. It seemed to me that there was an exceptionally large number of children present, conspicuous among whom were Uncle Guy's, whose eldest daughter I recall being passed over the coffin three times. Neither I nor my brother and sisters were, because my mother would not have approved.

All the men seemed to be mopping their brows with white handkerchiefs – did they perspire more profusely than the women? Many women were attired in mauve, a colour generally regarded as unhealthy, a symbol of foreboding. They walked like sinister orchids among the black- and white-clad mourners. Unlike the gathering two nights ago, when the visitors hardly moved from their chairs, there was now a constant flow of bodies, of groups dissolving, of children being taken up into adult arms and being put down again, of embraces and expressions of condolence. And in the midst of all there was my mother, sitting on a straight-backed chair beside the coffin, weeping unashamedly in an uncharacteristic display of public emotion. Several women went up to her and placed an arm on her shoulder, but she did not once look up.

All of a sudden I found myself looking towards the door, in

pursuit of a scent that overpowered me, the same scent of flowers about which I had spoken to my mother in the carriage. A man was trying to steer two large wreaths through the open door and there came to mind those small signs on the white-painted paling fences of certain houses in New Garden Street, bearing the inscription, 'Flowers for Sale'.

And in spite of these vivid recollections I can call to mind nothing of the coffin being borne out of the house. Perhaps the incidents that spring to mind are all connected directly and, in some curious way indirectly, with my mother sitting alone, marking the end of an epoch with a copious flow of tears. My grandfather had fallen into the possession of the Pale Insomniac, who must have been watching, unmoved by such grief and the paraphernalia of death, garments in black, mauve and white, the colours of decay and mystery.

Grandfather's procession must have moved off before the electric bulbs were lit and street lamps went on, before darkness fell suddenly over the crossroads where traffic was brought to a standstill and men stood on the pavement with their hats against their chests out of respect for a body parted from its soul.

I was to attend many funerals, and often wondered about the reality behind their manifold symbols, at the evidence of posture and silence which, though readily interpreted by some, is entirely lost on others.

Was my mother's isolation on her chair an indication of the tenuous relations between herself and Grandfather's second family? Later it became clear to me that she and her stepmother disliked each other intensely, that Sonny's banishment from the Queenstown house soon after the death might have been as much an expression of that dislike as the action of a widow now obliged to fend for herself.

CHAPTER 8

A Moral Collapse

Sonny came home, a sullen fourteen-year-old. He did not conceal the fact that he felt out of place in the tiny cottage. More than four years older, he was impatient with me, except when we played cricket in the yard. But as his contempt for me grew, so did my efforts to emulate him. I regretted not being left-handed, as he was. I copied his laughter and even practised walking like him. I longed to go to secondary school, where he must surely have learned his superior walk.

None of us suspected how much the break from my grandfather's house – where he had developed a close friendship with Hilton – distressed him. His moodiness amongst his own contrasted sharply with the enthusiasm he showed for his school mates, who frequently came after classes to play cricket in our yard. Since my mother did not come home until six o'clock and Sophie did not think that she dared interfere, from Monday to Friday of every week Sonny, his assembled friends and I did violence to the landlord's paling fence with a soft ball.

Almost invariably, when it was my turn to bat I would be ignored, and without a word of protest I would take up my fielding position again, hoping that the next time round one of Sonny's friends would stand up for me.

Ah! Cricket on those sunny afternoons! The shouts of satisfaction when a wicket fell, the quarrels that followed doubtful decisions, the ecstatic sensation after a well-executed stroke. We lived in a way we would never live again as adults.

Frankie, the Portuguese boy living in the back yard, used to hurry past me after Sonny came to live with us; and I, luxuriating in the protection afforded me by my brother's presence, took to taunting him about the way he went around searching in dustbins for any vegetable waste which might be sold as pig feed: 'Potagee! Potagee! Dustbin Potagee!' I would call.

In our first encounter he had attacked me for no reason whatsoever. Now that he had an excellent reason he could only shrug his shoulders and hurry by. So intense was the satisfaction I drew from my immunity, I was inclined to curse him even more extravagantly; but by then I had fallen in love with his younger sister Eileen and decided to marry her when I grew up.

One afternoon – the day before Sonny sat his public examinations – I became alarmed when I saw him walking in circles under the house, muttering to himself. But I told myself that he might have been playing a kind of game or even repeating some passage from his revision work. Besides, there had been until then no evidence of instability in his behaviour and, at school, from all accounts, he was disciplined and respectful towards his teachers. He had never once struck me or my two sisters, nor displayed any hostility towards my mother. Yet now there was something uncharacteristically whimsical in the way he hopped about; and on seeing me he made no attempt to adopt his dignified gait. I asked him if anything was wrong, but he ignored me.

'Anybody coming round to play cricket?' I pressed on, hoping for some reassurance that all was well.

Receiving no answer I went upstairs, more than ever disturbed by the new situation. What would my mother say when she came home? Would he answer her? How long could he go on circling an imaginary centre before he became exhausted?

The next afternoon I learned that Sonny had 'broken down' in the examination room; and I was left wondering why he chose that particular time and place to relinquish control over his good conduct.

In the days that followed, my thoughts became preoccupied not with Sonny's misfortune as such, but with its possible effect on my mother, for nothing existed except in relation to her. Grandfather was no longer there to protect her, to appear at the last moment and put things right.

Events come to mind, like a pack of illuminated cards which can be read singly and present a record of disaster, disregarding the narrative convention of time. My mother lies on a bed surrounded by women with solicitous expressions. Her right hand, as though holding a pen, writes furiously. A letter to whom? . . . She arrives home, pushing her bicycle before her. Sonny and his friends are playing cricket with a hard ball. They all stop as she comes through the gate. Then, without warning, Sonny throws the ball at her. It misses her head by a few inches and there is a great void in the afternoon. Did this happen before or after his breakdown? . . . Everyone, including my sisters, is up at two o'clock in the morning. Sonny is not in bed. At dawn Uncle Dolph brings him back on his bicycle. He had been throwing stones at his house in Queenstown, a good three miles from our cottage . . . Sonny appears at my primary school during the midday break, bearing a photograph of himself when a small boy. He seeks out Aunt Edna, with whose family he had lived for so long. She refuses to receive him. I see him climb the banister of a stairway, sit astride it, then give a creditable imitation of a horseman on his mount. There is no embarrassment, only distress at his unusual behaviour in front of school children younger than himself. I am led home by the teacher of the Scholarship Class, who mutters comforting words, and I am no longer distressed, as though all the pain had been imagined.

Nights of anguish, listening for every noise; marauding bats, dogs barking in the distance. I have my first bout of insomnia, thinking only of my mother and the terror of silence. Could she not shout out, 'I am not myself!'

1988. A young woman relates a dream she had. She and her husband . . . she *or* her husband . . . lock their cat in a cupboard, on purpose. Weeks later the cupboard door is opened and an emaciated animal, barely recognizable as their pet, totters out. She, the dream-teller, is the offended cat, we both decide. And this tale seems to carry echoes of these gloomy days fifty years ago. Yet Sonny's condition was not similar. The echo persists, nevertheless.

A few days after Sonny's breakdown I sat watching a group of municipal workers clearing the gutters with long poles. My chin resting on my hands, I followed their progress while looking out for my mother, who should arrive as the sun went down. I now know it was not the hot afternoon sun which kept her, but rather that she had never got over my father's death and put off her return to an 'empty' house as late as possible before sunset. Every afternoon she visited Mrs Harper, who shared so much with her and whose family still lived in Agricola.

I saw her in the distance and went downstairs to take in her bicycle. What must she have thought of my attentiveness? I had determined never to cause her pain again. Yet, only a short time after Sonny was taken to hospital, my Aunt Clara had to lecture me on the need to behave well and spare my mother, an admonishment that was to be followed by others at shorter and shorter intervals, because the effect of each wore off more quickly than the last. I had become insufferable, for no apparent reason. I did not want to come upstairs at meal times. I was rude to Sophie and could not bear being scolded by my mother.

One Saturday morning, while playing alone in the yard, a policeman appeared at the gate and asked if I was Roy Heath. I could hardly answer for fright.

'Why aren't you at school?' he demanded. On certain Saturdays members of the Scholarship Class were required to attend school for extra lessons. I knew at once that my mother had enlisted the help of someone at the local police station to bring me into line.

The officer gave me three minutes to get dressed for school and I complied with an alacrity that did no credit to my reputation as the terror of the family. If the policeman had ordered me to touch my toes I am certain I would have succeeded, although I have never managed to get below the upper part of my shins.

I fled past the gloating young arm of the law and up the road to the hated school which took away my Saturday morning freedom. From then on I was careful not to push my mother too far and conducted my guerilla warfare against authority with more guile than courage.

Since my infant school days – when I 'flew', according to my mother – I had never recovered that enthusiasm for learning, and the sound of the school bell for the end of lessons was always a call to liberty. Now I took part in the ritual of lining up and bidding goodbye to the teacher with a relish that was a kind of vengeance on the whole police force of Guyana.

Under the L-shaped building of Government School were the infant school, the janitor's living quarters and the room where children's caps and hats were left. There were also drinking taps, a unique feature in furnishings, justifying the school's reputation as a show-place. Another brand-new idea, imported from the United Kingdom, was having two separate gates for boys and girls. As befitted an educational establishment, its pupils were meant to discover the moral advantages of sexual isolation, at least while entering the gates of our educational purgatory. But the arrangement did not stop the children from mixing while in school, thus providing them with a useful example of the need for futile ritual in their everyday lives. The silly rule of entry had no effect on them whatsoever, for the fifth standard saw many love matches. Boys came back from breakfast a good half-hour before the bell went for the afternoon session, to meet their girlfriends in the fifth and sixth standard classrooms. One couple, who had become inseparable since they were nine, had taken possession of a corner overlooking Broad Street, and no one attempted to oust them from their vantage point. No such nonsense could have occurred in Catholic schools, which solved the problem of a dangerous proximity of the sexes by introducing the single-sex school. This oddity never caught on – except in two Government-sponsored secondary schools – to the credit of Guyanese realism. If our parents admired their colonial masters, they, nevertheless, wanted no truck with their sexual obsessions.

The oft-repeated remark that school days were the best days has always puzzled me. School was not simply tedious. I knew, even in primary school, that my development was being held back in ways I did not understand, but felt. Not being gregarious, going to school 'to meet my friends' had little appeal for me as an idea. Besides, cricket in my yard and other yards in Drysdale Street provided me with ample opportunity to meet my friends.

'Why can't I go to school two hours a day and concentrate on English and arithmetic?' I once asked my mother. She reminded me of the East Indian children in the countryside, whose poor attendance left them semi-literate and only fit for selling mangoes at the wayside in coastal villages. (The East Indians are now the wealthiest and best-educated section of the population.)

I would have preferred to seek out relatives my mother never spoke about and discover what in their life style or their past made them an unfit subject for conversation. My destiny was, somehow, tied to theirs, to the activities that excluded them from our precarious middle-class existence. They had surely fallen into the pit on the edge of which our class hovered, continually beset by money problems and the tensions of blood relationships. In short I was interested in nothing that could earn me a living.

My mother told me about one of these relatives much later, when, in fact, she was in her nineties and seized by an urge to unburden herself of her last secrets. Her eldest brother, Clement, while studying for his pre-med. exams, which would qualify him to enter medical school in the United Kingdom or Ireland, confided in her that his ambition was to own a gun and a dog. 'What would you do?' 'Go and live in the bush. You hardly need any money there.' My mother started to cry, because he was the favourite of her two brothers and the favourite son of her father.

'You can't take a joke!' he teased her.

His examination results confirmed his consistently fine school reports and my grandfather made him do the rounds of relations and wealthy acquaintances who might make some contribution to his forthcoming trip to a university abroad.

One night my uncle admitted to my mother that he had been serious about his 'gun and dog' and would take enough money from what had been collected in order to realize his ambition. Faced with his imminent departure she was torn between loyalty to him and the need to forestall a crisis in the home; but she remained silent. A few days later, after my grandfather had informed the police that his son had disappeared and might have been the victim of an accident, he received a letter from the Northwest, in which Uncle Clement explained that he could not bury himself in medical studies for seven years. The forest had attractions he could not resist and he intended living there the rest of his life. Distraught, my grandfather cursed his solicitor brother for 'putting ideas into the boy's head'. Life was not all about playing a musical instrument and discoursing with friends. The brothers never spoke to each other again.

Much later, when my grandfather learned from an acquaintance that his son was living in squalor with an aboriginal Indian woman in a village near Morawhanna, he made the journey, taking with him gifts of money and powdered milk. According to my mother Uncle Clement spoke as if he had only seen his father the day before. He broke off the conversation several times to shout orders to his lady, a creature of such docility that my grandfather believed his son could never live in town again and become attached to a townswoman. Clement died of tuberculosis the same year.

My mother claimed that there was a self-destructive streak in the de Weever nature. I pointed out that both Grandfather and his brother lived full lives and were legends in their lifetime. She replied, 'Something happened in the next generation.' She was right, for in quick succession her half-brother Guy and her half-sister Beryl fell prey to mental breakdowns, two years after Grandfather's death. Within three to four years the de Weever clan was to experience a kind of moral collapse, as if the death of its head, Peter Moses, had left it rudderless.

CHAPTER 9

The Reluctant Bridegroom
and Other Tales

The development of consciousness involves an awakening to the awareness of death, relations between adults, and much else, long before the apprehension of one's self. It was about this time that I found myself listening avidly to stories concerning adults. And of these, the most remarkable seemed to concern marriage and death. Just as, nowadays, I am often plagued by the delirium of words, so I took to listening to adult talk in the same feverish state. In those days the concern for excluding children from grown-up conversations was less great. Besides, the very architecture of the houses conspired with this laxity to facilitate eavesdropping.

One of the memorable stories concerned a couple who had set the date for their marriage and made all the appropriate arrangements. Custom required that the bridegroom should be at the church a good fifteen minutes before the bride; but on this occasion the bride and her numerous relations arrived first. Half an hour later her intended had still not appeared and the bride began to weep on her father's shoulder, while her brothers openly threatened the absent groom. An hour after the appointed time the seven cars containing the bride and her numerous relations drove away to ambiguous applause from the onlookers. And almost immediately afterwards a cry went up as two youths dragged a young man out from under the church, his elegantly cut suit covered in dust. From his sheepish expression the onlookers guessed that he was the defaulting bridegroom. The men among them burst out laughing and began making ribald remarks concerning his lack of resolution; but the women, incensed to the point of hysteria, took up the threats of the would-be bride's departed brothers. Finally, exasperated by the men's flippancy, they attacked the hapless groom with their umbrellas, driving him out of the churchyard and up the road.

A more bizarre incident occurred a few years later. After the much publicized matrimony of a well-known sportsman and a more obscure lady, the two went off to the reception where they both drank heavily, to the surprise of their table companions, mostly personalities from the sporting world. The bride, who became more and more indiscreet as the rum got the better of her, kept rising and proposing toasts to various sportsmen, each time in a tone of voice more gruff than the last. Then, as her headgear slipped, all doubt was dispelled and she stood revealed as a man. This notorious homosexual wedding came as a surprise to many people, who considered homosexuality to be a joke and were not even sure whether it was simply a pose confined to men in the art world, who had travelled and become 'infected'.

Other tales which made a great impression on me came from the extensive lore to which every racial group – apart from the Chinese and Portuguese, who make up only a very small proportion of the population – has contributed. Baku, the man in the bottle, is of African origin, and merits serious study as an early apprehension of the force of the ego. The unexplained wealth of many families has been ascribed to Baku, a tiny, anthropomorphic creature who lives in a bottle and, on being let out, disappears for days on end, to come back laden with jewels. It is essential that he should be well fed; if neglected he is capable of harming his owner and family, and has even been known to set fire to a house.

There are many illustrations by European alchemists of humans and animals in bottles, as though the bottle were an enclosed world where any number of transformations take place. The bottle, evidently a successor to the jar, is an archetype, a projection of the womb, where the foetus becomes a fully developed human, capable of surviving in a

non-hermetic environment. It is entirely appropriate that the
bottle should harbour the dangerous ego, helper and des-
troyer. 'Rational' town-dwellers are all too ready to dismiss
Baku lore as absurd, forgetting that it is a symbol for
something that has a rational explanation. The limitations of
rationalism represent no more than the failure of rationalists to
come to grips with the function of symbols and, by extension,
to the function of myth.

Stories drawn from country lore were never told in our
home. Sophie must have been familiar with them, but would
not have dared relate them to us, knowing my mother would
have disapproved. School, visits to the house next door and
the occasional road encounter yielded much in this connection; so that I came to realize that I, like Baku, was living in a
hermetically sealed environment which purported to follow
the dictates of a class. 'You're keeping bad company', hardly
understood at first, only served to make the despised company
more attractive when I came to appreciate the family's class
position – based on nothing more than wish-fulfilment and an
addiction to education. The fundament of our class attachment – money – was conspicuously wanting.

Many lore figures, like Bush Dai-Dai and Masacurraman,
were the creation of the aboriginal Indian tribes, the Caribs,
Warrau, Akawoia, Arawaks and others. Most of them share a
belief in the existence of Kenaima, a force in the guise of an
animal, a human, or even an inanimate object, which equalizes
a wrong. In the absence of public justice – before these cultures
had to submit to European rule – the idea of an equalizer
flourished and became embodied in physical representations.
The jaguar that devoured a member of the clan had rectified a
wrong he had committed. Kenaima was said to be recognized,
in the case of a human agent, by the way his feet were turned
inwards. Many piaimen*, believed to possess the power to
turn themselves into jaguars, were, for that and other reasons,
feared by clan members.

The acute reaction to wrongdoing is characteristic of

*shamans

aboriginal Indians. People from other cultures have been struck by their capacity to harbour resentment for a very long period of time, sometimes for years. When an opportunity arises they will avenge themselves in an appropriate way, not stopping at murder. It is interesting that South American Indians whose culture is intact do not see a slaying as the worst wrong. Selfishness is infinitely more vile, since it threatens their way of life more effectively than killing does. In fact outsiders were, in the sixteenth century, astonished at their passion for disposing of non-clan-members, more often than not out of vengeance or in fighting over women.

Of course, much aboriginal Indian lore is not meaningful to other racial groups, because it serves a specific survival purpose. Yet, there were those living in and around the bush, charcoal-burners, porknockers and storekeepers, who accepted some of the lore as fact and even claimed to have had experiences which confirmed such stories. One porknocker related how he and an Indian came upon cow deer while walking along a river bank. The Indian told his companion to remain still as he slipped off into the undergrowth. His friend saw the animals look up and then bound away, pursued by a jaguar. A while later the Indian came back, dragging a dead deer behind him. He never offered a word of explanation and the porknocker never doubted that the Indian had changed into a jaguar in order to kill the animal.

Another man working with a timber grant swore that he was followed by an ape-like creature with burning eyes and only escaped by hiding behind a buttressed silk-cotton tree.

In Guyana, public storytelling is mainly the preserve of creoles (descendants of Africans) and aboriginal Indians. Two houses away from our home in Agricola, friends and relations frequently congregated after dark to listen to tales old and recent. The sight of a practised storyteller performing can be an unforgettable experience. The voice, only one of his or her instruments, often gives way to gestures. Hips, shoulders, head, arms, hands and feet are all brought into play in a display of virtuosity. And the voice itself has a repertoire as comprehensive as the tale-teller's gestures, so that sounds like the chirping of crickets can be rendered with bewildering accuracy. The written word has impoverished storytelling, just as a wide range of instruments has robbed the drum of its ancient power.

Among the aboriginal Indians, stories are almost invariably traditional, as though there is great reluctance to add to their lore. Unlike the creoles all their legends are *real*. If the Macusi relate with terror in their voices that at a certain phase of the moon a giant bat comes down from the Kanuku Mountains and carries off one of the tribe, it is because they are convinced that this event is repeated month after month somewhere in the region. Disappearances are attributed to the marauding bat, in the same way as unexplained deaths are laid at the door of Kenaima among the Arawaks.

My godfather – my godmother's husband in truth – and I were to have long discussions on the function of storytelling which, he claimed, originated in our dreams. Although I was in my late teens I understood nothing of the statement and still harboured my mother's mistrust of talk concerning dreams and everything that had to do with the unconscious.

He believed that our passion for gossip was no more than a perversion of a storytelling need and drew attention to expressions like 'tale-bearer' and 'you're telling stories'. The latter means in creolese, 'You're telling lies.' The human psyche reveals itself cruelly in stories and jokes, he insisted. 'The English tell hundreds of anti-Irish jokes,' he said, 'and the Germans hundreds of madhouse jokes – *Irrenhauswitze*.' (He had worked in Venezuela, where he had met many German immigrants.) 'The English need to confirm their superiority by running down the Irish, while the Germans project their geo-political anxieties into their laugh-stories.'

At Government School one teacher stood out for his irrepressible behaviour. We learned very little arithmetic from him, but he provided us with a reason for attending school. He told stories with the facility of those professional orators who held forth at funerals. Taking advantage of his captive audience, he regaled it with an unending stream of fantastical tales, figments of an irrepressible imagination, as well as tales of porknockers who had created a lore for themselves based on their experiences in the bush. We liked the latter best of all. Time and time again, when bored with one of his embarrassing essays into teaching, we would demand a porknocker story. Our favourite was 'Ocean Shark' who, travelling into the interior on a launch filled with other gold- and diamond-seekers, was thrown into the water when the boat failed to negotiate a notorious stretch of rapids. Ocean Shark managed to grab hold of a rock as he was being swept away. Another porknocker swimming towards him in a desperate effort to share his precarious hold, stretched out his arm towards Ocean Shark, who kicked him away with the words, 'If the Lord did intend you to live he would've send you here first! May Jesus have mercy on your soul!' Ocean Shark was saved, but his hapless mate drowned, along with most of the other passengers in the launch.

Another story we clamoured for told of a diamond-seeker who struck it rich and came to settle in Georgetown. At the end of a long journey from the interior he hired a carriage to take him to the most expensive hotel. 'Make the vehicle go forward!' he ordered the cabbie, who complied. 'Make it go backwards!' he then shouted gleefully. The cabbie's horse performed the difficult manoeuvre. 'Now,' said the porknocker, thrusting his head through the window, 'make it go sideways!' And at the word 'sideways' we all roared with laughter. We never tired of hearing these stories about a ruthless Ocean Shark and the whimsical porknocker, two men who, on reflection, seem to represent important sides of the Guyanese character.

The earliest stories I heard were full of repetitions. Why small children are fascinated by these oral refrains appears to be a mystery. If, at the age of ten, I no longer cared to listen to simple repetitions, something or someone in me demanded an endless retelling of tales that fired my imagination. Are we not connected in some curious manner by the stories that carry us away, stories that possess a secret ingredient which eludes analysis? And those tellers of tales from our childhood who led us down uncharted paths, did they not exploit our childhood sensibilities, affording us pleasures we can never again experience as adults?

Ocean Shark and the wealthy porknocker belong to that long line of trickster figures stretching back to neolithic times. They live on today in the villains of literature and drama, the men and women who turn our world upside down as we would, but dare not, the underground fascinators who provide material for our endless gossiping.

Built into the aesthetic of storytelling is a powerful wish-fulfilment need, particularly strong in European literature. Ulysses returns home, ousts the suitors from his house and is reunited with Penelope. Their long separation notwithstanding, they live happily ever after, the story implies. This blatant offence to realism fails to diminish the fascination of the story because voyage and return are two engaging archetypes. In the same cavalier tradition Robinson Crusoe plants wheat – successfully! – in the tropics, and is vouchsafed Friday's undying loyalty by a Defoe who dreams up the obsequiousness of a neolithic man, more suited to the psychology of the European urban wage-earner than to the free savage. Again, the exercise in wish-fulfilment succeeds on account of the tale's unerring archetypal interest. Crusoe's isolation – the pivot of desert island jokes – and the chilling effect of a footprint in the sand, guarantee Defoe's success.

Traditional West African stories are, frequently, centred around a deep anxiety. A man taking pity on an old woman offers to carry her on his back as far as his village. But when he reaches home the old woman refuses to get off and the poor man is doomed to carry her wherever he goes. This is in striking contrast to the European preference for happy endings, which, transplanted to the United States of America, became all but obligatory in films until the 1960s.

My godfather devoured novels as others read newspapers. He read, for the most part, American Westerns and detective novels, and had a partiality for the work of Dashiel Hammett. Convinced that his wisdom derived from these pulp-papered, limp-covered books, I would dip into one of them from time to time, only to be disappointed. I was not yet ready for such sustained reading. But I remember these abortive sorties into adult literature as extraordinary events.

Much later, when I began taking a serious interest in the genesis of storytelling, I learned of the entirely different approach to the art as practised by aboriginal Indians. The world of the Carib can only be explained (in stories) through a mythic rationale, inspired from archetypes, such as dismemberment. The dismembered body of a culture hero becomes a constellation, as often as not the Pleiades, whose appearance coincides with a plethora of fish in the rivers. (This archetypal preoccupation with dismemberment is encountered in industrial societies in the hallucinations afflicting very small children separated too early from their mothers, and is not an infrequent content in infant psychosis.)

Among the more technologically advanced Arawak and Warrau tribes, however, stories have progressed beyond this stage and record historical events, like the Carib penetration into South America, when the Orinoco delta was 'awash with the blood of Carib warriors'. And this development in the art and content of traditional tales taught me the invaluable lesson of a relativity implicit in aesthetics, which rests ultimately on the exigences of technological time.

CHAPTER 10

Legacy

A few months before moving from the tiny cottage in which we were living – I was then ten – my mother bought a piano. She had told my sisters and me that if on returning home Sophie reported to her that we had been good she would have a surprise delivered. Avis, Lynette and I sat on the front stairs watching the road and exchanging guesses as to what the surprise might be. I thought we were going to have a dog; Avis was certain it would be a visitor, perhaps from abroad; while Lynette, then little more than eight, could not imagine it would be anything other than sweets. We only ate sweets at Christmas time or when a rich visitor dropped in, and agreed that the most worthwhile of the three would be the sweets. After Avis pointed out that a visitor from abroad was likely to give us no less than six cents each, we all hoped for someone from America, perhaps Mrs Dolphin's sister, my mother's first cousin who had emigrated years before.

When the dray cart stopped in front of our house, a black piano secured to its top with ropes, and my mother went out to meet the two men standing next to the donkeys, we looked on, dumbfounded. Only rich people owned pianos. Would my mother be keeping the instrument for a friend until it was called for? The umbrella mender had repaired our umbrella only a few days ago; and soon we would be moving into the bigger house at the corner. If we were convinced of anything connected with our status it was that we were poor. Whenever my mother did business she proclaimed her widow-hood, thus attempting to claim some financial advantage. How then could we afford a piano? I found out later that my grandfather had left her a small legacy, to the chagrin of her stepmother.

A third man appeared to help the two dray cart men get the piano up the stairs, a manoeuvre they achieved by turning it on its side. As the enormous instrument tipped over, all its keys began to hang out, and I, fearing the worst, closed my eyes, certain that my mother had been duped by an unscrupulous dealer. I took refuge in one of the two bedrooms and only came out when I heard the miraculous sound of piano music in our house. My mother, sitting on a raised stool, played as though she had done so every day for years, and we watched her, open-mouthed with admiration, witnesses of yet further proof of her magical powers.

Two of the children next door came to look through the window, attracted by the sound of the piano, and probably as surprised as I was that its keys functioned. I went outside to join them.

'That's my mother,' I said, foolishly. After all, they could see clearly through the window.

She played for a very long time, immersed in that same deep satisfaction the instrument was to give me in years to come.

We exchanged houses with a Portuguese family living at the corner of Drysdale and Ketley Streets, who could no longer afford the rent of their larger cottage. The grandfather, who suffered from tuberculosis, continually spat through the window, and my mother wanted to have the house fumigated before moving into it. However, arrangements she had made to leave it vacant for a few days fell through and we were obliged to take over the dwelling as it was.

Obscured by a large, mature sapodilla tree (the chicle-producing tree from which chewing gum was originally made), our new cottage could barely be seen from Ketley Street. Around it grew lemon, soursop, almond, coconut and dunc trees. We only shared the vat which supplied our rainwater with the adjoining house. Above all, neighbours did not have to use our yard as a way of necessity to reach the street, since our cottage was separated from the neighbouring ones by fences.

My mother revelled in our move. I can remember no particular thing she said or did, but I know, by that infallible instinct peculiar to children, that she had changed, that she had shed a burden I associated with her from our time in Agricola. It is strange that, although she could not do without Grandfather while he lived, his death finally liberated her.

Our move acted on the family like a blood transfusion. In a larger house, with new neighbours, with our mother in better spirits, everything about us seemed to glow. I received news that I had been granted a scholarship to Central High School. Sophie, who had been sent away because she had been expecting a child, started visiting again. And suddenly more people began to drop in to see us.

The function of a dwelling place is much underestimated. The mature personality is the product of a number of formative influences, including house and landscape. When I think of my neighbours they seem, in some peculiar way, to represent their houses, as dogs resemble their owners. Of course this view is highly subjective, since we connect people with their houses anyway. But I am certain there is more than a modicum of truth in it. I cannot imagine Mrs Bourne – a new next-door neighbour built like a Japanese Sumo wrestler – emerging from a tiny range yard room; nor the sea captain's thirty-two-year-old daughter living in the house on the eastern side of ours, in anything but a dimly lit cottage, where she seemed to be confined. There are loquacious dwellings and reticent dwellings, sick houses and houses of rude health; there are houses of temporary occupation and houses whose inhabitants see off generations of occupants to their long home. There are expansive cottages and cantankerous ones, cottages on high pillars with long-legged owners. A prescription against a violent nature should be a home built on a generous ground plan. Are we not less in control of our fates than philosophers would have us believe? The Guyanese murderer almost invariably inhabits accommodation of meagre proportions, and only once have I heard of a murderer from a two-storey house.

Mr Bourne, husband of the Sumo wrestler, was a proud man of about fifty. An employer would describe him as having a chip on his shoulder, because he did not possess that all but indispensable qualification for wage-earning, namely compliance. All his stories about jobs he had had spoke of humiliations endured at the hands of superiors. One departmental head had insisted on calling him 'boy', he once told me. His objections ignored, he gave in his notice, to the annoyance of his father, who reminded him that they had to eat.

I do not think I have met many people with Mr Bourne's sense of excellence. Having been dismissed from several jobs he set up on his own as a maker of fine guava jam, and within a few years he presided over a thriving export business. However, the very success of his undertaking caused the price of guavas to rise, to the point where his excessively high overheads made the business unprofitable. He then turned to joinery, which he practised for many years, and could reel off a list of houses where his pieces of furniture lived.

'I guarantee they will last a hundred years,' he boasted.

Nothing pleased him more than to describe the care with which he had applied layer upon layer of beeswax to a table in order to seal the wood and impart to it an admirable sheen. Being a poor businessman he preferred to accept commissions from other joiners, who did not pay him enough to live on.

When we moved into our new home Mr Bourne was practising as a lampshade-maker, competing successfully with the importers of lampshades sold in the big stores. His beautifully made constructions ensured that he never went short of work. I suspect that he survived as a lampshade-maker, in spite of his poor business sense, because his wife dealt with the customers, negotiating prices and making excuses for him when he failed to meet a delivery date. She was an utterly charming lady.

The Bournes had one child, an attractive daughter of about twenty-one, as distinguished as her mother. I once fell in love with her for a week or so, after I escorted her to some home she was visiting on a foul, windy night. My voice kept failing whenever she addressed me and several times I had difficulty in mastering my bicycle, bumping into hers and causing her to swerve dangerously into the middle of the road, accidents which drew forth an 'Ooh!' or an 'Ah Roy, be careful!' Which only made matters worse. I blamed the wind.

Finally we arrived at the mansion in High Street and I waited dutifully for her in the drawing room while she disappeared into the back of the house with the lady she had come to see. On the way home she suggested that I go on ahead of her, no doubt aware of the difficulty I had in controlling myself. The season of storms, during which I hoped to be called upon to perform further escorting duties, was brief. And so was my passion. After that I could see her leaving the house without experiencing that feeling of collapse in the pit of my stomach.

The other next-door neighbour – the sea captain's daughter – was a solitary, secretive lady, who was under her father's thumb, I learned. A curious expression, it strikes me. Why not 'foot' or 'hand'? Anyhow, her father, an even more secretive man than his daughter, had an incestuous relationship with her, according to one of many paid servants my mother employed after Sophie went away. I once caught a brief glimpse of him on one of his stays in port. He was furtive and excessively ugly, the ideal 'mysterious neighbour'. I could not imagine what power a gentleman of his appearance could exercise over a lady, in or out of uniform. But then stories of incest are usually marked by an irrational stamp, as if their very extravagance provides their unwonted rationale. The relationship of father and daughter appeared all the more odd as she was an attractive woman. But, according to my informer, while he lived she did not look at another man, in spite of his frequent, protracted absences. His schooner worked the islands, from Trinidad to Jamaica, transporting ground provisions and other perishable goods the large steam and diesel boats, with their long sojourns in harbour, could not carry profitably. All this I learned from my informer, whose remarkable propensity to gossip was as appealing as the stories she recounted. I got to know more about the sea captain and his daughter, to whom I never spoke, than about the Bournes, whose house I frequently visited.

Next to the Bournes lived Dr Bailey and his family. His surgery was unusual in that a pharmacist worked for him, so that only occasionally did the nearest drugstore benefit from one of his prescriptions. Like all physicians Dr Bailey lived in a large mansion. My mother told me that my father used to play the flute in the doctor's amateur orchestra. Nevertheless, what struck me about the medical man's house was not his orchestra – long defunct – nor his pharmacist, but his garden, the only one worthy of the name in Charlestown, a district distinguished more by its tenement yards than for its opulence. Walking past his house at four or five in the morning, one became acquainted with the seductive scent of roses and other flowers he cultivated, though not for wreaths, as was the case with many other garden houses.

I have described Ketley and Drysdale Streets here and elsewhere at some length because we were to live in the area for fifteen years before I went abroad. I remember the district, not with the romantic attachment of Queenstown, nor with the vivid recollection of wild happenings at Camp and Regent Streets, but with that calm recall of a portion of one's life when one has already been overtaken by a fuller consciousness.

Sophie came visiting from time to time, always with a present for me, practising a favouritism of which my mother evidently approved. I repaid her with visits to her range yard home in Lombard Street. Once my mother made her a present of our dog in response to her complaint that she was afraid of being

alone at night when her young man went to work in the
Georgetown foundry. When the bitch gave birth she brought
the newborn puppies one by one to our house and deposited
them by the pillar where she used to sleep. The next morning
we found the five animals dead, side by side. We never
discovered how their mother managed to get through the
closed gate or the paling fence. Moreover, no one understood
why, having brought the puppies to her former home, she did
not stay herself.

Whenever I went to Sophie's room I found her alone. I did
not ask about the child she was supposed to have had. She
frequently spoke of her young man's temper, which she feared
might cause him to lose his job. Were there many Mr Bournes
about? Was this impatience with wage-earning a Guyanese
characteristic? The generations born in the wake of dramatic
change always see the new state of affairs as normal. It is worth
recalling that in ancient Rome working for a wage was
considered no better than slavery. Most Roman males aimed
to carry on a business, to have their own bakery or to be
wheelwrights or practise one of the numerous trades that
flourished in an expanding empire. Nearly all the work for
'other people' was done by slaves. If in the advanced
technological societies wage-earning is the ineluctable rule,
we should not forget what we have given up in personal
dignity, a loss that has had a profound effect on the psyche.
Once we appreciate the significance of our position it will be
easier to resist yielding to a misplaced contempt for primitive
people who, when they have not been tampered with, retain
an enviable dignity and freedom.

Sophie's young man lost his job at Sproston's foundry a
year or so later, forcing her back on her own resources once
more.

But until that event I thought that, all in all, Sophie was
happier than she had ever been. Enjoying the sort of freedom
she could only have dreamt of while living with us, she went
out when she was disposed to, handled her money as she saw
fit, cleaned her own place, washed her own clothes and

received her numerous relations. At this time she smiled as she never had in our house.

Yet Sophie claimed that her education at my mother's side had been indispensable to her later success in life. Where is the truth? I could have pointed out to her much later – more than forty years later – that the influences of our household had not been entirely beneficial. My mother's tendency to isolation, for instance, had become for Sophie an ideal, reflected in her suspicion of 'mixing', a standpoint most Guyanese working people would find abhorrent. Yet I did come across the same attitude when Sophie herself took me to see a family in Mocha, the village of her birth. We found the daughter, a young woman of about nineteen, scrubbing the floor, and her brother reading in a corner of the room in which we were received. Their mother, a small woman with an authoritative air, proclaimed her aspirations for her children, especially the daughter: 'I don't allow her to mix!' She was determined that her children would do better, materially, than she had. Her son was destined for the ministry, while the daughter would become a pupil teacher. The two exceptionally obedient children spoke only when spoken to, but with a strangely unconstrained manner that belied their mother's authoritarianism. I have no doubt that the young man did become a parson and his sister a teacher.

Long after I went away I came to understand the influence Sophie had had on us, certainly on me. In our home, as a servant who only used the back door, she followed the prescriptions of behaviour suitable to her condition as my mother saw it. Yet behind the ostensible child–nanny relationship there had developed bonds of immense durability between herself and us children, and I often think that Sonny might have benefited from an attachment unsullied by the ambivalence of his Queenstown experience.

My mother disapproved of my visits to Sophie and continually asked if she was pregnant. (She did not mind the former servant's visits to our house.) In the seventies and eighties, during my frequent holidays in Guyana, she still wondered why I kept going to see Sophie in Peter's Hall, a village where she owned her own house. And on the eve of my departure from the country Sophie would arrive early in the morning laden with presents and, not forgetting her training, would always use the back stairs. She was better off than my mother, spoke with the same assurance as she did, but still saw fit to perpetuate their absurd relativity of status.

During those hours in Sophie's room when I was barely eleven, I learned much about my family, the snobbery, my father's womanizing, my relatives whose view of my mother and her dead sister's affected superiority caused much family friction. Nothing is ever what it seems, and what Sophie revealed made me wonder whether I knew my family and background at all. I got the impression that her disclosures were not made out of malice; rather, she was trying to treat me as a grown-up, in the same way that my mother began doing when I reached the age of fourteen or fifteen. I was flattered but a little confused, being unable to play the part expected of me. Besides, should I pretend to be shocked at what I heard? Truth to tell, I was supremely indifferent to what I learned regarding my dead father, a remote, romantic figure, represented visually by a single faded photograph. His non-existence must have left its mark on my character, albeit in a negative way, for since the age of eighteen or thereabouts I have never been able to tolerate an excessive show of authority.

The truth about my family was harder to take. The confirmation of my mother's excessive snobbishness informed me of a flaw about which I would rather have remained in ignorance. My dream of the perfect mother suffered, not for the first time, a severe setback. For all that, these wounds healed so swiftly and well that the dream remained intact. Sophie must have noticed my disapproval of her gratuitous revelations, for they ceased abruptly and I felt able to go and see her without imagining that I was betraying my mother.

Apart from Sophie I began looking up grown-up acquaintances, mainly those in the habit of giving me money. In fact Sophie was the only one I visited without expecting anything.

Receiving no pocket money from my mother I cultivated older people, almost all women, having soon discovered that men were unusually tight-fisted. I also came to the conclusion that men did not care much for me – with the exception of my godfather, who occasionally would give me a coin. But Godmother proved to be my surest source of money when I wanted to see a film, and like Mrs Cambridge and Mrs Bourne next door, made many of my Saturday afternoons worthwhile.

These women thought highly of me, and through them I discovered a quality in myself appealing to some. I also learned that it had the effect of disturbing others. On more than one occasion I was taken aback by an unusually violent reaction to my behaviour, all the more unpleasant because I could not explain it. Now, older and somewhat wiser, I can see that that had been precisely my mother's experience with people.

At the age of eleven I began going to the cinema, almost always sitting in the bug-infested pit, which cost only four cents for children. I had made friends with G., an East Indian pupil who had attended the scholarship class at Government School with me. There, he used to sit at the back. But at Central High School, where the atmosphere was more relaxed, he sat in front and immediately made an impression on the maths teacher. Our acquaintanceship strengthened into friendship and I took to going to his home in Lombard Street, in which his mother ran a cook shop. Through a half-concealed gate you entered a long passageway which led onto an open space where large iron pots were perpetually on the boil under a narrow roof.

G.'s mother, tall and strapping, hardly ever seemed to lose her temper, so that I never hesitated to go and ask if G. was in. Sometimes, if he was out, I would wait for him, sitting on one of the long benches ranged against tables placed side by side. The customers, many of them East Indian beggars, belonged to the abjectly poor of Georgetown, and came to G.'s mother's eating place because of the exceptionally low price of the food. For a large meal of fish and rice they paid six cents, and were able to hang around and talk long after they had eaten. I used to sit in a corner taking in the unusual scene with an avidity that suggested an interest much deeper than mere curiosity, perhaps compounded of a fascination with the Indian community's life style and G.'s mother's work as both cook and waitress.

Contrasting with the moving picture of the beggars' deprivation was the elegant, motionless figure of G.'s great-grandfather, a bearded old man forever bent over a Sanskrit text, who took up an unusually large space in the centre of the dining hall and drew absently on his houka from time to time.

G.'s father, a good three inches shorter than his wife, worked at the Pedasco cycle shop. It appears he had little, if anything, to do with the running of the cook shop. Yet, when G. borrowed a ping pong table and invited his friends round to play, I was certain that *he* objected to the intrusion, rather than his wife. Time and again the celluloid ball would fall into one of the pots; time and again Mrs N. would fish it out without a word of protest, when Mr N. would glare at us, not bothering to conceal his annoyance.

In G.'s yard we developed our skill at table tennis, just as we were to do in my yard, for cricket. And from this time, while in the first form at secondary school, we became inseparable, sharing money – his money – and secrets. He was worldly wise; I was not.

Against all expectations my mother liked G., and he, it seems, admired her more than he did the mothers of other acquaintances. It is possible that their mutual respect helped to cement our friendship more than anything else. I felt that I was growing away from her. The very fact of attending secondary school provided me with yet undiscovered resources with which I could struggle against a dangerous feminine influence that threatened to become all-embracing. What I had not noticed as little as a year ago became painfully apparent now; and on being told that I had to attend shorthand and typing classes I refused, only relenting when promised my own bicycle in a year's time. I, the only male student, endured these

Wednesday classes, but took care not to mention to G. what I did. As it turned out typing proved an invaluable accomplishment in later life.

G. paid for our visits to the cinema and it did not take me long to realize that business was more lucrative than the professions. Most professional people were creoles – apart from the local and expatriate whites, who held down the best-paid jobs – while most business people were East Indians, Portuguese and Chinese. G.'s mother's cook shop did well enough to provide him with pocket money to go with me to the pictures once a week *and* eat a sumptuous meal of pepper pot and rice in a low Regent Street dive. On those occasions we took the precaution of hiding our ties, the only evidence as to the school we attended.

These meals gave G. a particular pleasure, since they contained pork, a forbidden meat among Hindus. Neither G. nor his parents were practising Hindus; nonetheless the taboo was strong enough to be respected in their home. Like mice on a foray beyond their burrows we always watched the door in case one of our teachers should take it into his head to do what we were doing. But in time we became careless, sat where we liked and neglected to keep an eye on the entrance. Once, as we were both laughing out loud at some scene from a film we had just seen, I felt a hand grip my neck and at the same time noticed the swift change in G.'s expression. He got up slowly while the vice-like grip swivelled my head round and upwards to face my tormentor, the young geography teacher, regarded by the pupils as the most incompetent master on the staff.

'So! This is where you do your homework!'

He took us both by the ears and brought our heads together. Someone at a table opposite our own laughed out loud, mocking us.

I do not remember the outcome of this incident. G., far more resourceful and enterprising than I, must have promised to perform some service for the teacher. The fact is that he ignored us from then on. It is also possible that our knowledge of his secret visits to the lower depths guaranteed us immunity from his attentions.

Few school children went to the cinema as often as G. and I. We enjoyed fights on the screen as we enjoyed real fights in the pit. If we could have afforded to go into the dress circle, twice as expensive, I doubt whether we would have exchanged it for the pre-show entertainment amongst notorious pit-squabblers. When I began going to the pictures on my own G. and I would recommend to each other films we had seen and liked. I judged the worth of a movie by the number of fights it featured, a minimum of three being essential to arouse my interest. Needless to say I went to see all of Errol Flynn's films, for they consistently pandered to the taste of youngsters like myself. G.'s tastes were wider. He liked musicals as well and could not understand why I avoided them, even when he offered to pay for me.

At the age of sixteen, when I began to work, the heroic movie lost its magic for me. In fact, I gradually developed a resistance to the Hollywood production line, yet went to the pictures as frequently as before; for when I liked a film I took it into my head to see it several times. *The Picture of Dorian Gray* was one of these. The androgynous hero who never grew old, his endless seductions, the portrait in the attic, the old man playing Chopin's D-minor prelude in an opium den, the elegant, if mannered language, the London mists, all contrived an atmosphere so potent I became convinced that my destiny did not differ from Dorian Gray's. His features were angular, like mine; he played the piano, as I did; his subconscious life was potent, as mine was. Therefore my destiny was similar to his. I had never shared my fantasies with anyone. Dorian Gray's life *was* a fantasy, a descent into a sensual, extravagant hell, in which vice became pleasure, through an arbitrary, but not for me, implausible metamorphosis.

I found secondary school as boring as primary. Its organization seemed wrong, 'upside down', as I thought. Even my preference for certain subjects was 'upside down'. I liked English, in which I often got very poor marks, and trigonometry, where my performance was so deplorable the mathematics master did not even bother to mark my work. A line across each page of my exercise book – without so much as a comment – was apparently all I deserved. In one exam I got *three* per cent in trigonometry, accompanied by the sarcastic comment, 'You have excelled yourself!' Alas!, I was beyond suffering. At least G. regularly received eighty to ninety per cent.

Some children suffer far less than parents and teachers imagine. Or perhaps humiliation leaves tiny, invisible scars whose effects are not verifiable. I navigated through the perils of geography, history, mathematics and a variety of other subjects, armed with the considerable weapon of indifference. If school seemed a hell for some and 'best days' for others, it reminded me of a fog, an impalpable impediment one had to overcome in order to reach the luminous afternoons where cricket beckoned.

But from time to time a comic or untoward event relieved the boredom of school. 'Difficult' boys in the fourth and fifth years were caned. One large boy, sent to the headmaster to be punished, did not appreciate the unusual distinction and objected to being struck 'like a cow'. The headmaster, ignoring the offender's plea to be dealt with in a manner more appropriate to his age and size, took the cane from the cupboard and ordered the pupil to bend down. Now, Mr Luck, the headmaster, measured about five feet two inches, no more than his wife. The protesting boy was all of six feet.

'Bend down, I say!' ordered Mr Luck.

'Make me, ne,' said the giant boy.

According to him, at that moment a teacher knocked on the door and offered Mr Luck help.

'Help!' he shouted. 'To handle a boy! I don't need help!' he protested angrily. Thereupon the teacher left the room.

'Bend down, I say!'

In answer the boy lifted up Mr Luck and thrust him bodily through the window, where he hung by his armpits.

'Help!' he shouted, kicking desperately.

A passer-by jumped off his bicycle and ran upstairs, but by the time he burst into Mr Luck's office the teacher who had offered help had come in and persuaded the boy to drag the hapless man inside.

Mr Luck was not an unpopular head teacher; nevertheless, the delinquent lad became a hero with the pupils, and when he was expelled we all felt we had suffered a loss.

G. told me the following story which I believed only too willingly because, at the time, I had it in for the boy concerned. In the fourth year, most of the boys were secretly – or openly – in love with a very attractive girl. X. was so smitten he used to follow her about, at a discreet distance. One night, after he dreamt that he went roller-skating with her, G. urged him to declare himself, saying that the dream was a good omen. X., flushed with G.'s advice, came to school early the next morning so as to catch the beloved as soon as she arrived. G., knowing full well that X. did not have the slightest chance of success with her, came to school early as well, determined to witness his rebuff. If G. was generous, he was also brutal in the way he schemed up practical jokes. Poor X.'s humiliation at the girl's hands put him off roller-skating for good.

Another time G. sent X. up a ginip tree in a yard we had never raided until then, while he and I stayed below to catch any fruit he might throw down. But no sooner had X. got half-way up the tree than a dog came bounding out from the back yard. G. and I fled through the open gate and watched X. clamber up the tree faster than we thought possible. We laughed noiselessly, but took care to show a doleful expression when X. reached a safe branch and turned to look at us.

'What am I going to do?' he pleaded.

'I dunno,' G. shouted back from the road. 'That vicious dog won't go away.'

'Why not crawl to the end of the branch and jump down on

the road?' I asked, knowing full well that the branch would
break and he would be delivered to the slavering brute.

The owner of the house came home about two hours later
and released X. from his misery, after warning him that the
next time he would let him remain on his perch all night.

On the way to X.'s home we decided to tell his mother a
concocted story, to explain why he was late, for we knew her
as a forbidding woman, the disciplinarian in her home.

'You go up first,' X. urged us. 'She'll hit me if I go first.'

'No, man,' G. objected. 'Everybody knows about your
mother's biceps.'

We waited at the foot of the stairs, the agreement being that
G. should tell the story as soon as X.'s mother appeared. After
a timid knock on the door things happened so swiftly G. had
no time to say a word. A massive arm shot out of the open
door and dragged X. inside, and at his screams we kept
repeating to each other, 'Pai! Pai! Take that and that and that!'
mimicking the mother's masculine voice. Neither G. nor I had
experienced such treatment at home and our opinion of X. as
an acquaintance who did not dare strike out for his independence was confirmed by that drubbing at sundown. Poor X.,
one of six children, envied us our freedom to come and go as
we pleased. It is obvious, from this distance of time, that that
provided one of his excuses for disliking me. On the other
hand he seemed incapable of bearing resentment towards G.,
who continually thought up ways to embarrass him and only
offered the most transparent excuses for his conduct.

CHAPTER 11

A Street of Pawnbrokers

At the age of about twelve certain changes became noticeable to me. The repairer of iron pots no longer walked the streets shouting his incomprehensible invitation to repair. People now bought the new aluminium ware, cheap, easy to wash, light and no less durable. The disappearance of the umbrella mender a few years later appears to have been the result of a larger volume of money circulating during the war, which, in turn, increased the demand for new umbrellas.

My mother would have been lost without her umbrella, goloshes and bicycle. During the rainy season rain would fall for hours on end, and I used to worry so much about the loss of these possessions, so indispensable to her connection with work and the outside world, that they became for me guarantors of her security. Goloshes, like iron pots, disappeared too — but for no apparent reason — contributing to that imperceptible sense of a changing world which overtakes us long after the actual loss.

No kitchen was without its mortar and pestle, their chief, sometimes only, use being to make foo-foo from plantains, which until 1900 was the staple food of Guyanese until supplanted by rice.

In the late thirties, the period of conservation, you could point to absurdities in dress which would not have escaped the attention of visitors to the country. People wore felt hats, closed shoes, jackets and even waistcoats. An uncle of mine attended his daughter's marriage dressed in a cut-away coat! We aped our masters, abetted, no doubt, by the economic machine which benefited from the importation of these goods.

The most dramatic changes came later, with the European war. Currency reserves piled up from British purchases – of aluminium, for example, which increased Canadian demand for Guyanese bauxite from the then British Guiana. Also, imports were reduced to a minimum, with a consequent beneficial effect on our balance of payments.

By 1943 the Government could grant civil servants large pay rises. Teachers did not get theirs until 1945.

In 1939, at the outbreak of war, I was thirteen and in the second year of secondary school. War scares had actually begun in 1937, while I was still at primary school. A rumour that German planes had dropped poisoned sweets brought many mothers to Government School to see if their children were still alive. They congregated outside the school and some demanded to see their offspring. One mother, the spitting image of her son, came to his class brandishing an umbrella that had lost its shape. The boy went out to her and in her relief that he had eaten no German sweets, she smothered him in kisses. The poor youngster never lived down the incident. Why the Germans would want to bomb the country and how they would manage to cross Africa and the Atlantic never occurred to the parents.

As we found out during the war our position as a colony caused many to harbour a deep resentment at being automatically embroiled in a conflict that did not concern them. They pointed to Dr Giglioli, an expert on malaria, to Dr Remitti – his valuable work at the Georgetown hospital was widely admired – and to a German engineer sent to maintain very expensive machinery bought by a businessman, whose internment as enemy aliens was a disaster for the enterprises for which they worked. Many people backed the Germans in secret, apparently willing to exchange one yoke for another.

On a personal level it is interesting to note the effect imprisonment had on the three men. Dr Giglioli took advantage of his enforced leisure to collect plants and pursue his interest in research, while the German made several fruitless attempts to escape. Dr Remitti, an Italian like Dr Giglioli, committed suicide, unable to tolerate his isolation on the edge of the forest.

If the war conjured up a drama of international proportions, Sonny's hospitalization was, for our family, considerably more significant. He had been kept in the pauper ward of the General Hospital, where I took him oranges and other fruit. In the beginning I was afraid of him, for he would grab my wrist and question me, about school especially, his great worry being the neglect of his education. After a few visits he began treating me more kindly and I would sit on the edge of his bed and hold long conversations with him on cricket, about which he was very knowledgeable. I then looked forward to seeing him, flattered that at last he dealt with me as an equal. Then one afternoon when I arrived, anxious to put down the fruit which had burst its paper bag, I saw that his bed was empty. A nurse promptly ordered me to follow her into the yard where there were rooms with bars visitors stared at as they went by.

Sonny was standing in one of the rooms, watching a man distributing enamel plates of food to the inmates, exactly as in a zoo. He grabbed his, then promptly threw the contents on the floor.

'Sonny,' I said, approaching the barred cage as closely as I dared. But he took no notice of me whatsoever. Retiring to a corner he sat down on the bare floor with a blank expression.

Reporting to my mother what had happened she repaid me with a resounding slap. I guessed at her shame and did not protest.

Soon afterwards Sonny came back home and immediately took up his studies again, to my mother's alarm, for she attributed his breakdown to too much reading. I have often wondered whether she appreciated the effect of his being sent away to live with relations. Be that as it may, Sonny's studies had thrown him into a state of depression and she never ceased repenting of it.

My mother insisted that my brother take his meals with us, in spite of his odd behaviour. He deliberately overturned cups and glasses, so that Avis, Lynette and I hated meal times. I do not remember how long he stayed with us, but one afternoon, on returning home from school, I learned that he had been taken away to the New Amsterdam mental hospital. I was not to see him again for several years.

'Sonny is the sacrificial lamb to the family's well-being,' my godfather said, in an effort to console me.

The tale of children being shunted from one home to the other is common among the working class and does not seem to produce such disastrous results. I am certain that every psychological 'truth' is relative to class and culture. A psychiatrist would no doubt emphasize Sonny's weak personality, his family experience and the de Weever vulnerability. How would he or she explain the fact that depression appears to be unknown in Africa? Psychologists from the former colonies are becoming increasingly aware of the limitations of European psychiatric practice, and transcultural psychiatry, still in its infancy, has thrown up important material, which should serve as the basis for a more comprehensive view of confusional states and mental illness in general.

In my opinion it is harmful to split off the study of psychiatry and its practice from that of anthropology. Women, who for nearly all of human history were never separated from their mothers – the men to whom they were attached came to live in their clan – now, for the most part, live apart from their own parents. This changeover, recent in the historical time scale, must have an incalculable effect on their behaviour. A study of anthropology can only illuminate much that we try to explain in psychological terms.

Perhaps the great truth is the elusiveness of truth. It is not for nothing that the 'search', in the guise of a journey, is an archetype.

I have good reason to be afraid of hospitalization and cannot abide the scent of oranges. Life goes on, bearing the flotsam of our experience as great rivers carry away detritus.

Gradually Sonny was forgotten by us children. I know my mother thought of him often; but in a couple of years she began to laugh again and we were glad because we could not bear to see her unhappy.

A great-uncle, Thomas Durant, his wife and two teenaged daughters came to live with us. My mother never explained why. My uncle was stone deaf, which did not prevent him and his wife from quarrelling. She, frustrated by his lack of reaction to her words, became wild with anger whenever he said, 'Woman, don't shout!'

She would then lift her bosom with both hands, always a preliminary to another volley of words.

As soon as he came home she would launch into an account of the day's events, articulating her words carefully, but to little purpose, since his lip-reading was almost as defective as his hearing. They could not do without each other and it is possible that his deafness contributed to the overall harmony of the relationship.

Uncle Tom seemed to prefer his younger daughter to the elder, a charming, considerate young woman, who, however much she tried, was incapable of pleasing him. And while at times Aunt Lena, his wife, appeared to share his preference, at other times his open favouritism irritated her and she did what she could to make up to Elaine for her father's unpardonable conduct.

Aunt Lena believed that no one had ever been wrongfully imprisoned, because God would not have it. Once, when my mother made an untoward remark about her unusual opinions, she took offence and started stacking her furniture, vowing she would move out the next day. During the years the family lived with us we witnessed this scene so often it came to lose the meaning it was intended to convey. Yet the passion Uncle Tom's lady brought to the task of stacking her chairs and the violence with which she raised her bosom while contemplating the pile carried such conviction, any visitor to the house would have feared for a permanent rift between our family and hers. In fact the two families lived together for more than ten years, until Uncle Tom died and the others emigrated to the United States. In spite of her strangeness, I remember Aunt Lena as someone whose life was dedicated to the service of others.

My grandfather's legacy did not sustain us for long and once more my mother's debts began to pile up. When I was about fourteen she sent me to one of the numerous pawnshops on Lombard Street to hock her only piece of jewellery, her wedding ring. At month end, on receiving her salary, she gave me the money to redeem the symbol of her attachment to my dead father. And so it was to be every month. On or around the fifteenth I would take the ring to one of the three pawnshops – usually the one at the corner of Lombard and Hadfield Streets – sign a form which allowed me to regain possession on repayment of the loan plus a few cents, and take away five dollars. I became familiar with the interior of these loan shops, the bicycles suspended from the ceiling as if by magic and the display of East Indian jewellery in plate-glass cases. Every object bore its numbered label, like those ciphers identifying prisoners, many of whom would one day be released.

I enjoyed my furtive trips to these emporia of the indebted, largely because they took me into the adult world of responsibility and loss. How many necklaces, foot-rings, earrings, bangles, bracelets, mute historians of women's decline! It was as though the shops divided themselves into two sections, one devoted to men's fortunes and the other to women's. The men, represented by their bicycles, were left suspended, while the women went on display, laid out with studied care.

Portuguese businessmen owned all the pawnshops in Lombard Street. The shops were to be found nowhere else in Georgetown. The Portuguese, a less dynamic community than the East Indians, nevertheless managed to secure a monopoly or near monopoly in certain activities, like baking. Having come over from Madeira as indentured labourers, a few families succeeded in breaking out of the contract trap and made good. Because they first came to the country as labourers they were not considered to be white and therefore enjoyed none of the benefits reserved for Europeans. The Georgetown Cricket Club and the Georgetown Club, for instance, did not accept them as members. There was one exception to this practice, however, which allowed a wealthy Portuguese regarded as being 'distinguished' to penetrate these exclusive circles.

Popular prejudice supported the low status of Portuguese, characterizing them as 'ignorant', a word that is more potent in Caribbean English than in the American or English variant and can mean 'stupid' or even 'unable to spell'. And few things haunted ambitious Portuguese more than their inability to put on their aitches in the right place. In Latin languages the h is usually redundant. In French it is occasionally used, as in the theatre, where (h)aie (hedge) is sometimes pronounced as *h*aie, in order to give the word body. In Spanish (as indeed in French) there is a guttural which is not far removed from h. It is therefore easier for a French or Spanish national to cope with the difficult sound than it is for a Portuguese. Many Portuguese compounded the problem by attempting to add the aitch sound to words beginning with a vowel, so that one frequently heard 'horange' and 'hegg'.

Creoles generally regarded the Portuguese as a gentle, easy-going people, and the case of Mr Brazõa and Mr Hack, an East Indian, was often cited as an illustration of this view. Mr Brazõa sold his land with its mansion, fruit trees and large aviary to Mr Hack, who within a few months had the trees cut down and the aviary dismantled. The following year two houses were erected where the fruit trees had stood, and only a year after that a smaller house joined the two recently built ones. Mr Hack was the businessman, Mr Brazõa the aesthete.

CHAPTER 12

The House in South Road

If in the beginning I felt I belonged to a group larger than the immediate family, later, with my grandfather's death, came the realization that my boundaries extended no further than my own family. When I was about fourteen the apprehension of myself as separate from the family surprised and unsettled me at the same time. Of course this awareness represented the culmination of a process that had been going on for years; since I started attending secondary school, it seems. I began making decisions for myself; my pride was easily wounded; and above all, objects no longer possessed their once great powers. For G. and myself the emergence of this new personality brought no overt conflicts. In fact it surprised us to find that a number of our acquaintances did not have a smooth transition to this unusual state, poised somewhere between childhood and adulthood. One boy's father demanded that he come home every evening by eight o'clock, and for this alone he conceived a hatred which concealed a mortal dread for the man to whom he had felt attached until then.

But most conflicts seemed to arise from a fanatical desire on the part of the child to demonstrate what neither parent had challenged in the first place. Some found it necessary to promote this ritual revolt at all costs, and a single ill-chosen word by a parent, or a meaningless gesture, sufficed to arouse bad feeling in a stable family.

On the whole, most families accommodated themselves to the sudden, subtle shifts in relationships brought about by the irrational behaviour of their maturing offspring. I have often wondered how I would have fared with a strict father. I never forgot the policeman who nearly made me foul my pants and forced me to attend Saturday morning school for months afterwards.

I was developing a growing admiration for my god-mother's husband, due in part to his generosity on the rare occasions he was in work, but clearly, as well, to my search for a substitute father. He designed houses, and like most architects of the time had never been formally trained. Whenever I went to see my godmother the likelihood was that he had either just sat an examination or failed one. His optimism must have come from his birth sign, she thought, for nothing, in her experience, suggested that he was capable of passing an examination. On being informed that he had to sit one on such and such a day she would look at him blankly or pretend she had not heard. At first I could not understand why someone, normally kind, should be indifferent to her husband's morale at so crucial a time. But I came to realize that, in fact, he got off lightly. After all she had been successful enough to keep him in style.

The fact is, my picture of Godfather had been built up on the basis of his view of himself. Stories of his excellent designs, trips to the interior in which he had distinguished himself by his courage, pictures of him with his right foot placed on the head of an anaemic jaguar, narrow escapes from herds of peccary, had shown him to be hero and intellectual, exactly what I, in my heart of hearts, already strove to become. If I did not possess the staying power to be an intellectual, Godfather had problems in this connection as well, I came to learn.

Godmother owned many houses. I have no idea how many. Creoles were usually reticent about their wealth and a modest cottage might be the home of a substantial property owner. Indeed, many people felt they courted disaster by acknowledging any kind of good fortune. Godmother com-plained to my mother that Roy – my godfather and I shared the same name – who was responsible for collecting the rent from her houses on a Sunday, never brought home the money equivalent to what was due. Some tenant or tenants did not pay, a claim proved to be false on many occasions; he had dropped a dollar note while putting the money in his pocket; or he simply had no idea where the missing coins or notes could have gone.

Godmother had defied her family to marry him. Her parents, aunts and uncles had asked to see him, at the instigation of an uncle, who thought the young man should be given the opportunity of proving himself. But the meeting only served to confirm Ruby's parents' distaste for an unemployed future son-in-law who sported two prominent gold teeth and whose numerous inventions interested no one except himself. One aunt insisted he was up to no good. Why else did he keep inventing things? Why was he so restless?

The assembled women declared one thing to be in his favour: he did not drink. But the uncles' reaction to this abstemiousness proved to be so unfavourable, my godfather regretted he had not admitted to being a tippler, which he most definitely was.

My godmother's account of this confrontation of generations was so amusing I would frequently ask her to go over it when she appeared to be out of sorts. She had borrowed an ill-fitting suit for the occasion from one of her brothers, with braces too short for Godfather's trunk. The gap between his trousers and feet was so wide it could only be an omen for disaster. During the interrogation Godmother's mother thought she recognized the suit. 'My son's got a suit just like that!' she exclaimed. 'How could it be, Fanny?' her husband asked. 'It can't be in two places at the same time.'

Since good manners required that a lady should not be present while her intended attempted to justify his application to become a member of her family, Godmother listened to the interview from the other side of the partition. Judging that any enquiry into the ownership of the suit would have been fatal for her and Godfather, she let out a piercing scream, which brought her mother and three aunts rushing into the bedroom.

'There!' she said, pointing to a spot under the bed. 'A centipede! It walked across the floor while I was reading.'

The women shifted the bed to the other side of the room, but found nothing under it. Godmother's father came to help and he, in turn, called the two uncles, to no avail.

By the time they called off the search the suitor's garb had been forgotten and Godfather received the advice from his future father-in-law to come back and see him when he had found a decent job. But he and Godmother went ahead and got married in the time it took to publish the banns in the local Methodist church.

The story is all but unique in the twenties, when few educated women would have dared face the opprobrium consequent on defying their parents.

My mother disliked Godfather, whom she regarded as a poor example of manhood. But her lectures on his unsuitability as a model made little impression on me. His inventions, his dead tigers*, his capacity to discover a way out of a scrape were all eloquent of a magnetic personality.

Occasionally I did find him working at his desk with its sloping top, guiding his slide rule expertly across his mysterious plans. Once or twice I accompanied him on a visit to a client, either to collect money owing him or to submit the designs of a commission for which he must have charged a fraction of a better known architect's fee.

Immature, impressionable, I was completely taken in by my godfather. Besides, he was a genuinely warm man. That is why his wife loved him and could forgive him endlessly.

One day I went to their house and the door was opened by Godmother. I saw a pregnant girl sitting on a chair. About sixteen years old, she wore full bridal dress and held a small bouquet of artificial flowers in her hand. My godmother introduced her to me as a niece, but the girl would not look me in the eye. Godmother went inside to busy herself with some sort of preparations she must have been engaged in before I arrived, leaving me alone with the bride. *She* would not address me, I knew. *I* could not address her, for anything I said would be interpreted as an impertinence. She sat with bowed

*The Guyanese word for 'jaguars'

head, both hands grasping her bouquet, while I cast sidelong glances at her, trying to call to mind whether I had ever seen a pregnant bride before. Unbelievably naive, I did not imagine that a pregnant woman would ever be permitted to enter a church. Then I wondered whether my wife would be in that condition when we married. She would most certainly not be as surly as the girl before me. I caught her looking at me with such hatred in her eyes I had no doubt I was the object of an unspoken accusation. Of silence, maybe. I thought of something to say.

'You've just got married?'

In answer she directed towards me a long, hostile look, defying me to speak again. When the chauffeur of a hired car came to the door the bride leapt up and went inside, and almost immediately she and Godmother came out, each carrying a suitcase. I had told the chauffeur to wait on the landing.

'Say goodbye to my godson,' Godmother urged her.

'Goodbye,' she muttered.

I heard the car drive away. Godmother came back and sat down as if fatigued.

'Thank God that's done,' she said.

Her niece had been put out by her parents when she became pregnant. They had warned her not to associate with the young man. Godmother had stepped in to help with money. I knew that her smile meant: 'This is my story over again, but I didn't get pregnant.'

She attributed to me a greater understanding than I possessed. But so did her husband, the barbershop habitués, Mr and Mrs Bourne, who lived next door, and so many others.

Both my godparents, so different in character and education, shared what seemed to me an uncanny talent: they were able to detect the most carefully concealed lie in any account I gave of a person or an incident. I had mentioned G. to Godfather several times and he appeared to be interested in him because he did well at mathematics. That a boy should have no difficulty in mastering a subject which had defeated him in so many examinations perplexed and intrigued him. More than once I compared my weakness in maths with G.'s facility, and each time I noticed that Godfather was strangely silent. The more emphatic my professed admiration for G. the cooler Godfather became. If Godmother was discreet in dealing with others her husband preferred the blunderbuss, and for that reason I became uneasy at his coolness whenever I spoke of my best friend. Then one day he asked after G. I replied somewhat guardedly that he was well. Godfather went on to tell me a story, an allegory he must have saved up for a suitable moment.

Envy stood before his extensive wardrobe, wondering what outfit he should wear to the Dissemblers' ball that evening. His favourite costumes, Hatred and Disdain, he felt to be inappropriate, as the fête in question was bound to attract many wise people, for whom either disguise would be all too transparent. Suddenly it occurred to him that he had never worn a certain outfit, which, indeed, he had never thought of wearing: the costume of Admiration.

When I confessed I did not understand the point of the tale Godfather declared brutally, 'You're too envious of G. You ought to be ashamed.'

I was deeply hurt, being convinced he had misjudged me. G. was my closest friend, and I kept praising him because my admiration was genuine. For months afterwards I avoided the house in South Road.

In truth, Godfather had hit upon a trait I refused to acknowledge in myself – even decades afterwards – which assumed manifold disguises, but lived within me like an independent person whose existence I repressed with varying success. Perhaps the price of that success is my intense dislike of all kinds of dissembling in other people and my conviction that intellectual dishonesty is the meanest of faults.

Inevitably, I returned to Godmother's house with its rocking chairs and quiet certainties, and was disappointed whenever Godfather was not there. I came to know many of their secrets, the constant, if subdued bickering over missing money, her suspicion that he was drawn out of the house not only by his drinking cronies, but by women of doubtful character; and above all by the way he suffered on account of his thwarted ambitions. Theirs was the only house I knew without children, and it might have been aptly named the 'House of Absences'. For almost no one save Godmother and her husband ever entered it. And even the bride seemed, in her hostile way, to be apologizing continually for her presence, in spite of her blood relationship to Godmother.

Thirty years later, Godmother was still chiding her husband for his foolish claims to some revolutionary invention. His legs had curved to such a remarkable degree that he walked only with difficulty. They were both housebound, he because of his bone disorder and she on account of a heart condition which had declared itself in her sixties. It was strange to see them face to face, in perpetuity, as it were. More often than not, in the old days, I saw him on his way out or at his work desk, rarely in a sitting position. Now, both chair-bound, one could no longer confide in me when the other was out. And this contrast, between their new life, in a different house, and the old one, evoked arbitrary images of a joker among the playing cards, of dilapidated buses racing each other in competition for passengers along South Road, of rocking chairs at rest, of the forties when Godfather eventually found permanent work at the American air base as an engineer, of a voice from inside enquiring who was at the door, and of intense longings for a father. The past was as immediate as the present. Rather, the past was incorporated in the present, in such a way that a new, undifferentiated time emerged, neither past nor present. The effect of this fusion of time was no doubt heightened by the fact that I had not seen them for twenty years, and therefore had not witnessed their decline. Their ageing – however palpable the evidence before my eyes – appeared less real than my recollections of them as people in early middle age, and like the magical transformations brought about by Wu-Li-Wong, the Chinese magician, the very astonishment evoked by the change was an invitation to disbelief.

I have always harboured the guilt of never having assumed the role of godparent. The institutionalized sacrifice is so much a part of the culture in which I grew up there can be no satisfactory excuse for such a neglect. My godparents had a duty towards me until I became an adult: should my family fall on hard times they were expected to take me in and complete my education to the best of their ability. They were, in fact, potential surrogate parents. Few godparents would lightly evade their responsibilities, and most took them very seriously.

The institution has its roots, I would think, in the avunculate of ancient societies, in which the maternal uncle discharged certain responsibilities towards his nieces and nephews. Godparenthood appears to be an attempt to meet the dangers of a shrinking family. It is curious that in a country like Guyana, where blood relations assume these obligations, the institution should still flourish. It is even more curious that the alarming erosion of family ties in industrial societies has been accompanied by the gradual weakening of godparenthood, so much so that the word godfather has taken on, in the United States, a sinister connotation, deriving from the power of a Sicilian Mafia potentate.

CHAPTER 13

Norma

Prejudices pile up like soiled crockery, tiny prejudices so small as to challenge awareness; large prejudices that weigh one down, like the old woman the young man was obliged to carry on his back the rest of his life. Prejudices, false assumptions that nestle in the mind and pass for independent thoughts, began to worry the growing awareness of my early teens. A family that ate from enamel plates and drank from enamel cups could not be regarded as 'decent'. Many a time I made a silent judgment of such a family while eating as a guest at a strange table. There was the prejudice of colour, perhaps the most corrosive and degrading of all. If its origins lay in the master–slave relationship, it was fortified by the experience of Indians in India, where it flourished as well. The light-skinned clerk, assured rapid promotion in the civil service, could avail himself or herself of innumerable advantages not available to his or her dark-skinned colleague.

Another prejudice concerned dining out: as children we were not allowed to report what we had eaten. By the age of seven or thereabouts the childish urge to disclose details of a strange meal was no match for the rule that it was 'not done'.

Another rule forbade servants to use the front door. Indeed, any neighbour could deduce the relative status of a visitor from the door she or he used.

I tried to discuss these absurd rules with G., but he took the view that if I disliked them I need only ignore them. I could do nothing about who used which door and should not waste any time thinking about the matter.

The fact is, I had become very fond of our maid, a young

woman of about twenty, who used to speak to me at length about her home and her young man. Instead of rushing back to school to play table tennis I would seek her out in the kitchen, where I remained until a few minutes before the afternoon session of school began. Uncle Tom's wife did not approve of the friendship and came into the kitchen on the flimsiest of excuses when she would normally be having her afternoon siesta. She would look round the kitchen, raise her bosom with a swift gesture, turn and leave, as if that were enough to bring the conversation to an end. But usually the maid paid her no mind.

Norma told me that her young man, a pilot, brought in the ocean-going ships over the bar. He had a telephone. A telephone! Yes. A ship might have to be brought in at night, so it was essential that the harbour master be able to get in touch with him at once. She described to me how her young man went out to the lightship by motor launch. I remembered standing on the beach at night counting the seconds when the light of the lightship would flash and then disappear as it revolved on its axis. Only last night her young man was on duty and might well have been called out to bring an ocean-going vessel through the channel.

Norma's young man was not a pilot at all and if I was taken in by the circumstantial detail and the apparent sincerity of her account, I could not hold the fabrication against her when I caught her out. The need to provide herself with a profession-ally qualified lover was touching.

I taught her long multiplication and she taught me how to make sorrel drink with sorrel she gathered from a plant she herself had grown in the yard.

Norma wore glasses on grand occasions. Her eyes were in perfect condition and like myself she could read the finest print. But when she attended church on communion days or went to visit someone in hospital the crowning touch of a magnificent turn-out would be her pair of glasses with plain-glass lenses. Her description of her arrival in a hospital ward, where the bedridden old men would rise miraculously from

their mattresses, reminded me of the times I went to visit
Sonny and could not get over my surprise at the visitors'
sartorial display. According to Norma, the old men had to be
restrained by the nurses from getting out of bed when she
walked between the rows of patients.

Norma's fantasies were reserved for men and the effect she
had on men, yet there was something chaste about her
character.

Once I went to her range yard room to collect six cents she
had promised me for the cinema. One partition of the room
was dominated by a picture of Christ with his bleeding heart
exposed, while another featured other pictures, of film stars
and vaudeville artists. I expressed surprise that she was a
Catholic, to which she replied that so were all her relations.
She always attended the church of the family she worked with,
so as to make an impression. It turned out that she also
belonged to an obscure sect which believed in passionate
worship, and whose members practised the laying-on of
hands.

To me Norma was an enigma, simply because I had no idea
how the working class lived. And what passed my understanding appeared absurd. Why should someone belong to a
single church? The Japanese might marry according to
Buddhist rites and be committed to the other world in a Shinto
ceremony. I learned that Norma was one of a large number of
people who sit in the back pews of the officially approved
churches – Catholic, Anglican, Methodist and Scots – on
Sunday mornings, yet worship in the more inspiring atmosphere of a shadowy building on the outskirts of Georgetown.
The approved churches could not contain their ardour, which
drew on an African past, long thwarted in the middle-class
creole.

The Catholic Church, supported by an intellectual élite
priesthood not notorious for its spirit of compromise, nevertheless found it expedient to permit dancing in churches of the
then Belgian Congo. Anglo-Saxon churches, on the other
hand, have never even recognized that a problem existed. The

Normas, reluctant adherents of a pale religious practice, found a far from satisfactory solution in multi-faceted worship.

Nothing illustrates more clearly the gulf that separates Roman Catholicism from the Anglo-Saxon sects than the successful synthesis of Christianity and African religions in Haiti and Brazil, where the Yoruba gods Ogun, Eshu and Shango figure as prominently in worship and possession as Christ and the Virgin Mary. I suspect that this has been achieved not only through the tenacity of Yoruban slaves, but also through the perspicacity of the Catholic élite, who recognized, unconsciously, perhaps, that Christianity is not a one-god religion. Like Hindus, who pray to Lakshmi, Ganesha, Kali, Manassa and a host of other Hindu gods, Catholics pray not only to Christ and his virgin mother, but to numerous saints as well. Even with the benefit of a sophisticated, broad-minded priesthood, Protestant churches, encompassed in a narrow ethic, could not conceivably accommodate themselves to the wealth of possibilities offered by the Yoruba religion.

Not the least of its riches is a powerful, comprehensive poetry:

> Ogun kills the owner of the house
> And paints the hearth with his blood.
> His many gowns he gives to the beggars.
> One to the woodcock who dyes it indigo
> One to the egret who leaves it white.
> Ogun scatters his enemies.
> When the butterfly comes to the place where
>   the cheetah excretes
> They scatter in all directions.

Such praise poems are found, not only in Nigeria and Benin (formerly Dahomey), but also in Brazil.

It is in the countryside that culture is preserved in its primitive, purest form. (Urbanization, on the other hand, is tantamount to the kiss of death.) Its demise is hastened, needless to say, where there exists a system of censorship,

overt or covert. Norma attended the Methodist church
because it was good for her to be seen there by Mother.
Nevertheless, she worshipped at night among her own on the
edge of town. But even her ardent worship was no match for
the dances practised in the comfa possession cult of the deep
countryside of the Courantyne and Berbice. Norma's religious involvement represented the link between town and
country, the last, if impressive, fluttering of the fowl whose
head has just been severed. Seduced by the cult of urbanism –
wearing glasses on special occasions and cultivating a 'superior' walk – her roots stirred sufficiently to draw her away
from the centre towards the crossroads, where opposites are
reconciled.

I did meet Norma's man friend eventually. He took an
immediate dislike to me and never tired of making disparaging
remarks about my short pants and the fact that I was still at
school. I felt flattered by his jealousy, but at the same time
envied him his manhood. If he was no pilot he certainly looked
the part. His swaggering gait matched his tailored sharkskin
suit, which fitted him so well I despaired of ever finding a
tailor who could do as much for me when I came out of short
pants and started to 'build' a wardrobe.

It was a curious fact that many working-class men spent
more money on their clothes than their middle-class counterparts who, in many cases, had few opportunities for showing
them off, apart from church on Sundays and the odd wedding.
Norma's young man was almost certainly an expert dancer;
and in the public halls where dancers' backs became soaked in
perspiration within two or three hours, a small wardrobe
would be a serious handicap. Very often, the first expensive
acquisition was a serge suit, wholly unsuitable for a tropical
climate, but a symbol of worth and, in any case, indispensable
in a country where death worked so assiduously.

At my remark that her young man did not like me, Norma
said, 'Good. It serve him right!'

They were both in love with each other, but did their utmost to make each other jealous.

If I learned much about life in my godparents' home, I learned from Norma that there was much more to life than I had hitherto imagined. My godparents never quarrelled, at least, not in my presence. Godmother, especially, would have been unable to face me if I had heard her voice raised. Norma, on the other hand, gave as good as she got whenever her young man attempted to lecture her. Once, his exasperation at my presence led to a quarrel and he struck her. She left the room without a word. He and I remained silent while we waited for her to return. And when she did, about a quarter of an hour later, she was carrying a piece of wood about three feet long. She stood in the doorway, barring his escape. (Each room of the range yard had a single door.) Adopting a conciliatory posture, he began pleading with her, hands raised slightly and palms turned towards her. His manner, incongruous in his immaculate get-up, made no impression on Norma, for she continued advancing towards him. Then, like a boxer, he pretended to lunge towards the right, drawing Norma's first blow, which cleaved the air as he dived in the opposite direction. Before she could recover he leapt towards the door and out into the yard.

The silence was unbearable. Disappointed at her outburst, in such contrast to her usual gentleness, I could not look at her, lest I discover something else.

'You want me to go?' I asked.

'No. I want you to do something for me.'

'What?' I asked, anxious to do anything which might lessen the tension.

She asked me to go to her mother and tell her she would be sleeping there that night.

I set off, keeping the directions she had given me in mind. My elation at being able to do her a service was not of a piece with the feeling of disappointment at seeing the ugly side of her nature. My experience of women had convinced me that they possessed a temperament more predictable than that of men. The simple fact was that I knew very little about men and generally had never been at ease in their company. Besides, in my view, they either died or ended up in the mental asylum. The world of women, on the other hand, seemed full of certainties, high resolutions and ideals that derived from an inviolate moral code. Norma represented something new and utterly mysterious.

Her mother lived in Kingston, an expensive quarter of Georgetown, scarred here and there by some of the poorest range yards in the city. I knocked on her door several times before she opened it and asked gruffly who I was.

'Norma send you? Come in, ne.'

She would not hear of my going back at once, after delivering the message. When I arrived she was just about to eat the bambye from the midday meal, but she offered to cook for me instead. I dared not say no in the face of such hospitality.

Norma's room, poor, but well maintained, had spotlessly clean glass windows. Here, the windows were unglazed, with brown paper stretched across them. A kerosene lamp high up on the wall gave off a weak light which barely redeemed the living quarters from complete darkness. For the first time I had come face to face with that poverty of the interior suggested by exterior conditions in range yards throughout Georgetown. The room, scrupulously kept, as Norma's was, flaunted its dilapidation, like a gaunt, wild-eyed woman who steps out into the street in a carefully laundered frock.

The kitchen was a makeshift structure just beyond the three steps descending to the yard, and from there Norma's mother attempted to make conversation. Was I still at school? When did I expect to go into long pants? Her grandmother used to be in service, like Norma. She took her to market every day, so that she learned to balance a tray on her head while walking and talking. Norma had it easy, because nowadays the mistress often became friendly with her servant.

'Long ago was different,' she said simply.

She talked of the old days, of old Georgetown, of how people stood up for one another when she was young. If someone punished a neighbour's child she was thanked for it.

'Now you touch a child an' is police story.'

The community was perishing before our eyes and we described it as progress. She expressed contempt for the new ideas discussed in the newspapers in connection with proba- tion for delinquent children, since they only meant that the responsibilities of the community were being eroded.

'How much chil'ren know what a third cousin is? I got seventh cousins an' all I got fo' do is pick meself up an' go to the Essequibo where they live an' stay as long as I like.'

I was overwhelmed with talk of family and community, concepts I had never heard discussed, except perhaps in my grandfather's house when still a small child.

Her solitary life belied these preoccupations; yet I felt I understood her nostalgia for the past, which brought to mind the time when Grandfather was alive. Had his death been a landmark?

I had once again come across an old lady with whom I had hit it off. Mrs Cambridge, the keeper of doves, and Mrs Bourne, our next-door neighbour who lectured me with impunity on my violent behaviour towards my sisters, were only two of the large number of elderly women whose friendship I cultivated. If I once blamed my mercenary nature for this unusual bent, it could not explain the impression made on me by Norma's mother, who possessed little.

I began my meal about an hour later; it consisted of sliced fried plantain, salt fish and rice, which I ate while worrying about what Norma must be thinking. 'Tell her I'm coming tonight.' At this rate she might arrive and find me there. I could not leave as soon as I had eaten. In fact, an hour at least must elapse before attempting to go away, I told myself.

During the meal my hostess sat on the bed watching me without a word. Puzzled by the lack of conversation, I decided to get her talking again. But she ignored my question, asking in turn how it was I associated with Norma. I knew why, but had no idea what to answer. Seeing my confusion, she said that her question had no importance, for there was much in life she did not understand; she never bothered to go into things deeply. Norma resembled her in that respect. Did I see any resemblance between her and Norma? Yes, I replied. But I could not say what.

I preferred it when she talked incessantly, when her voice seemed to come from another world that reached back into the last century, trailing indistinct memories of iron pots, mortars and pestles, when ministers of the church set aside at least one day a week to attend to the needs of their flock, writing petitions and letters of representation, when extravagant behaviour was permitted to the extent that every street had its entertainer, some woman or man born to make people laugh; when every well-off household had its lowly woman friend, who always entered by the back door, but stayed all day because she was indispensable to the mental health of the mistress, imprisoned in the home like a caged animal.

When she relieved me of my empty enamel plate I attempted to count the minutes to the moment when I could say I was leaving without causing offence. Shadows thickened in the yard beyond the open door, where I tried to follow her with my eyes as she disappeared with the plate. I heard the water from the standpipe and knew that she was washing it. All this trouble for a stranger, I thought. My mother had never washed up a teaspoon in her life. Worlds within worlds. The pest of class. I wanted to embrace this woman and flee her at the same time. Would she judge me to be arrogant, as so many people had? If only they knew how shy and uncertain I was! That the appearance of arrogance was not even a pose, but something that had settled upon me like the downy blight afflicting our lemon tree.

Norma's mother came back, placed the plate and spoon in the kitchen at the foot of the stairs and joined me once more.

'You got nice eyes,' she said, looking at me in the darkness. 'But you so fine! You mus' lift weights.'

Her remark had struck home, for I was over-sensitive about my thin frame.

I confessed to the belief that I would never be able to go into long pants, on account of my frailty. She laughed so heartily I felt offended. But she promptly made up for her cruelty by telling me about her husband, who was as thin as a rake when she married him. I only had to see him now!

Norma's mother, inexplicably, fell silent again. Her elbow propped on her lap and her head cradled in her hands, she just stared at the floor as though enveloped in a private grief. I waited once more for an opening to another bout of conversation, whilst keeping an eye on my internal clock, when suddenly she asked me what I thought of Norma's young man. Everything she had said and done until now seemed to have been a preparation for this question, and I could only stammer that I didn't know him well. My skill at dissembling had deserted me. Her silence appeared to convey that she had cooked for me, I had eaten her food, made work for her and been entertained by her, and all she asked in return was an honest answer to her question. Caught between loyalty to Norma and an acute sense of shame I chose the former. Did she sympathize with my predicament? The fact is she did not embarrass me with further questioning, but at once told me of a dream she had had a few days after Norma brought her young man home and introduced him to her. She dreamt that while walking along one of the main roads she noticed a crowd in the distance. Hurrying up to discover the cause of the gathering she elbowed her way past the people on the edge of the circle. Further and further she pushed towards the centre in a seemingly endless journey, until she realized that she would, in all probability, never arrive there. She turned round with the intention of making her way back to the edge of the crowd and looked up at the faces around her. To her astonishment the women and men all had identical faces. Panic-stricken, she thrust forward, using elbows and knees, shouting that she did not belong there, that she had mistakenly entered among them. At that point she woke up in a cold sweat and heard an infant crying in the night with a nightmarishly high-pitched voice.

'That man goin' do for Norma,' she said simply.

I felt I had let her down in my pretence that I had formed no opinion of Norma's friend, whom I detested from the bottom of my heart. I had no idea what the dream meant, but agreed inwardly that harm would come to Norma, through her association with the young man.

Finally I said goodbye and promised to look her up again. She accompanied me through the yard to the street, seeing me off with the obligatory 'Walk good!'

I walked through the night with thoughts jostling one another in my reeling head. Why had Norma not yet arrived at her mother's when so many hours had passed? Was it only the working class that took dreams seriously? In our home no one bothered to recount a dream, much less suggest that such night experiences might have any significance. If I could not resist this forbidden world, I had no idea that I was storing up potent tales, to plunder them years later to the advantage of a fiction that drew on a well dug in those formative years. I had struck out from the abundantly signposted road, down which my sisters were drawn as if by some gravitational force.

And what should I make of Norma's mother, who confirmed my opinion that women were more interesting than men, that they possessed a secret which alienated and attracted at the same time? A friend of later years dismissed the notion of a 'secret' as romantic. The alienation I spoke of was a natural state between men and women. The secret, on the other hand, was none other than the attraction between a sperm bank and an egg-laying machine. Be that as it may, it has spawned a lore so remarkable and extensive it cannot be discounted by a mere scientific observation.

On entering Norma's yard I could hear loud music coming from the first room. Its door was wide open and two men were standing in the doorway. I said goodnight and went past. The door of Norma's room, the middle one of the range, also stood wide open. I stopped in surprise at the foot of the stairs, unprepared for what I witnessed. Norma and her young man, locked in each other's arms, were dancing to the music that came from the radio in the first room. I waited until the changing steps brought her face to face with me. But whenever this happened she ignored me completely, just as though I were an inquisitive passer-by. Disconsolately, I made for home, dismayed at the turn events had taken. No one who noticed me, in short pants, skirting the grass verge, would have seen anything but a thin, long-legged youth returning from a visit or an errand. An accurate observation indeed, but far short of the essential truth.

The next day when I came back from school at midday Norma was her old self and behaved as if nothing unusual had occurred. In the presence of my sisters she was always deferential, and I had to wait until I left for school before I could see her on her own. She was standing under the house, where we had many of our conversations to avoid Aunt Lena's disapproving looks. Apologizing for having sent me on a pointless errand, she wanted me to accompany her to her mother's room on Saturday. Her mother, a 'talk-general', could entertain us for hours on end, she said. Tempted to ask if her young man would be there, I said nothing.

A few days later a neighbour found Norma in her room with a broken neck. Her young man was arrested the same afternoon, but released the following day for want of evidence on which to found a charge of murder.

Even now, it is unimaginable that someone so unique, so 'own-way' as her mother described her, could be lying beneath the gravel of Le Repentir Cemetery. For years afterwards I compared every young woman I courted with Norma, in a futile attempt to repatriate her presence, her gestures, her wrong-headedness.

Since my late teens I have been conscious of the working of symbolic forces, without being able either to identify them or to define the content of their influence. Now, in retrospect,

Norma represents 'activity', the opposite of the passive woman. Her young man is a type readily recognized by Guyanese, the impeccably dressed dandy, widely, if secretly, admired, but whom we also fear, knowing that the flawless, butterfly exterior conceals a personality in turmoil.

I was also to discover that these symbolic forces are readily recognized and defined by primitive people. Depth psychologists have difficulty persuading those who deign to listen that night represents for humans a feminine principle. There are aboriginal Indian groups in South America which actually live out this conviction, so much so that at night men urinate in a squatting position, while by day – following the converse idea that day is masculine – women urinate in a standing position. The Desana, a clan of the Tukano tribe who live in the Amazon basin, *know* that the anaconda – the largest snake in the world – is feminine, because its habitat is water; that honey is masculine since its viscosity recalls that of sperm. Perhaps they display an original capacity for apprehending the symbolic power of images. Every object exists on two levels, Carl Jung claims, the material and the symbolic. The importance of this remarkable statement can never be underestimated. Like many a truth it is demonstrated to us on every side, not least in our dreams, which speak to us in that oblique but compelling language of the psyche.

Those who are unaware of the power of symbols are in danger of being overwhelmed by them. When the moment of ritual revolt came it was directed against my mother. I had no idea what had overtaken me and floundered from one quarrel to the next, convinced that I was misunderstood. I recall the period as a struggle with some terrible power.

CHAPTER 14

Essequibo

Christmas, 1940. I was feeling a growing unease about this season which, until a few years before, had meant no more than presents and the traditional fare of York ham. One morning – it must have been the 21st or 22nd of December – I found Avis, Lynette and Mr Savage under the house sandpapering our chairs with a view to varnishing them for Christmas. They were surprised when I offered to help. I had interrupted Mr Savage's account about the history of schools and schooling throughout the world. He had not worked for more than ten years and kept body and soul together by doing the rounds of families he knew, helping to repair where repairs were needed and collecting a meal for his pains. His appetite, like his independence, was legendary. Unlike the army of hangers-on who ate at the tables of those to whom they were not related, he had not attached himself to a single household and boasted openly about being a man of the road, a wanderer.

His information came from Europe, he said. And, for Europeans, Europe was the world, so we had to accept at the outset that their description of the history of schools and schooling across the globe was biased. One of the first European countries to turn its back on the beating of school children was France where, in 1840, a schoolboy stabbed the teacher who had struck him. The teacher's death provoked a debate on the justification or otherwise of striking pupils and finally led to the abolition of whips, sticks and other such means of encouragement.

Mr Savage went on to tell us of the time when he was a pupil teacher at a school in Queenstown. Once the headmaster left him in charge of the top class of his primary school, urging him to keep the children working while he went to the Education Department on the edge of town. The boys begged Mr Savage, then in his seventeenth year, to take them out into the yard for a game of cricket. Not wishing to get on their wrong side, he did. But in the midst of the shouting and excitement, when a batsman had just lofted the ball over a fence, the headmaster appeared in the gateway. The pupils lost no time in fleeing back to their benches, leaving Mr Savage standing alone in the middle of the school yard. Following the pupil teacher inside, the headmaster took his cane from the cupboard with great ceremony, and in front of the assembled school of pupils and teachers, he ordered him to bend down before treating him to six hefty strokes on his backside. Then, in the interest of the latest ideas on democracy, all the offending boys were chastised in the same manner.

Mr Savage read everything he could lay his hands on. If leaflets were being handed out on the street he never failed to take one, when other passers-by made long detours to avoid the distributor. He read posters carefully, as he did the synopses of films to be shown in the coming weeks, displayed in the foyers of the great picture houses. The arcane Court notices of land sales, normally ignored by a paper's readership as if by a tacit, universal conspiracy, were consumed avidly, as were the births and deaths columns, the accounts of funerals with their lists of mourners in order of status, the information on high tides and low tides, as well as the phases of the moon. Not for Mr Savage the regulation hour for perusing a newspaper. Every weekday he could be seen at the public library annexe from 10am to 1pm, bent over the *Daily Chronicle*, and from 2pm to 4pm in a similarly devout posture above the *Daily Argosy*. In my opinion it was not Mr Savage's desire for liberty that allowed him the time to read so widely, but rather his passion for reading that obliged him to claim his independence.

Mr Savage showed us how to apply the varnish in thin layers. He accused me of hating to work with my hands – which was true – and of looking down on him – which was not. He told us that in China the nobility had to cultivate the habit of looking forward, never downwards, so that they should not notice their dogs and lackeys. The sarcasm was not lost on me and I wondered what had offended him in my actions. Could it really be because I disliked using my hands? Or was it that I appeared to be less attentive than my sisters when he spoke? At that age – I was fourteen – I had begun to take other people's opinions of me seriously. I liked Mr Savage, but could not stand open-mouthed at his pronouncements, something he expected, it seemed to me. Years later, the indifference developed to strangers' opinions of me might well have been a reaction to my desperate attempts to understand why I offended some people and, equally mystifying, why I made a favourable impression on others without trying.

'It's true you hit your sister?' Mr Savage asked me.

Overcome with shame and hatred I felt trapped between my sisters and this stranger who had learned my secret. I felt certain he was referring to an incident that had occurred one April, in the kite-flying season, when I set out with Lynette for the seaside where I would have no difficulty in raising my kite to compete with the scores of others. Whenever I took my younger sister out alone I became imbued with a strange, protective instinct towards her; but especially so on this occasion, possibly because I knew that kite-flying in Guyana was confined to Easter, the time of Christ's resurrection. On arriving at the appointed place I told Lynette that as we were earlier than I expected I would go and look up a family nearby, who were once our neighbours when we lived in the yard with three houses. I asked her to take particular care of the kite. None of the family was at home and I came back in less than ten minutes, to find Lynette crying. On catching sight of me she pointed to the kite lying on the ground beside her, now damaged beyond repair. A passing youth, once assured that it was being guarded by a defenceless little girl, had stamped on it before moving on. I reacted to the story by striking her a blow on the back and warning her that she need not wait on me to take her home.

I had struck her several times during a quarrel without experiencing any regret. But what caused me to suffer whenever I recalled the kite incident was the fact that I had let her down as a protector. I prayed for another chance to show that I was sincere in my wish to stand between her and danger. That Mr Savage should rake over the ashes of this incident seemed unforgivable, and the strong feelings it aroused in me provided my first clear recollection of vengeance harboured against someone outside the family.

'It's true you hit your sister?'

I answered defiantly, pretending that I did not care that I did, and received a gratuitous lecture on cowardice and the fate of males who struck women. Unable to bear the humiliation any longer I dropped the wet varnish brush and rushed upstairs to get away from Mr Savage's accusing voice.

There were occasions when my rage was like a fire that had got out of control; and afterwards, when the anger subsided, I would marvel that no irretrievable harm had been caused. Only between the ages of fourteen and fifteen was I afflicted in this way.

Some weeks after this incident I became involved in an altercation with my elder sister, Avis, the most retiring member of the family. Seizing a jug in a fit of exasperation she brought it down on my head. And even before the full realization of what had happened, I felt the warm blood trickling down my face. Someone fetched my aunt, who came running upstairs. But the only thing I recall of the sequel to the incident was my shame at having to explain to F. A. Danny, one of the pharmacists at Cendrecourts Drugstore, how I managed to split my head open. I had fallen. On the top of my head? No, I was standing on my head on the bed and slipped. It must have been a very tall bed. Mercifully, he let up; and then, touched by his discretion, I nearly confessed everything – my intransigence, my bad temper and all the faults of which I had been accused at one time or another. My disgrace at being hit by a girl, then at having been exposed as a liar and, finally, at being called over by Mrs Bourne, who said nothing about my wound, but a great deal about my disruptive conduct in a 'decent' household, was too much to bear. I decided that the time had come to find some means of escaping from the house of women and of mixing with males on a regular basis.

I confided in G., who had no hesitation in suggesting that we join the Y., the single letter used to describe the Young Men's Christian Association. He had been there, he assured me, and members were not required to take part in religious services, nor even declare their affiliation to a church. And so began a fierce competition in games between myself and G. Unable to outdo him in any subject at school, I offered the challenge in billiards, table tennis, bridge and tennis. And the six wonderful years that followed, during which we achieved a degree of excellence in all these games, were a memorable landmark in our development. I lived for games and even took my studies more seriously because of them, fearing that the idyll could be brought to an end by some officious male relative, who might use my failure at an examination as a pretext to lay down the law as a supplement to my mother's more brittle authority.

I imagine my joining the YMCA was followed by a collective sigh of relief in our home; and when I passed my Junior Cambridge examination I knew that the exercise of my freedom was, from then on, guaranteed. My sleep became haunted by dreams of cannoning billiard balls and smashes down the forehand; and on hearing from an acquaintance that he spent much of his spare time doing Latin unseens I judged him to be much deprived.

The YMCA grounds, situated in the northernmost section of Georgetown, took up part of an area in which there were only sports grounds and educational establishments. This curious bias was the result of a condition in a deed of gift which passed the lands to the Georgetown municipality, soon after the abolition of slavery in 1832. The then owner, an ancestor of Quintin Hogg, the former British Lord Chancellor, could turn the estate to no account in the face of the ex-slaves' refusal to continue working. Up and down the coast estates were abandoned, and most of the once thriving sugar lands lay derelict for want of labour. To this day, acre upon acre of north Georgetown has the appearance of a vast park by the sea, bounded on the west by Kingston and on the east by Vlissingen Road and the village of Kitty, now part of Greater Georgetown.

Soon after I passed my first public examination my mother presented me with a bicycle which she had bought for a song from my Uncle Dolph, who still lived in Queenstown. It took me less than fifteen minutes to ride from my home to the YMCA, so that within an hour of leaving school G. and I met there to hog the small billiard table reserved for beginners. I became possessed by the idea of wielding a cue and making large breaks. And so swift was our progress both G. and I qualified to play on the full-sized number two table within a matter of weeks. When, somewhat later, I got permission to play on the number one table, with its darker green baize and ivory balls, G. lost interest in the game and confined his attentions to table tennis. Later, we were to bring the same passion to tennis, in which a more uniform progress allowed us to maintain our mutual competition for about three years.

I came to realize that my docility at school was no more than a pose. I had to give the impression of being innocuous, a nothing. At times I stirred myself, to demonstrate as much to myself as to my teachers that a different person stood behind the passive pupil who did no homework, asked no questions and became nervous when noticed. Once, deciding to test my ability to concentrate throughout a whole period, I chose a history lesson taken by Mr Adams, who also taught French. Two days later, while distributing the marked homework, he gave me mine, with the remark that I was a 'canary that could whistle when it wants to'. I had got full marks. Mr Adams had recognized what I always knew.

Not so the teacher of English, who humiliated me in front of the class when, having ordered me to read my composition aloud, declared that I had copied it from a book. In my experience as a practising teacher this accusation is not uncommon. My reaction, however, was. Far from being angry or dismayed at the injustice, it only served to confirm my belief in myself. 'Copied from a book' meant that it qualified to be included in a book.

Many teachers are trapped in the conviction that a pupil's capacity can be deduced from his or her academic perform-ance, just as they equate the ability to learn readily with a general intelligence. In fact, the pupil is in a better position to assess the teacher's intelligence than the teacher the pupil's.

My growing self-awareness, perhaps a function of puberty and my age, was facilitated by my performance on the billiard and table tennis tables, I am certain. Now confident that I could put off my commitment to studying until a few weeks before the Senior Cambridge examination, I settled to the business of enjoying my evenings.

By the time the signs of puberty showed, the hardening nipples and night emissions, I felt I had become an adult in many ways, seeming to be in control of my destiny. A job in the civil service was well within my grasp. Beyond that lay the freedom which comes with the resources of money, and an infinity of pleasures.

So many changes in so short a time! In the way of the secret metamorphosis within a cocoon, I was becoming a different person. To think that my elder sister Avis had a similar tale to tell, that she had become a woman without my noticing, is extraordinary.

The new certainty of my powers resembled those dreams of flying I had from time to time, in which I soared with utter confidence above the roads and fields. Nothing appeared too difficult to master; and if I continued to treat mathematics with disdain, it was perhaps because I could not forget the humiliations heaped on me by a teacher who deluded himself into believing that skill in calculating was the sole qualification for entry into a distant, intellectual paradise. Having revised my theorems and crammed the essential algebraic formulae a week before the Senior Cambridge, I appeared in the examination room and sought out G. We talked until the invigilators arrived, when we chose places as far from each other as possible, faithful to a tacit agreement of long standing.

Certain I had done well, I accepted an invitation to spend my holiday with an Essequibo family presided over by a woman. Her husband, an Irish estate manager who had died several years before, had amassed enough wealth to build himself a mansion on an extensive coconut estate. At the slightest hint of revolt from one of her sons she would threaten to leave him nothing in her will. I learned much later that the two eldest sons had abandoned her some time before and were living in Trinidad. She ran little danger of being defied by the two younger ones, twenty-four and twenty-one years of age respectively. A., the elder of the two, ran the estate, while B., with the sensibility of an artist and the aspect of a sleepwalker, preferred to take the boat out on aimless trips along the coast.

Mrs E.'s two daughters, fourteen and sixteen years old, were as different from each other in temperament and appearance as two sisters could be. Strangely abstracted, both gave the impression of being aliens in this world, and what is more, the one always seemed to know where the other was and what she was doing, displaying a mutual sympathy that belied their contrasting characters.

Perhaps my tendency to be readily smitten had passed, for I was not in the least attracted to these young women, in spite of the four weeks spent in their company. Perhaps they were too large-boned, too tall; as it turned out, I preferred small, slight women.

I arrived at Suddie when a forest fire on Tiger Island – an island near the mouth of the Essequibo River – was burning itself out, and a rain of ash drifted down on the boat; but no one appeared to take any notice. A., who had come to fetch me, explained that he preferred the ash to the flames which, although the island lay more than a mile away, had delivered an intolerable heat across the water and caused the dogs to howl in broad daylight.

On arriving at the house Mrs E. told me that dinner was at seven, but I could have a bun if I was hungry. She must have noticed how quickly I ate it, for without being asked she brought me another. I felt ashamed. Indeed I came to discover that hunger was practically unknown – as far as I could judge – in the Essequibo, especially in the northwest, where people had huge appetites and were taller and healthier than other coastal dwellers. I realized that there existed a special urban deprivation, which hung around street corners, slept on pavements and spoke in a shrill distracted voice.

I liked Suddie at once. Now fifteen, I no longer saw holidays away from home as a kind of deprivation. Besides, Suddie reminded me of Agricola, with its palms and shame-bush beside the trenches.

The house boasted the unusual feature of sliding doors. The largest bedroom, furnished with a dozen beds, was reserved for guests. But the kitchen impressed me most of all. Standing apart from the house, it was connected to it by a long passage, a feature left over from one of the oldest mansion designs, now all but defunct. A vast drawing room gave another clue to our way of life, the passion for entertaining.

An arsenal of eight rifles enclosed in a case of highly polished glass hung from the drawing room wall, opposite the partition against which the piano stood. No one ever gave me a satisfactory explanation of the need for so many rifles, and the family's reticence in this respect left me with the impression of a secret, whose source lay in the lifetime of the dead father. Mrs E.'s sister, who lived in a cottage not far from the house, never lost an opportunity to run down her wealthy sibling, yet would say nothing about the unusual collection of rifles.

The path leading from the back of the house opened out, some one hundred yards away, onto a beach of dun-coloured sand, from which could be seen part of the twenty-mile-wide mouth of the Essequibo. The family's small sailing boat, used more often than not without its sail, floated beside a newly built landing stage.

The boat and arsenal alone justified this, my first free holiday. Yet only once did anyone fire a bullet during my stay, when a young woman was bitten by an alligator while she washed clothes in a canal. A., the eldest son, agreed to take a shot at what the villagers thought to be the same animal. I accompanied him to the canal, where he pointed out an object that looked to me like a leaf floating on the stagnant water. Resting the gun on my right shoulder he took aim and fired, and before the report died away a crimson bloom began to spread out from the centre of the canal where the leaf had vanished below the surface.

None of the onlookers would venture into the water to retrieve the animal, out of fear that it might only be wounded. Finally, however, a young man, urged on by a woman standing beside him, waded in, and we all applauded as he came back out, dragging his booty by a leg. A man who had witnessed the scene from his house on the other side of the canal offered to tie up the apparently dead animal with a length of cord and only just missed having his leg broken when, while attempting to put a noose over the alligator's head, it lashed out with its tail. The people who had gathered round leapt back in alarm, only approaching again after A. had fired another bullet into the alligator at close quarters.

I often went to another canal to see the alligators sunning themselves on the bank. A. explained that they climbed out of the water, not for the warmth of the sun, but to ensure that their skins did not rot. There was a lake in Berbice, he said, where the caimans grew to a great length, gorging themselves on an unlimited supply of fish.

We were on the edge of what has been called 'the paradise of eternal repose', the impenetrable forest between the Orinoco in Venezuela and the Amazon. And the people who inhabited the region, even those on its borders, appeared to be endowed with a peculiar indolence. Boat and paddle, as appropriate to this world as cars and cycles were to town, became invested with a mystery in those long, unclouded days. I learned how to paddle without scraping the side of the boat, how to control it when in sail; I also learned enough to understand that men were capable of being seduced by objects and even devoured by a landscape, as my Uncle Clement had been. Many of them came, ostensibly in quest of diamonds, but, as they discovered later, in pursuit of their souls. So Mrs E.'s sister would have me believe.

She hated her sister, who had, she said, given her a cottage on the estate with the sole purpose of punishing her. But the effect of this obsessive resentment was relieved by her willingness to instruct me in matters hidden from Georgetonians, whose fancied superiority concealed their ignorance of anything outside the capital.

One evening after the sun had gone down I saw a corial approaching on the river. To my surprise there were four aboriginal Indians in it. Only the day before I had tried to sit in one of these canoes, without success. At each attempt I fell over in the water, unable to keep my balance. Now, before my eyes, a whole family was travelling in this fragile craft. I watched them with the same interest I watched country waifs tread water in the Demerara River, as naturally as G. and I rode our cycles.

The fleeting picture of a family using the ancient highway was instructive in ways I could not imagine. Before Europeans came, the basic social structure among Indians was the clan. Families only moved about as a unit in times of crisis, when, for instance, threatened by an epidemic. I had witnessed the truncated image of a people caught in a crisis which had destroyed the Caribs and reduced surviving tribes to a collection of families. The once powerful Warrau, technologically one of the most advanced tribes of northern South America, were now the most degenerate and the most despised.

No institution for the study of Indian history and technology exists in Guyana; none is planned, to my knowledge, or even deemed desirable. A study of Indian psychology alone provides

invaluable insights into the condition of man. What, might
one ask, is the value of a Euro-centred psychology, which has
only just got around to an enquiry into transcultural psychology as an appendage to its introspective concerns?

While the scale of inter-clan fighting among so-called non-
acculturated Amazonian groups has attracted much attention,
it has provoked little thought about its historical significance.
The violence is, for the most part, caused by attempts to
abduct women, a well-known theme in the history of every
continent. It is significant that matrilocality is still regarded as
the norm where clans have not been destroyed; the man who
becomes attached to a woman in a pairing marriage goes to
live with his wife's clan. An abducted woman is obliged to
stay with her 'husband's' clan, a blow to the very foundation
of an organization that prevailed for most of man's history. I
have no doubt that the function of war among early planting
groups is to initiate patrilocality, a process that must have
spanned countless generations, and which is even now far
from complete.

Many questions regarding matrilocality and its demise need
to be answered. Why, for instance, was it necessary for
humans to hold to matrilocality for so long? The answer is
likely to be found in the exigencies of a life style based on
hunting and food-gathering.

The male's view of his mother-in-law is not derived solely
from personal experience, but also from the primitive experience of matrilocality. The respect accorded a mother-in-law in
ancient times has been institutionalized in certain more
modern cultures. In parts of West Africa a man may not eat in
his mother-in-law's presence. Finally, respect has changed
into resentment with the devaluation and disappearance of
matrilocality.

We made many excursions along the coast by boat, using the
sail for long distances. Interesting as these were, I remember
best the trip to Tiger Island, where we went to hunt for crabs. I

was surprised at the speed we worked up, paddling in unison. As the boat with its complement of ten – most of them invitees – coasted along the shore looking for a suitable place to land, we could hear tiny explosions, the cause of which mystified everyone, including the aboriginal Indian member of the party. They seemed to be coming from the trunks of massive trees growing near the water's edge; but on looking up towards the canopy, it seemed equally certain that the noises came from the buttressed roots instead. Soon we found a beach, and once ashore had no difficulty in spotting a line of large, pink-backed crabs. I imitated the others, who began throwing them pell-mell into the boat.

The operation had taken no more than fifteen minutes, and thinking that the men would be reluctant to go back so soon, A. suggested an expedition across the island to search for iguanas. Armed with a cutlass he walked ahead of the rest, hacking a path through the dense vegetation. Nothing was as I expected it to be in this fantastical world. I had learned at school that only the Indians knew where to find monkeys, yet overhead a troupe of about a dozen sakis was leaping from tree to tree, when we must have been about halfway across the island. Around the foot of an enormous tree whose crown had disappeared above a forest of leaves there lay a scattering of blue flowers in a perfect circle, as though some hand had placed them there.

On the white sand of the other shore we noticed the spoor of an iguana, which we followed to a tree hardly twenty feet high. No one managed to spot the lizard, even after the closest examination of its branches. And then, suddenly, I saw it, motionless on the lowest limb. A loop placed over its head was wrenched tight and the animal fell to the sand at our feet. Several days later I was still puffed up with pride at my success in spotting the iguana, when seasoned hunters had been unable to pick it out, camouflaged against the identical green of the leaves.

We set out in the boat with five iguanas and about two score red-backed crabs, which two men kept at bay as we paddled back to the E.s' beach.

The next night, the family, with the boatmen as their guests, feasted on iguana flesh, crab claws, boiled rice and pepper pot. I was the butt of many jokes because of my small appetite, which failed me after the second helping.

Our joys often find no recognizable expression. I sat and watched without taking part only because I felt shy in the midst of strangers who spoke about things of which I had little understanding.

A.'s younger brother, who usually remained on the edge of his seat and behaved like someone about to bid his family goodbye, proved to be as companionable as A. and his mother, exchanging good-natured remarks and laughing heartily when amused. He it was who initiated the discussion on people's kinna, food shunned by someone because it did not agree with him. In fact, kinna has a deeper significance. Originally it meant 'food you dared not eat because it was taboo for *you*'. B., the younger brother, told us of one of the maids who would not eat or even prepare manatee (sea cow).

'In Georgetown a lot of people won't eat iguana,' I put in.

A stunned silence. I had spoken! When the Indian burst out laughing a general uproar followed, a long series of guffaws. Then, infected by the general merriment, I began laughing myself, only to see many of the men pointing at me, no doubt pleased at the evidence that I was human after all. One day I might even develop an appetite, the man who had remained behind to prevent the crabs from escaping suggested.

After Mrs E. and the girls retired the conversation became more robust and B. began telling obscene jokes. I thought back on the genteel conversations of my relations and their preoccupation with grammar.

We all listened attentively to the Indian boatman, who related how his brother, an Arawak piaiman, would cure people by blowing across their bodies or sucking out the foreign substance that had lodged itself in them to cause the illness. The Macusi Indians blew on their enemies to cause them harm. When a grown man, I recalled his words and people's passion for pulling at cigarettes, for blowing out the smoke through mouth and nostrils, and wondered whether we understood the significance of smoking or the distaste it is capable of arousing. Smoke, fire, blowing and the propensity to suck, all oblique, enduring symbols that disturb and comfort in turn.

Speaking in the singsong drawl of people from the Essequibo, he told us how his father, offended by a visitor, harboured his resentment for more than twenty years before killing him on a path near his clan home. He spoke of the Caribs, who used to track down runaway slaves for the slave-owners, and received an annual reward of gifts from Government agents. The practice having ceased after the abolition of slavery, the Caribs went into rapid decline. Now, only a handful remained in the upper reaches of the Waini and a few other rivers. Yet the Arawaks still dreaded the sound of their name, carrying within them the memory of their depredations along the coast when they irrupted into South America. There was a place where two rivers met, which they, the Arawaks, still avoided, because at a certain time of the year – when certain constellations appeared on the horizon – Carib men once gathered there to hold a council of war.

He talked without a show of emotion, stopping neither to take breath nor to search for a word. He spoke of sickness, death, paiwari celebrations during which some of the men would hallucinate, regressing to a childhood state; of the absence of marriage among his people, since there was nothing to celebrate. Baptism he regarded as being even more absurd, because even if the family were Christians, the infant was not yet a person.

All this I learned when I myself had become aware of certain changes operating in me. I listened to this man, believing he had come to instruct me specially, and that the holiday was no more than a pretext, as had been the crab-gathering and iguana hunt on the island of two shores.

That night, after the boatmen had dispersed and the family gone to bed, I remained at a back window to look out on the river with its dark islands. I went over all I had heard that day, believing that not to do so would be to incur a loss.

Even now, I write this with some caution, being suspicious of the reliability of recollection. In 1987 I watched a film on television which I had already seen at the cinema in the 1940s. The climax featured the hero, a violinist, playing an arrangement of Wagner's *Liebestod* from *Tristan and Isolde*. I recalled his rapt expression while he played beside the ocean, and the ocean backdrop to this wonderful music. What I saw on television, however, was quite different. The hero was performing in a concert hall, not at the seaside, while the heroine walked into the sea to drown herself. If the astonishing transposition has its own logic it also calls into question the validity of memory as a source of factual recall. Yet much of what I heard was to be confirmed by the same man when I visited him on my first trip back to Guyana after twenty years abroad.

The day before I left for home, Mrs E.'s sister invited me to her cottage and gave me presents of fruit and a cake she had baked, and told me although I had been kept from the house by her sister – this was untrue – she had not held it against me. Did I know that Mrs E. only got married after she bore her second child? Her husband even had to teach her how to wear stockings. He spent hours reading to her every night so that she should pick up the semblance of an education. Did I not notice how she had lost her Essequibo drawl? Her husband had drummed it out of her by making her repeat sentences endlessly. She could tell me much that would cause my eyes to pop out of my head with disbelief. The next time I came on holiday she would do so and I would be able to judge for myself whether she spoke out of malice or a sense of injustice. Her nephews were gentlemen, but the girls! They would only greet her if they passed within touching distance of her; and even then you needed the hearing of a crab-dog to detect whether it was a grunt or a greeting. To think that in the first years of her sister's marriage she used to keep her company in that big house when her husband disappeared for days on end without an explanation! As the children grew up they saw less and less of each other until, out of shame, Mrs E. had built this cottage for her, at a 'safe' distance from the mansion.

As she spoke I kept thinking how well Mrs E. had behaved towards me.

She fetched her leather-bound bible from inside and read for me, to demonstrate, I thought, some kind of superiority over her sister. But as soon as she began I understood the extent of her bitterness against a sibling who had sustained her for so long.

'There is an evil which I have seen under the sun, as an error which proceedeth from the ruler: folly is set in great dignity and the rich sit in low places. I have seen servants upon horses and princes walking as servants upon the earth.'

In my early childhood I had become familiar with the corrosive power of envy, outside as well as inside the family, and I know of the lies it engenders, its silences and disguises. And I know of the sway it holds over ambitious men and women who cannot even bear the mention of a particular name, or dwell at length on the failures of others.

When I got up to go I promised to come back on holiday, knowing full well that in a year's time, at the age of sixteen, I would be a very different person. Although this was the first holiday I had taken by choice, it also was likely to be the last of my childhood, for in the event of success in my examinations I would immediately look for work.

I had done much during the weeks in Essequibo, but there is much I have not written about: the parrot-shooting sortie on the estate, for instance, which had to be abandoned because I made too much noise; the meal of tiny birds placed before me at midday after I had boasted about the nine birds I had shot with a borrowed air gun; the well whose water rose and fell mysteriously.

I set out for Georgetown one sombre morning while the sea was calm but rain threatened continually. As usual when travelling alone, I descended to the lower deck where bunches of plantains jostled with chickens tied together by the feet and people suffering from the exceptional humidity were fanning themselves with broad-rimmed hats. Then I went back upstairs and leaned over the railing, only to find that the shore had receded so swiftly the stelling was only visible on a blurred, uncertain shoreline.

BOOK 2

'When I lay aside my mask
I am not myself.'

CHAPTER 15

Across the River

I had passed my Senior Cambridge examination, and being only fifteen, received a bursary of ten dollars. Nevertheless, I had to remain at school another year, since I had not done well enough to be exempted from Matriculation.

My stay in the Essequibo had changed me, making me aware of another horizon, a world other than that of asphalted streets and an ordered existence in which tensions took on a razor-like sharpness. It seems to me that the dissatisfaction that drove me to go abroad dates from this period when, following my holiday, I became infected with a craving for books, which could not be satisfied by what I took out of the public library.

G. had begun to read a good deal earlier than I; but he confined his interest to fiction, which had no hold on me. I borrowed an encyclopaedia from the husband of a cousin of mine – Uncle Tom's niece. He lent me the volume reluctantly, claiming that he could not afford to replace it. Dissatisfied with what I read I took it back to him and felt flattered when he challenged me to a discussion on the theory of knowledge.

Knowledge itself contained many pitfalls, for in imparting it one applied, necessarily, a certain censorship. He opened the encyclopaedia, pointed to a building and asked me what I thought of it. I answered that, like many other Gothic cathedrals, it was beautiful.

'Beautiful? It's not beautiful. It's impressive, but not beautiful. Muslim architecture is beautiful *and* impressive.'

He then turned a few pages and showed me how little space was devoted to Mohammedan architecture in an article which purported to deal with architecture throughout the world. He

asked me whether I still thought knowledge was a simple
matter of gathering facts. Of course I did not! Knowledge, as
abstract as the idea seemed, could not be separated from the
culture which attempted to impart it. He cited example after
example, until my head reeled. I had not been educated, he
claimed, I had been assaulted. Ashamed at my interest in table
tennis and billiards, I nevertheless knew that I was not yet
ready to be instructed in serious matters.

About a year later he was arrested when he failed to answer a
call-up to the militia. His wife told me how he had been
marched away in his pyjamas, having been refused permission
to shave or get dressed. When I saw him again he related how
he had planned and executed his revenge on the authorities,
who had impressed him into guard duty in the interest of a
conflict thousands of miles away, to which he was indifferent.
One night while on duty at the Cable and Wireless building he
challenged the occupants of a staff car, which failed to stop.
From his experience most of the vehicles driven by white
officers ignored the order to stop. Before the car could gather
speed on the drive he plunged his bayonet into one of its rear
tyres. Throughout the investigation into the incident he stuck
to his story that he had done his duty, and was discharged
from the militia, to the mutual satisfaction of his superiors and
himself. He insisted that they would have found some way of
punishing him if they thought that he had some influence over
other militiamen. They preferred to see his back before others
thought of emulating him.

I often looked him up, especially when I wanted to learn
about the war and America's involvement. A natural teacher,
he always went back to 'basics' and to the need to *think* in the
particular subject. His specialization was history, which, in his
view, could only be properly understood in global terms. The
idea of the history of a particular country was, from an
intellectual standpoint, an absurdity. In French, of which I had
grown particularly fond, he explained the need to understand
the function of base words, prefixes and suffixes, and to
practise elucidating the meaning of new words before consul-

ting a dictionary. How many English words had I looked up in a dictionary? Very few. Yet my vocabulary kept growing, because I deduced the meaning of words from their context and the base word contained in the elaboration.

Had I met him when I was eleven or twelve I have no doubt I would have made a success of mathematics, the nightmare discipline. What was this nonsense about disliking maths, the most elegant and satisfying of all subjects? Like chess it was capable of teaching one about life. He would never tell a class about tan, sine and cos before giving it a thorough introduction to the *thinking* behind trigonometry. The higher a structure to be measured the greater the angle from the position of observation. Retreat from the spot and the angle changes in relation to the height. The subject dealt with angles and distances, a statement which descended upon me like a revelation made in a half-waking state. He taught me how to read contours, cleared up the mystery of the extraordinarily fertile land on the coast and generally managed to make geography, 'that prince of bores', not only palatable, but exciting.

My mother, far from being impressed by what I reported of his ability, dismissed her cousin's husband out of hand. Eventually she told me he had caused Aunt Beryl's breakdown. It was he who stole her heart, she who knew nothing about men, having been confined to the house like a recluse from the age of sixteen. Her visits to his home to receive extra tuition in mathematics had proved fatal. This was the first I heard of Beryl's illness which, evidently, had been concealed from me and my sisters.

I could not forgive her seducer either. Had he offended Edna I could have forgiven him, and might even have applauded. But Beryl! To go back to his house would be the betrayal of an affection. I had attained the age of morality, when a broken promise was an abomination; the age of exaggeration and of monsters to be overcome. I imagined the teacher I admired had plotted Aunt Beryl's ruin and, in spite of his talent, bore the mark of a villain.

★

A year later I took my examinations once more and applied for
a position in the civil service in anticipation of good results. In
December, 1942, I was offered a post with the special board
which had been set up to control prices of essential goods.

I cannot adequately describe the difference working made to
my life. The freedom I had won seemed paltry compared to
those I now could claim. I smoked, took my girlfriends to the
cinema, attended dances, played billiards at the Park Hotel and
had suits of expensive cloth made by a good tailor. When
boredom drove me out of the house I could decide to see a film
on the spur of the moment without the need to borrow or beg.
I stopped reading and devoted my evenings to the pursuit of
pleasure, as though I had been presented with the opportunity
to assuage a longing that had been denied me since birth. The
confidence I had gained over the last year could now be
'engaged'. I now played billiards better than ever and could
gamble on my skill with my own money, in contrast to the
days when I played truant and frequented billiard rooms in
Tiger Bay, where stevedores backed me because they could
not reconcile my size and short pants with the mature game I
played.

Nothing gave me more pleasure than to meet acquaintances
from Tiger Bay in the Ice House, a notorious drinking place
opposite Stabroek market, where the reek of stale rum
engulfed its clients in a thick, invisible haze. The night I came
home blind drunk my mother was out. My Aunt Lena helped
me to bed as solicitously as if I had been a member of her
family. Touched by her concern, I began buying her presents.
Perhaps I did so, as well, to make up for my boorish conduct in
the past, when I could only see her in opposition to my
mother. I tried to confide in her, but she preferred to know
nothing of my doubtful associations, thinking, I am sure, that
loyalty between parents would oblige her to disclose what she
knew, in order to save no less than my soul. She had once
described me to her husband as erratic and reckless and might
not have been prepared to endanger our improved relationship.

I still had my hair cut at the American barbershop in Lombard Street and could now establish the difference between the working class I knew through my visits there and the very deprived of the Ice House, some of whom wore their whole wardrobe wherever they went. Among the frequenters of the Ice House were undoubtedly scholars and self-made men, but many also who would cut your throat in a quarrel. There were thieves who specialized in stealing from wharves, house thieves protected by the police because they were informers, men who boasted of the number of times they had contracted venereal disease and pimps who kept a vice-like hold on their women. There, deals were struck between policemen and criminals, between criminals and criminals, who valued the privacy of a conversation guaranteed by the tumult of a hundred voices.

I revisited the Ice House in 1983 and nothing has changed, except that above it one can now eat in an elegant restaurant which caters for people who would not even dream of walking past on the pavement below. Its entrance is in Brickdam, and although just around the corner from the Ice House, gives the impression of being a great distance away. Here, it seems that proximity has been abolished by the simple notion of opposites.

What was a matter of pride to me – that I could readily frequent two contrasting milieux – caused my mother much anxiety. Difficulties had already arisen with regard to the amount of money I should contribute to the household each month, and we both took care not to widen the rift by making unnecessary demands. A tacit understanding required that she should not mention my smoking or drinking, while I would be silent about the demands she made on our cooks who, at a time of difficulty in recruiting labour, rarely remained with us longer than a few months. One night she broached the subject. It had come to her ears that I had been seen in certain places in unsavoury company. Incensed at the intrusion into my private affairs – all the more irksome as I now earned my keep – I replied that whoever had seen me must have been frequenting these 'certain places' as well. Yes, she said. It was a policeman whom she had taught at school and who could not stand aside and see me ruin my health and my prospects. By way of an answer I treated my mother to a torrent of abuse, and in the heat of the outburst I could see myself as another person, distinct and separate from myself, a judge who had decided not to intervene, but rather to look on in disdain while I exposed myself with no prompting from anyone. I spoke of my contempt for her opinion, all the more so because she was 'no more than a woman'. I spoke of her treatment of Sophie, whom she had exploited ruthlessly and who was still obliged to use the back door when she came visiting. I spoke of my embarrassment and humiliation at being made to endure her pleas that tradesmen reduce their prices because she was a widow. I dragged up small matters to add to the enormity of all the ills I had suffered and would like to have suffered in the interest of a ritual revolt whose force I had experienced months ago, but successfully held in check. I said things I did not wish to say, barely resisting the impulse to lay my hands on her and fell her to the ground. I saw my other self now laughing openly at my rage and, driven on by his opposition, I redoubled the abuse on my mother, who stood opposite me, refusing to be intimidated.

The price I paid for being left alone was shame at my lack of self-control and guilt vis-à-vis my mother. Even then I refused to engage in a dialogue with my other self, whose presence I was now more aware of than at any other time. I detested his surveillance and thought, at times, that my feelings of guilt had more to do with him than my mother.

It was either at this time or a few months before – I no longer recall the sequence of events – that I began to suffer from insomnia. I told no one except G., who advised me to see my doctor. He prescribed a barbiturate concoction, which worked very well for a week or so, after which the insomnia returned as a regular affliction. I rarely fell asleep before dawn and in the morning could only be awakened by someone shouting in my ear. Rather than lie awake or look out on a deserted road I took to walking the streets after midnight. Oddly enough, if I went out after two o'clock in the morning the stray dogs would run away as I approached, whimpering, as though I were an apparition. Between midnight and one o'clock they were aggressive and snarled at me, and even snapped at my heels at times.

While a small child I woke up on several occasions under the couch in the drawing room, having gone to sleep in my bedroom. This only happened in my grandfather's house where, on the face of it, I had always been happy, since I never went there except in my mother's company. My doctor could not see a connection between my sleepwalking years ago and my insomnia now. The former was a condition common to many children. I should try exercising before going to bed, he suggested. If that did no good I should count horses rather than sheep, which were such stupid animals I would probably be bored with them before I dropped off. My doctor was clearly bored with his profession and I interpreted his facetiousness to mean he could do nothing for me, that I must take myself off and consult someone else. I followed his advice about exercise and began to sleep well some nights. But two years passed before I began enjoying a regular good night's rest once again.

After an apprentice week in a Georgetown office of the Control Board I took up my post at the District Commissioner's Office in Pouderoyen, a village on the opposite side of the Demerara River. Every morning I crossed the river by ferry, disembarked at Vreed-en-Hoop and walked the half-mile or so to the Commissary Office, which shared a compound with the Public Works Department. I enjoyed leaving the boat in the company of fellow workers bound for the Telephone Exchange, the Public Works Department, the Magistrates' Court, the match factory and various schools. The rush to find a taxi or a bus by those going farther afield than Vreed-en-Hoop or Pouderoyen, the clanging of cycle

bells, the much larger crowd waiting to embark for Georgetown, became part of my day, a habit, like my acquaintanceship
with the office furniture, clients, fellow workers, the dust
stirred up by vehicles, animals wandering about the compound
yard, the vast mansion where the District Commissioner lived,
courida bushes, women selling produce at the roadside, a
forlorn cinema set back from the road, Hindu funeral processions, my signature on a blue salary form at month end, a
barbershop that accommodated only a single customer at a
time, conversations in Hindi or Urdu, prayer flags adorning
long bamboo poles in front of East Indian houses, an overgrown churchyard with an imposing but derelict church, a
solitary cherry tree by the wayside, the match factory with
workers whose hands showed stains of a blood-red dye, an
endless procession of images that rooted in the mind.

Commissary Office employees represented the Customs,
Control Board, Forestry and Local Authority departments,
and the Poor Law Department. In addition, it was responsible
for issuing licences of all sorts, checking weights and measures
in shops the length and breadth of the West Coast and West
Bank, supervising the use of money provided for maintaining
drainage and generally administering the area between the
Demerara and Essequibo rivers. District Commissioners
represented the Colonial Authority and were Oxford or
Cambridge graduates. Of the two qualifications, graduate and
Oxbridge, the latter was the more important; and if anyone
had any doubts on this score they were settled during the war
when, the preferred graduates being in short supply, the
Colonial Authorities appointed Oxbridge undergraduates to
fill vacancies as they arose. If District Commissioner Gerard,
an affable, capable man, was what the authorities had in mind,
his successor, Mr Niven, was quite the opposite. Hardly past
his forties, his lack of confidence became apparent to anyone
who spoke with him. His hand shook continuously whenever
he raised a cigarette to his mouth, to display three fingers so
badly stained with nicotine someone with defective eyesight
could readily believe he wore yellow gloves.

Mother's first cousin, Mrs Dolphin, *c.* 1930

Mother (sitting) with two friends, 1957

Mother, aged 96, with two
of her music students, 1988

Lynette in 1970

The Public Buildings, Georgetown, *c.* 1924

Water Street, Georgetown, *c.* 1924

Both District Commissioners were liked, because they never attempted to be over-assertive. But poor Mr Niven soon passed on, transferred to some other post where he probably remained until his weaknesses attracted too much attention.

My work consisted of issuing gasoline coupons to owners of motor vehicles: buses, cars and launches in the main. Having verified that the vehicle in question carried a certificate of fitness, I gave out coupons to the value entered in my record book. There was little to do, except on Fridays, when taxi drivers and launch owners came to collect their rations. One Friday, about three weeks after I began working, a launch owner came for his twenty-four gallons' ration. I had never seen him before and wondered why he had let two weeks go by without collecting what was worth so much to him. Two or three weeks later Ramoo, one of the two revenue runners, catching sight of the launchman waiting in a corner while I served other vehicle owners, came over and whispered that I should ask him for his certificate of fitness.

'Can I see your certificate of fitness, please?' I asked, when his turn came.

He protested angrily that I had not asked before and when I insisted he pounded his fist on the counter.

'You lil' red-skin cunt!' he shouted, seeing I had no intention of giving in.

Then, very calmly, Mr Ramoo said that if he did not leave at once he would see that the Commissioner made him return the coupons he received while his launch was off the river. He turned and left, screaming that we were all sons of whores.

According to Ramoo I had let him have nearly one hundred gallons worth of coupons, which he must have sold. On learning that a youngster had taken the place of the previous employee he had seized his opportunity to test his vigilance.

Ramoo warned me to say nothing to Mr F., the Chief Clerk, who would pretend that my blunder was of little significance, but would not forget it. From then on I never neglected to demand a certificate of fitness.

At month end, old people qualified to receive Poor Law pensions flocked to the office in such numbers that most of them had to remain outside until they could squeeze through the doorway. In my first working months the sight of this ill-clad throng jostling and tugging at one another to keep their place near the door or advance towards it seemed degrading. Even the most dignified-looking among them would direct threatening looks at anyone who dared push past, or grab him by the hair and drag his head down to a level where it was difficult for him to keep his balance. At times, the haggard faces and open, wasted mouths presented a terrifying, other-worldly picture of destitution and suffering, like a nightmarish glimpse of the possibilities of ageing. Month after month this scene played itself out in front of the counter and in the yard, yet I could never bring myself to relate it to anyone, not even to G.; perhaps because nearly all the pensioners were East Indian. Nor to my mother, since the moral of the occurrence would not be lost on her; my complaints were insignificant compared to the lot of the poor.

Many pensioners could not sign their names and had to put their thumb prints where the signature would have been made. Never before had I met illiterate Guyanese – aside from aboriginal Indians. Like most Georgetonians I believed that illiterate people lived in the forest and beyond, on the distant savannahs. Here, just across the river, people were placing their fingers on an ink pad, after satisfying the Chief Clerk about their identity.

Every Wednesday a special court was held on the ground floor for the descendants of immigrants and old immigrants themselves. Described as a Crosbie Court – the first of these courts had been set up by a Mr Crosbie, an Immigration Agent General – it was the responsibility of Mr U., who also made up accounts for the Forestry Department on the basis of lease money collected by the Forest Ranger. Clients who brought their problems to Mr U. – the Crosbie – paid no fee nor availed themselves of a lawyer's services. The procedure being informal, clients soon realized they could speak freely and often did, sometimes to the great amusement of us employees on the lower floor and even the usually unsmiling Chief Clerk, Mr F.

More frequently Mr U. dealt with domestic problems, complaints about lazy or recalcitrant wives and unpaid dowries. One of the most serious domestic problems rarely figured in the cases I heard, namely the oppressive rule of wives' mothers-in-law. Newly married couples – in the East Indian community – frequently went to live with the bridegroom's parents, the tradition being reinforced by the fact that many did not have the means to rent a house of their own, while others expected a legacy from a father who might die in the foreseeable future.

It soon became clear that in husband and wife cases nearly every complaint came from a husband. The much vaunted Crosbie Courts, on the face of it a great asset to East Indians, had few advantages for women, and in fact confirmed their husbands' domination over them. Of course, quarrels between neighbours or matters of debt alone justified the courts' existence; but the blatant disregard for women's inability to gain access to them exposed in some measure the unsavoury side of public institutions.

Some of the cases I heard, some of the clients I saw, belonged to that fund of unlikely people and stories on which writers drew for their more striking tales. One wife whose husband complained bitterly of her behaviour supported everything he said, however disparaging it sounded, and even gave independent evidence to back up his accusations against her, raising a laugh every time she spoke. Her husband, bewildered by the lack of resistance, became more and more distressed until, unable to continue, he asked Mr U. to drop the case.

'Do you insist?'

'Yes, sah!'

'Well say it yourself.'

'I insist,' the man declared, impatient to get away from the place where his wife had turned the tables on him. He had thought to humiliate her publicly and now found himself begging the court to bring his dilemma to an end. Mr U., who needed several minutes to quell the disturbance caused by the man's capitulation, was evidently pleased at his success in bringing a smile to the Chief Clerk's face.

An observation of the Crosbie Court at work provided all the evidence to support the view that law had two functions, a regulatory one and an unavowed aim to preserve the status quo. East Indian women would have understood the second readily.

Decisions made by the Crosbie were not binding, so that a party who felt aggrieved might still pursue the matter in the official courts. But this rarely happened – at least in cases heard in the Pouderoyen office. Apart from Mr U.'s reputation as a fair and exceptionally competent Crosbie, the social pressures to accept the court's decision proved strong. One shopkeeper who sued his neighbour officially, after having been told by Mr U. to return tools he claimed the neighbour had sold him, lost his case. The result not only confirmed the unofficial court's competence, but also lowered the complainant's esteem in the community's eyes. He always insisted that custom had fallen off because people had it in for him.

The Crosbie Courts appear to have been a direct result of pressure put on the colonial authorities by the government of India, then still a colony itself. To qualify for a hearing at a Crosbie Court the complainant or defendant had to show that he was a first- or second-generation immigrant. East Indians were acknowledged to be severely disadvantaged in Guyana. Some of the older ones spoke no English; a large number could only find seasonal work in the cane fields; and whilst illiteracy among creoles was less than three per cent throughout the country, the figure was more than twenty per cent in the Indian community. If there were objections to the Crosbie system on the grounds of preferential treatment for immigrants, I heard none.

Mr U., a whimsical man with a sunny nature, was out of place in the Chief Clerk's company. The latter seemed to be forever brooding and I used to look forward to the time when he went out on his rounds with the two revenue runners, Mr Ramoo and Mr Hanif. I admired Mr U. for his gentleness and his extraordinary mastery of language. Fluent in Hindi and Urdu, he spoke English with an unforced eloquence. During Mr Foster's absence I would go upstairs to help him with his forestry accounts and occasionally discuss his work as a Crosbie.

Once, while we were talking of the duties performed by the Forest Ranger, who made long journeys into the bush that took him away for the greater part of the year, he suddenly asked if I would coach his sixteen-year-old son in French. My exam results, which had come out the week before, had evidently impressed Mr U. – especially the Distinction in French. I accepted, and visited him in Laluni Street twice a week, where I became acquainted with the mystic side of his character he kept carefully hidden at the office behind his banter. He could not resist engaging in a discussion on the existence of God or the history of religion, and I expressed my surprise at the ease with which he could give an objective analysis of religion while professing a belief in a God inspired by the status of chief and shaman. The apparent contradiction only appeared strange to someone with an excessive respect for logic as we understood it, according to him.

Mr F. said nothing about my results, but invited me to have lunch one Sunday and meet his family. Like Mr U., I felt uncomfortable in his company. Not only did he hardly speak to me, but I caught him looking at me severely more than once. Had he heard that I spent much time upstairs when he was absent? He could not stand Mr U. In the beginning I believed he envied him his work as Crosbie; but later I learned from Mr Hanif that two of Mr U.'s daughters were notorious prostitutes, information I did not readily believe, remembering his attractive drawing room hung with Oriental rugs, and his cases of books in three languages. Mr F. apparently knew of his daughters and thought it proper to despise this man so manifestly his superior in every way.

The following Sunday I crossed the river and went to Klein Pouderoyen, a village adjoining Pouderoyen, where Mr F. lived with his wife and many children, all girls except for a boy of fifteen whose physique was that of a man.

On my arrival Mr F. introduced me to his wife, who then summoned the children. He lined them up and introduced them to me one by one, while I nearly fainted with embarrassment. I am not certain whether there were six or seven.

Apparently, as soon as Mr F. learned of the results of my last exams he took it into his head to present me as a model to his children, all of whom were dunces, he informed me. They were made to bring their school exercise books and sit with me, after which I had to give him my opinion of their work. Mr F.'s son kept winking desperately in my direction. I had no way of knowing that, for him, his father was the embodiment of terror and that the favourite punishment of this, his only son, consisted in standing over him while he kneeled on a kitchen grater. Time and time again he had run away from home, only to be brought back by a solicitous policeman, concerned that the youngster did not fall into bad company! I took his book and after a cursory examination of it gave my opinion. Only his son's handwriting was weak.

'Then you know less than I thought!' Mr F. snapped.

The children dismissed, Mr F. led me to the dining table, laid only for two, where I sat opposite him while we were served silently and unobtrusively by his wife and eldest daughter. For several minutes no one spoke and I listened to the sound of cutlery on our plates, wishing I had declined the invitation. When Mr F. finally spoke he enquired whether I had a girlfriend, to which I answered yes, suspecting that he reserved his discretion for his superiors, like the District Commissioner, whom he always greeted with a broad smile and a bow. Did I like my girlfriend? Did my mother approve of her? Had I any intention of marrying her? A young man had to be careful whom he married. He and his wife had known each other at school. His advice should not be ignored. The more pleasant Mr F. showed himself the more I felt disturbed.

Would I have to come back to the house of this superior whom no one liked? Should I tell him that I went out at weekends and could not accept any further invitations?

I spent four hours answering questions and enduring the silence of my hosts in turn. Mrs F. had joined us after the meal, but said nothing, only rewarding me with a smile whenever I caught her eye.

Finally Mr F. asked me if I would coach his children twice a week. He must have seen the dismay in my eyes and corrected himself right away. Once would be sufficient.

'I can't!'

'You what?'

'I'm sorry, I can't.'

'He can't!' he exclaimed, turning to his wife.

And from her expression you might have thought *she* had refused to comply with a request he made.

Rising from his seat, Mr F. urged me to think again; then, coming over to my side of the table he took me by the arm and showed me the door. I looked at his wife over my shoulder, but she had not moved from her place.

I heard the door slam behind me and descended the long staircase, angry that my will was still almost as impotent as when I attended school. Convinced that I should have handled the situation more expertly I went back in spirit and told him what I thought of him, that the worst thing he could do would be to try to intimidate me.

I confided in Mr Ramoo, the revenue runner. He said I should have told him before going to Mr F.'s house and advised me to let him know if the Chief Clerk tried to force me to tutor his children.

In the event Mr F. did nothing of the sort, but rather behaved as if I had never visited him, so that within a couple of weeks I felt no more oppressed than I had before.

One morning I began work by counting my stock of gasoline coupons and checking them against the figures in the account, only to find that ninety-six gallons worth were missing.

Several recounts only confirmed the shortfall. Mr F. invariably arrived about half an hour after I did, which gave Mr Ramoo the opportunity to help me turn my section of the office upside down.

On Mr F.'s arrival I confessed the loss of two sheets of four-gallon coupons, while Mr Ramoo stood by, intent on giving me what moral support he could. I was ordered to make one more search before writing a report which would be sent to Head Office, where my fate would be decided.

That night I lay on my bed reviewing my short span of time at the Control Board, a stepping stone to the civil service proper, which I intended to enter at eighteen, the minimum age, if possible. A career in one of the professions was out of the question, as my mother could not afford to keep me at school, let alone pay for studies and upkeep abroad. Oh my God! For twenty-four squares of miserable brown paper my whole future would be compromised. I had been earning less than a year and had just managed to fit myself out with a respectable wardrobe. Was that, then, the extent of my power over my fate? I decided that if I had to go down I would do so with dignity.

The next morning I went to work, determined to conduct myself as I would have expected G. to do in a similar situation. Mr F. began ordering me about as he never had until then. I was sent over to the match factory to check crates ready for shipment abroad, a duty outside my province. I even took messages home to his wife and went to the shops on his errands. But each attempt to humiliate me had the opposite effect, for the very fact of the injustice gave me a certain strength.

Convinced that I could do nothing to prevent my dismissal I threw myself into a life of pleasure, frequenting the forbidden haunts in Tiger Bay, attending fêtes in out-of-town dives that had sprung up with the opening of the American air base, twenty-five miles from Georgetown, or private parties given by black-marketeers who had never learnt to spend money and could not purchase imported luxuries, given the activities of German submarines in the Caribbean, which had sunk every ship of the 'Lady' line that once plied between Canada and Guyana. Not for the first time I met a crisis with a frenzied indulgence in some activity or other.

The crisis also stirred up old conflicts. I found myself fighting the same battles with my mother I had fought over the years; and then, on the point of leaving home, the case of the missing coupons was unexpectedly resolved. As I prepared to deal with the flood of vehicle owners early one Friday morning I noticed a coloured sheet jutting out of a massive register lying under a pile of old registers kept on the counter. I could hardly believe my eyes when Mr Ramoo pulled out the lost coupons while I lifted the books above the one in question.

My report having already been dispatched to Head Office I asked Mr F. to telephone the Chief Clerk there as soon as possible, but he refused. He would write the same day. Mr Ramoo stood aside, stony-faced. He would be drunk that afternoon and I decided to wait until then to see what I might get out of him.

That night I celebrated in one of my haunts on the edge of town and vowed never to give up my secret life.

Mr Ramoo became drunk nearly every day by early afternoon, when he would stand around in the office, dazed and red-eyed. I often wondered why Mr F. put up with it until I learned from Mr Ramoo himself that the Chief Clerk relied on him heavily in many ways, more especially to help him identify old East Indian pensioners, all of whom looked the same to Mr F. Mr Hanif, the other revenue runner, never volunteered any information to the Chief Clerk.

Mr Ramoo did not trust Mr F., fearing that once he knew how to work without his help he would threaten him with dismissal should he ever be drunk on duty. He told me that the Chief Clerk had never forgiven me for refusing to coach his children when I was already giving lessons to the brother of two whores.

Mr F. suffered from filariasis, Mr Ramoo said, the affliction of women who stood beyond the pale of marriage on
account of their swollen legs. His were covered by his
trousers, which, however, did not protect him from pain at
night, when he tossed and turned at his wife's side. He wore an
ugly mask, and behind it was an uglier face. What did he
mean? But even in his drunkenness Mr Ramoo would not tell.

When the news broke that Mr F.'s son had been arrested
for theft I could only recall his desperate winking, not being
able to imagine how he suffered.

Mr Ramoo and I became close friends, with a friendship
different from that between myself and Mr U., which existed
only on an intellectual plane. I felt my life inextricably bound
to theirs, but in what manner I did not know, for there could
be no two men more unlike each other. It may be that I saw in
them a humanity so profound I stood astonished at my good
fortune. They became for me in my early working life what
my godfather had been in childhood, hooks on which to hang
my projections of manhood.

CHAPTER 16

The Americans

The only woman employee at the Commissary Office was a shorthand typist and secretary to the District Commissioner. I sometimes spoke to her when I went to help Mr U. An old girl of my secondary school, the District Commissioner was fond of saying about her that she guaranteed the excellent attendance of officers who worked upstairs.

One Saturday I took a late boat across the river back to Georgetown and could not help staring when I caught sight of her in the company of an American in uniform. Transformed by heavy make-up, she might have been someone else. Even her behaviour had changed. Tripping along, she dragged her serviceman behind her, so that even if I looked the other way they would come into view on completing the rounds of the first-class deck. Apparently he could not keep up with her, and they disappeared from view until the boat docked in Georgetown.

My introduction to the American presence in the country proved significant, for it was in this light that Guyanese men viewed the airmen and other personnel who had come to maintain the base leased by Great Britain to the United States for a period of ninety-nine years: they took away our women! This preoccupation, far more important to many men than the signing away of part of our territory for three generations, became an obsession with some. They could point to the flourishing brothels in front of which jeeps belonging to the American Military Police often parked when they made raids. It was common knowledge that official American establishments existed where officers could meet light-skinned young

women who demanded a more elaborate display than sharing
a drink before being bedded.

American money in circulation rose sharply. A Trinidad
calypso, 'Rum and Coca Cola', one of whose lines ran, 'working for the Yankee dollar', provides an apt metaphor for the
period. Civil servants and Control Board employees received
a substantial rise in 1943; less than two years later teachers
were granted a similar increase. The effect of the American
withdrawal at the end of the war and the consequent fall in
dollars circulating brought about social and economic changes
which are still being felt today.

The calypso line quoted refers specifically to prostitution
and its massive expansion during the American occupation,
the common experience of Guyana and all the Caribbean
islands on which America built its air bases. Since the
independence of the countries in question the United States, in
the event of a war, would have to negotiate separate treaties
with each of the countries involved. Then, however, a series
of umbrella treaties with the United Kingdom, the result of
one set of negotiations, sufficed to bring about the desired
result.

A mythology of white superiority, carefully fostered by the
British colonial administration, was eroded as assiduously by
American servicemen. The only serious fault tolerated by the
British among their administrators was incompetence, an
understandable indulgence, since it had achieved the proportions of an epidemic. Vulgarity was another matter. Should
vulgarity slip through the net in the process of selection, on
discovery it was promptly apprehended, shipped home and
erased from the records. Where American zealots want to be
loved, their British counterparts demand no more than
respect.

American servicemen had a partiality for Sundays, when
defence priorities seemed to be at their lowest. They would
hire hackney cabs to drive up and down main roads, accompanied by local women. And sometimes one was treated to the
spectacle of a uniformed serviceman stroking the exposed

breast of a woman masking her face behind a raised hand, while their carriage rolled by under the broiling afternoon sun.

The large brothels like Mamus', at the corner of Regent and High Streets, brought their owners much wealth. But one prostitute, at least, became rich and attracted the envy and hatred of many women who indulged in fantasies of unbridled licence. Betty U., daughter of Mr U., the Crosbie, had inherited her mother's beauty and her father's gentle eyes. She illustrated the principle that the boldest opponents of a prevailing morality not infrequently come from a group which itself adheres to a much severer moral code. Muslim daughters were not allowed to go out alone, could not choose their husbands and, generally, lived far more restricted lives than Catholic girls. Betty broke out of her mould and made it easier for her younger sister to follow suit. But it was Betty who bore that mysterious, if invisible, sign, which seduces men to the point of madness. She was reported to have had countless offers of marriage, in spite of her work. Indeed, there are those who claim that her wealth had not been amassed from the practice of her profession at all. Rather, an admirer had married her secretly, submitting to the condition that he place no restriction on her freedom.

The U.s had a distinct advantage over their rival professionals: they possessed their father's refinement. Betty was said to have banished an American airman from her home, saying that while she would forgive him his defective grammar, his poor manners were unpardonable.

But prostitution had another, secret face, illustrated by a story told me only a few years ago. The son of a well-known and highly respected family who had gone to Barbados to convalesce after a bout of tuberculosis, returned in 1943 with a Barbadian wife and settled in a cottage by the sea, not far from Georgetown. One of the owners of the neighbouring house related how she and her sister, then in their early teens, used to turn off the light in their drawing room and look down into the adjoining cottage, where young women, many of whom were regarded as the most desirable matches by local men,

entertained uniformed Americans, walking about stark naked
while smoking and drinking freely.

The effect of the American presence was felt as far away as
the Interior. Aboriginal Indians sometimes worked for them,
acting as guides in the bush. Their intimate relationship with
the different types of terrain – jungle, savannah, swamp
savannah, sandhills and flood plains – made them indispensable as mediators between their hirers and an environment the
Americans saw as hostile. But many Indians knew nothing of
money and could only squander their earnings on rum.
Growing their own food, building their own huts and
supplying all their needs from the forest and savannahs,
money represented for them no more than a means to come by
unlimited quantities of cane liquor which, like their cassava
wine, opened the door to the teeming spirit world. Unlike the
purposeful ritual of drinking bouts when they consumed their
paiwari, the purchase of rum in a shop and its consumption on
the premises led to loss of control in an alien world dominated
by machines and the apotheosis of individualism. One of the
most moving scenes I ever witnessed on television, forty years
later, was of Australian aboriginals tossing from side to side
after drinking spirits, providing an almost unbearable image
of cultural genocide.

My rise in salary allowed me to give my mother more money
every month, to save for the purpose – unconscious at the time
– of breaking free from an environment I found to be
increasingly oppressive; and above all to pursue my life of
pleasure.

My mother was tranferred to a school at Nismes on the
West Bank, so we crossed the river together every morning.
We had never got on so well. She no longer remarked on my
comings and goings and I had come to appreciate that she was
a person in her own right, perhaps my most significant
discovery since childhood. I made it a rule never to come
home drunk and to keep my low life as far as possible from

Charlestown, where we lived. I suspect that my sisters knew of my associations, but a certain discretion had grown in our relationships. We had all matured, in short.

Yet I must acknowledge the egoism behind my compromises. Had either Avis or Lynette, or my mother, found out about my activities their reaction might have been disastrous for us all. Yet I indulged, with the vague hope that what I did would remain secret.

G. did find out. He was still at school, having decided to pursue his studies, with a view to taking a degree later. He himself had missed nearly a year's lessons because he had become involved with a fifteen-year-old girl. They spent much of the day lying in a hammock in the bedroom of the girl's home. Her mother approved, being of the persuasion that young people should enjoy themselves. I have no idea what brought him to his senses, but one day he came to my house to tell me he had returned to school again. A friend of the girl's family had told him I had been seen emerging from such and such a place, to which he had replied that the person was a liar. While listening to him I felt ashamed, simply because *he* was so ashamed he thought it necessary to defend me. I denied the report and the matter ended there.

Now I knew I had to go away. My shame at being discovered and the realization of the extent of my egoism in cutting myself off from the family in a matter profoundly important to them proved too much for me.

G. and I had always played the part of a mirror for each other's behaviour. I came to meditate on the different types of friendship, on resistances that grow within the family because it is the family, on sisters oppressed by brothers, on the burdens of parenthood, on the constant lying to oneself, like the dripping of a standpipe tap that leaves tiny erosions on the concrete below, of little mothers who go away because they are not of the blood, of lunacy lurking like a thief behind the forehead of loved ones, of rivers that silt up like a neglected conscience and clerks who systematically destroy a whole family in the shadow of some strange compulsion.

★

Since I could not go home by the ferry and come back to work on time, I took my meals at the Broodhagens', who lived on New Road, Vreed-en-Hoop, about ten minutes' walk from the Commissary Office. Mr Broodhagen's erect carriage reflected his long association with the militia. Once a clarinetist in the Militia Band, he promptly renounced all interest in music on retirement, declaring that he never wanted to set eyes on a woodwind instrument for the rest of his life. It seemed to me that the proximity of young people made him nervous. He did not ignore them, as many Guyanese men do; nor did he affect a misplaced bonhomie to conceal his unease in their presence. His manner appeared to mean: 'Look, I'll talk to you; but I'd rather you were a lot older.'

His wife, a half aboriginal Indian lady, sat down only at table or in the evening, preferring to attend to her poultry in the yard or work in the kitchen in an endless round of cooking. Like many people of aboriginal stock her knowledge of animals betrayed an instinct that must surely be put to rest by so-called progress. She described a new puppy – acquired to take the place of a dog which had died of old age – as a coward, although she had known it only a few hours. Grown up, the animal would run and hide from iguanas that came to attack the chickens. Once she told me she knew which visitors would be attacked by her dogs even before they came to her house.

I grew very fond of her. It has occurred to me that the middle-aged women I liked and cultivated never spoke ill of anyone; a curious fact when one reflects on the label of 'gossip' that attaches to women and is rarely applied to men.

Even after leaving my job at the Commissary Office I took to looking her up, usually on a Sunday, when the ferry boats ran half empty. The Broodhagen home was one of the most tranquil I have ever known. Filled with beautiful objects, books, a hammock strung across a recess adjoining the drawing room, oil paintings by Mr Broodhagen's daughter, Marjorie, clay sculptures by Mr Broodhagen himself, it gave off an atmosphere of time lived, an ideal retreat for reading or watching the road through a casement window topped with marabunta nests. I came to know all the yards along New Road, connected to it by derelict bridges spanning lotus trenches which overflowed in the season of floods. Shy East Indian women beating their linen, who rarely ever looked up, a mosque and a temple separated by two scores of cottages and tenement ranges and ubiquitous prayer flags defined Vreed-en-Hoop as an East Indian village, as Pouderoyen was a creole one.

At the point where the villages met lived the Forest Ranger and his wife. Responsible for collecting money from charcoal-burners, gold and diamond miners and other leaseholders of Crown and Colony lands, he accounted to Mr U. on his return from the bush. In the year and three-quarters I worked at the Commissary Office I only saw him in the office about half a dozen times. He hardly said a word to anyone. One rainy afternoon when I could do nothing except watch the Public Works Department lorries leaving the compound and guess at the identity of the distant figures hurrying past on the Public Road, he came and stood beside me, seeming at first to have positioned himself for a better view of the road. After a while he began to speak. He asked if I intended remaining at the Commissary Office with a First Class Senior Cambridge, adding that red-skinned people had all the luck. I looked up and saw him smiling, as though he had been testing my reaction. My lack of protest must have made a good impression, for in no time at all we were exchanging views, in the way Mr U. and I did at his home. I was much more confident than a year ago, when I became confused at the discovery that work was so different from school and that you were not expected to make any mistakes in whatever you undertook. Perhaps he never felt at home in an office from which he was absent for the greater part of the year and found it easier to talk to a newcomer. He confessed to living in dread of his wife, who never quarrelled, he said. Pretending to be indifferent to his domestic affairs I answered his question about my plans for the future, confessing in turn that I had applied to the civil service and hoped to be appointed to a good department. I

begged him to say nothing to anyone, fearing he must have
sensed my embarrassment at sharing his marital secrets and
avoided the subject until he advised me to study land
surveying. The months away in the bush would guarantee a
private life, a life apart, he said, so that in the last resort I could
look on the time at home as an interlude. I nearly replied that I
wanted no job that would keep me away from my wife for
months on end, but yielded to that cowardice young people
display in the company of their seniors in years.

While he spoke I became preoccupied by the hasty confession I had made, until he began speaking of the bush, the
hinterland where rivers took the place of roads. I urged him on
with a question and he asked if I would care to join him when I
took my two weeks' holiday. Yes, I said calmly, and hoped he
would not read the eagerness in my expression.

That afternoon, instead of crossing the river by the first
available boat, I went to his home where I met the terrible
wife. A gentle creature, who was so small she had to crane her
neck while speaking to him, she offered me a weak handshake
and asked if I would drink bush tea or green tea. Surprised at
my preference for bush tea she enquired what kind of bush tea
I had in mind.

'Lemon grass, if you have it.'

She said she had and left us to prepare the infusion of my
choice.

The Forest Ranger's wife came back with two cups on a
tray, one of which she gave me. She herself took the other and
placed it on the table beside her embroidery, at which,
presumably, she was working before her husband and I
arrived. I asked why he was not drinking tea with us.

'He doesn't drink.'

Her husband seemed pained by the revelation. He drank no
water, no beverages, no liquid of any sort, apparently.

I hardly knew what to say to keep the conversation going,
for fear of stumbling on some other revelation unwelcome to
him. Everything about the couple and their home was
unusual, the furniture, their attitude to each other, the

pervasive scent which one moment appeared to be vanilla, the other that of burnt hair, the witch-wife with her diminutive frame and seductive ways, the immaculate condition of things dusted to a fault. My discomfort at the pause in the conversation went unnoticed or was ignored, for they persisted in their silence, unabashed by my presence.

'Would you like another cup of tea?' she asked, even before I finished the first.

I said no; and sensing an opening I enquired about a framed pencil drawing on the wall, which turned out to have been done by a relation of hers, whose father had been responsible for the upkeep of the Bourda Cemetery. I told her of Georgetonians' fascination with this unlikely survival from slave days which, with its sumptuous tombs, stood near the centre of the capital, opposite Bourda market. I expressed surprise at its upkeep, remembering the long grass between the tombs; to which she replied by giving me a lesson in its history. Bourda, a wealthy sugar-cane plantation in the early eighteenth century, belonged to the Bourda family, who received permission to bury its members, relatives and slaves in a section of what was once their estate. At that time it was a suburb of Georgetown, then called Stabroek. Long after burials in the cemetery ceased many people would not live in its vicinity, put off by stories of sighing by night in the eastern section.

The Forest Ranger did not hide his pleasure at his wife's expansiveness and nodded from time to time. She, pleased at my interest, talked of slave days, of the terror runaway slaves sowed among plantation owners, a number of whom barricaded themselves in their mansions by night, surrounded by their aboriginal Indian servants.

I pondered on the emancipation of slaves in 1832 – absurdly attributed to the efforts of anti-slavery societies – and it occurred to me that those South American countries with extensive forests had already witnessed a number of successful revolts, when the slaves retired to the jungle, where the king's writ did not run, where they grew their own crops and

defended villages bearing the debris of vanished West African
cultures.

She would nod her head imperiously to indicate a direction
or emphasize a point. Having come to the conclusion, earlier,
that the Forest Ranger had fabricated the story of the dread he
felt in her presence – so impressed I had been by her diminutive
form and her gentleness – I now changed my mind once more
and judged his silence to be not only understandable, but wise.
She had never gone out to work, and with no responsibility
for children – the two she had borne both died of malaria – she
indulged her passion for reading. I was lectured on the history
of slavery in Guyana, on the rise of a black intelligentsia in the
years following emancipation, and the suppression of facts
concerning Africa's comprehensive influence on Europe in
ancient times. She professed to have nothing but contempt for
Guyanese mulattoes, who had little to show for the years of
collaboration with a philistine expatriate class but their
vaunted polish. She almost spat out the word 'polish'. It spoke
for itself, did it not, since its nature ensured a lack of depth?

The Forest Ranger offered me rum and, though I would
rather have eaten than drunk spirits, I accepted.

I remember little of what happened afterwards until I was
awakened by the unusual sound of a braying donkey. I was not
in town! A cool breeze filled the room, with its scant furniture
lost in the shadows. Then, while trying to get up I realized that
I had no clothes on and that I lay in a bed filled with bed linen.
(Since I lived in Agricola I had not lain in a bed with old cast-
off garments and torn cloth.) My head reeled as I made another
unsuccessful effort to raise myself on my elbows before
collapsing on the uneven bed surface. Now I recalled how I
had drunk rum from an unlabelled bottle and the Forest
Ranger's wife's unconstrained laugh across the table at which
we were seated. Slavery and laughter were the only two
prominent recollections of the previous night, recollections
connected solely with the Forest Ranger's wife. Anxious
about the whereabouts of my clothes I did not want to fall
asleep again. In my next effort to get up I placed my hand

farther from my body and felt it resting on soft flesh. Next to me, stretched full length on the bed, was the Forest Ranger's wife, as naked as I. Calmly turning away from me she drew up the blanket which had slipped towards the lower part of her body.

The Forest Ranger, as far as I could see in the dark, had bedded down elsewhere, probably in the drawing room, surrounded by objects associated with his wife's endeavours rather than his, pictures in mahogany frames, chintz window blinds, assorted magazines and unfinished embroidery.

I recall a deathly stillness following the unusual sound of a braying donkey on the country roadside. In town it would have been the dogs with their insatiable appetites.

'Go to sleep,' she said softly without turning to face me.

'Where's your husband?'

'He left for the bush last night,' she answered.

I stayed there three days, just two hundred yards from the compound where I worked and a stone's throw from the match factory, whose employees turned from their clattering machines and nudged each other when I arrived to check the batch of crates ready for export. Three days when I discovered what lay behind the veil of conventions so readily drawn aside to accommodate strangers from the air base.

In the three days, when we talked endlessly, I learned much about her and her family, West Coast people for several generations. With her second child she had been in labour for three days, when she *knew* her husband had prayed for her death. He should have married her elder sister, who would have brought him security, with her insipid personality and odd ideas on devotion. In fact, he had started courting this sister, only to get involved with her when he became an habitué of the house. From then on she and her sister began having their periods at the same time, to the dismay of her mother, who wanted to forbid him further visiting. In temperament, her father was just like the Forest Ranger, hence she was destined to marry him, which did not prevent her from entertaining fantasies about strong men. Too bad! In her family nothing ever lasted and nothing was expected to last. I must not grow to be a weak man or set any store by the future, unless I married, she advised me. The person who dared remain single enjoyed a unique, privileged state.

For the first time I understood how a man could be bewitched and why women with the capacity to bewitch were often plain. The Forest Ranger's wife, unremarkable in looks, was small, with my mother's build and the same air of utter conviction in her superiority, which attracted or repelled, but left no one indifferent. Like my mother she was a Leo, although *she* believed in planetary influences, an idea abhorrent to the de Weevers. Her discovery that my birthday was August 13th did not please her.

Three days, during which I did not even bother to let my family know where I was. In the morning I watched my mother going by on her cycle to Nismes, riding past the stragglers from the ferry, faithful to her habit of waiting till the boat emptied itself of all its passengers before leaving for school. In the evening we listened to the local radio station on the 49 metre band. Three days in hiding, from my mother and sisters, from G., the neighbours, acquaintances at the YMCA. The exhilaration of withdrawal imbued me with a feeling of power that aboriginal piaimen must experience in their mystical journeys to treat with the Master of the Animals, exchanging souls of the dead for beasts in a successful hunt.

She harboured obsessions about slavery, which she saw not only as an imposition from without, but as a connivance from deep within. Wishing to maintain the fire she had kindled I suggested staying while the Forest Ranger remained in the bush. But she refused, saying that three days was enough. She did not wish to be enslaved. Apparently disturbed by the turn our conversation had taken, she got up, offering to make me a cup of cogue . . . A painted window, derelict mansions in the rain . . . 'There are shadows round the moon,' she said, before clouds gathered low overhead. A scent of vanilla came from her kitchen and I visualized her pouring beaten eggs into a jug of hot milk over the edge of which hung two lengths of

orange peel. A scene from childhood, the diminutive personality lurking behind our anxieties of separation and loss, and
fear of the dark, to be metamorphosed into delusions of
power. I had read in some obscure magazine that my affection
for womankind was the very source of rape in a season of
terror, and that sexual love often became sexual antipathy,
especially in women. Did she once love her husband, the
Forest Ranger? Later I came to know women who could not
stand the proximity of their mothers, evidence of this strange
identity of opposites, which manifested itself in so much
around me. And such things made me doubt all the certainties
which had been so painstakingly inculcated in me and wonder
at our depreciation of the magical thinking in which children
indulge. The absence of a father had allowed me to cultivate
illusions of perpetual love in marriage, fed on the innumerable
stories my mother had told me about my father's unfailing
courtesy and the devastating effect his death had had on her.

I had dreamt more than once of two mothers, one instantly
recognizable as my own, while the other, though shrouded in
shadow, I confidently identified as Sophie, the lover-mother
whom I could undress, protected by the dispensation of
innocence. The Forest Ranger's wife did resemble Sophie with
her short hair and smooth skin.

I listened to the noises from the kitchen, indistinct voices of
inanimate things, restoring recollections of Agricola, the
house of awakening consciousness, and Hadfield Street,
where I was born, and from where my father's funeral set out,
unrecollected, yet known. She came back with two cups, one
in each hand, placed mine on the table and hers on the ledge of
the window where she had sat. I asked about the strong scent
of burnt hair during my last meal with her. It came from the
house next door, she said, in which her husband's sister ran a
hairdressing salon. I plied her with questions about everything
except what I longed to know. What was it like having a
father? For I could not help thinking that a father's absence
brought about a condition akin to statelessness.

I did remark how embarrassed I would be to spend a week in

the bush with her husband during my next holiday, but she could only say that it would provide me with a test from which I might learn something about life.

She accompanied me to the foot of the stairs, staring at me all the while as though I had been accused of some wrongdoing. And to my suggestion that she come as far as the stelling she declined by shaking her head.

'You're a strange woman,' I couldn't help saying.

'No,' she said, in turn. 'You are a strange boy.'

I left; and on arriving in front of the post office where I drew my salary at month end, I was taken by an urge to look back, to see if she had remained where I left her; but my pride would not let me, and I walked on, past the iguana-infested churchyard, the Telephone Exchange and District Council Office, until I reached the stelling forecourt where taxis and buses congregated.

Mr F. had left me in peace since the gasoline coupons were found. In fact he hardly spoke to me at all. I met his eldest daughter from time to time on the boat, when we talked about school. In my desire to show that I bore no resentment towards him for the way he had bundled me out of his house, I once enquired after the same daughter. He glowered at me and maintained his gaze until I looked away. In the early days he used to find the slightest excuse to criticize, even to lecturing me on my inability to spell Portuguese names like Veira and Pereira, which any ninny could write, he claimed. Now he would overlook my mistakes with no change of expression.

The employees whom I befriended had all invited me to their homes at one time or another, except Hanif, a Muslim like Mr U. A thin, doleful-looking man, he reminded me of those Christians in books I had read, who flagellated themselves as a penance for sins they had not committed. Having found out about my stay in the Forest Ranger's house and my proposed trip into the Interior, he advised me against going. I resented his counsel, because he had not a good word for anyone, not even Mr U., or perhaps on account of the hawk-like features that exaggerated his surliness. Nevertheless, I let him go on, and learned that one of the Forest Ranger's apprentices had disappeared while on a trip with him up-river. His body was never recovered.

'Why would he harm me?' I enquired. 'Because he must know of your stay in his house,' came the answer.

'How would he know?'

His wife would have told him everything by letter, down to the last detail.

'How do you know that?'

But he only tapped his temple as an answer.

I was more determined than ever to join the Forest Ranger.

My mother arranged for me to see Mr Kranenburg in the Colonial Secretary's Office, with a view to joining the civil service proper. Meanwhile Control Board employees had received a substantial rise, comparable to that of civil servants, which brought me up to thirty-five dollars per month. I anticipated a tussle with my mother about how much more I should give her. But the matter of my larger contribution to the household became, substantially more than a bone of contention, a matter for amiable discussion during which I suggested I give her twenty dollars, substantially more than the fifteen for which she had asked.

Surprised by my generosity, she invited me to go with her to a wedding reception to be held in Hadfield Street the following afternoon. Aunt Ethel's eldest daughter was marrying Wilson Harris, who became our most distinguished novelist. (The bride's brother, Jan Carew, was also destined to be a novelist, as was his daughter, Lisa St Aubin de Terán.)

The house was full of people standing with glasses in their hands. While the women made remarks about the bride's dress, the couple's good looks and matters connected with the wedding, the men's conversation seemed to shun such things deliberately. Since I had ceased going out with the family I had not attended a wedding or funeral, or any of those gatherings which, ostensibly private affairs, provided, in fact, a public affirmation of community bonds. In a way, my presence at this reception with my mother was an indication that my revolt against her had come to an end.

She left me to join Aunt Ethel, her life-long friend who, like herself and most of her close friends, was to live on into her nineties, protected by a mysterious immunity to sickness.

I remember nothing more about the function except our departure, after darkness had already fallen. We took the central pedestrian walk along which grew stunted crabwood trees, wretched imitations of the forest giants.

The pedestrian walk in Hadfield Street, like that of Main Street, was once a canal in which broad-leafed lilies thrived. I have never been able to tread either of these roads without imagining that I am walking on water, accompanied by a sensation akin to the exhilaration of flying in dreams. My mother remarked that I always drifted off while walking. To 'bring me back' she talked about weddings she had attended in the old days and how her Uncle Aloysius often said *funeral* when he meant *wedding*. And while she talked our shadows lengthened and shortened in turn under the lamplight and the drifting moon. And inevitably she came back to the subject of my father and their courtship, when he would visit with gifts he could ill afford. There had been other suitors before him, who came at the instigation of her landlady, a would-be matchmaker who deprived her of meat if she declined to be introduced to one of her visitors. In those days a man who looked up a young woman more than once would be asked to state his intentions, for fear that her reputation might be compromised, should his visits give rise to gossip.

In New Amsterdam things were reputed to be worse. A young man was encouraged to call again, not realizing that the object of his interest would be plotting to ensnare him. Men from Georgetown were advised against visiting when in New Amsterdam, especially if the girl and her mother appeared to be too accommodating. And in support of the warning a certain tale had gained currency in the capital, according to which a man became besotted with a seamstress after her mother had fed him pine tarts on which the girl's menstrual blood had been smeared.

Until then my mother had never talked to me about such intimate matters. I listened, taken aback by her candour, and wondered whether I was receiving oblique advice.

I recall this walk as a kind of crisis, even though my mother and I did not quarrel, and our conversation, the most agreeable we had engaged in for months, ran no danger of foundering on the reef of my latest resentments. It is possible that I expected her to broach the subject of my involvement with the Forest Ranger's wife, which, I assumed, she knew about. Had she spoken about it I would have been angry; now I was perplexed and disappointed at her silence on the matter.

Why do some occurrences, no more striking or important at the time than others, demand to be recalled? Like that of the young man leaning over a piece of furniture in our Hadfield Street house when I was less than two years old, or waiting for the tram while I wanted to urinate, this stroll down the pedestrian walk returns from time to time with unwonted force, obliging me to indulge in a video-like re-run of all its images, until we come to the crossroads with Camp Street and I look up at the darkening sky to see the shadows round the moon of which the Forest Ranger's wife had spoken.

In the event, the crisis foreshadowed by my anxieties and the image of a moon in distress did not materialize. Things fell into place and all doubts about myself and my position in the world were dispelled in a series of auspicious happenings. Apart from the rise in salary and the accommodation with my mother, I became involved with new acquaintances at the YMCA who, convinced that I was endowed with special gifts, lionized me in a way that recalled my early barbershop days when I was made much of by grown men. I thrived on such adulation, while consciously striving to justify it. I became obsessed with the idea of perfection in everything I did and, but for my pride, would have apprenticed myself to the man who had dismissed school education as an assault on one's psyche.

Having grown away from my mother and sisters I felt I was drifting towards the discovery of some new association, leaving behind childhood and youth which, like the double-headed needles of Tenerife lacemakers, seemed hidden beneath mementoes in some secret drawer.

CHAPTER 17

The Forest Ranger

Just a few days before my journey up-river to meet the Forest Ranger the memory of my stay in his house had become blurred to the point that I could pass under his window on my way to work without looking up. I no longer thought about the risk of his vengeance as Mr Hanif had warned, until the morning I set out with a full canvas bag and wondered if I would have the courage to cancel the trip should I become convinced of its unwisdom.

The small steamer started on its journey a few minutes after the American air base boat set out, laden with employees recruited locally. In spite of the large number of people on board our boat some passengers managed to sling hammocks on the lower deck, so that others moving around in search of shade or a seat had to duck under them to get by. I had been up the Essequibo, but never the Demerara by boat and, eager to see from the river villages I knew, I remained at the railing, only to find that – apart from an imposing koker where a creek met the river – I recognized none of the distinguishing features which would permit the traveller to identify McDoom, Houston, Agricola and other places connected with my childhood.

Before nine o'clock the sun had become oppressive and I sought refuge upstairs in the saloon, where a few first-class passengers sat on benches and chairs. I took a book from my canvas bag, but found it impossible to read, in spite of the unusual silence and the smooth passage of the steamer.

By the time we docked at Mackenzie, the bauxite township, many passengers were asleep. And when we set out again after

the bustle created by departing passengers and the embarking
of new travellers there followed the same pattern as before of
conversation eventually overtaken by boredom and silence.
Then, an hour or so later, someone shouted, 'Look!' And we
all got up and stared through the saloon glass. On a small
landing were seated people of all ages dressed up in fifteenth-
or sixteenth-century clothes, all staring down into the water,
as immobile as the jetty on which they were. I rushed out on
deck to get a clearer view of the strange group, but they soon
went out of sight as the boat took a bend in the river.

I spotted the Forest Ranger on the wharf. He rose above the
crowd, which emphasized the impression he gave of complete
detachment from his surroundings when not at home. But on
seeing me his gesture could not have been more friendly.
Pushing his way to the front of the crowd he stood there like a
foreman among workers he habitually commanded and
resembled in no way the diffident figure he made in his wife's
company. And I could only see this as a reassuring sign. All
would be well. In any case I could not go back now.

He took me to a tiny, dilapidated cottage near the water-
front, explaining on the way that we would leave early the
next morning for the charcoal-burners' hut, a couple of miles
inland. I fell on the meal waiting for us, which was served up
by a Portuguese woman whose deeply furrowed face held my
attention whenever she came in. It was common knowledge
that Portuguese women aged swiftly in the tropics, but she –
she could not have been older than thirty-eight – provided a
striking example of the decline.

That night the Forest Ranger and I spoke to each other
across the room from our beds. I had long given up trying to
detect any evidence of resentment in his voice or manner and
listened avidly as he related incidents from his life in the bush
which, according to the Portuguese lady, he knew like the
palm of his hand.

The name of the village escapes me, but its night sounds
were the most remarkable I had heard until then. Tiger Island,
which I had visited by day and left before nightfall, had not

prepared me for the shrieking and calling from the nearby trees, sounds which, in themselves, could have inspired the aboriginal catalogue of monsters and seductive women of the forest, who lure men to their doom. Then, within a few minutes, the wild, almost frenzied noises gave place to a curious stillness, interrupted by an occasional thud on the roof, as of a stealthy, diminutive walker, who was taking the greatest care to cross the corrugated iron sheets unnoticed.

'You don't talk much, do you?' the Forest Ranger asked, and I felt his eyes on me in the dark. 'That's what the wife likes about you.'

'But I'm the most talkative of all my friends,' I corrected him.

'Then how come you don't talk at the office?' He seemed put out that I was not the taciturn type he had imagined, as though he could only forgive his wife's interest in me if I were quiet.

'You're asleep?' he asked.

'No.'

Evidently relieved, he told me what we would be doing the following day. 'Scruffy people these charcoal-burners.'

As his deportment would confirm the next day, the Forest Ranger could have been one of those changelings of Indian lore. Nothing about him was the same except his figure and his regulation khaki uniform crammed with notebooks and money. Here, on the edge of the forest, the vast prison from which the German internee made many futile attempts to escape, the only truly *free* state on the continent, the Forest Ranger had staked a claim for his personality. The man who dared not look his wife in the eye could here speak authoritatively of encounters with the fearsome bushmaster serpent – 'susurucú', the Whisperer, 'lachesis muta', the Silent Death. He explained why the Indians, when they were given fine houses by a Government agency, made fires in them, apparently to no purpose, only because in the bush their fires never went out; that tigers – jaguars – were fascinated by fire; it was believed that they, originally, held the secret of fire-making and often came to reclaim what had been stolen from them.

I dreamed the same night I was bitten by a bushmaster and lay dying while a group of men continued with their game of cards. According to the Forest Ranger the dream meant that I should master my passions. But he made the remark in such a matter-of-fact way I saw no more in it than a spontaneous attempt at interpretation.

Our 'tea' consisted of chocolate on which thick blobs of fat floated, and white bread with tiny fried fishes. This, our invariable fare every morning, was the most delicious meal, because we never ate after breakfast – the huge midday meal – and came to table with voracious appetites.

I remember nothing of the journey to the charcoal-burners' hut, but for all that I recall vividly the heat as we approached and the shimmering air above the slow-burning wood. The barking of dogs broke out on our arrival and the Forest Ranger shouted back an answer to a challenge I had not heard. He shook hands with the two charcoal-burners, but did not bother to introduce me, which caused me no surprise; rather, the hand-shaking did, for it seemed more out of place than it would have been in Georgetown, where elaborate gestures of courtesy were not encouraged.

Almost at once the older of the two men went off to their hut to sleep for the rest of the day, for he and his mate took it in turns to watch the fire, which needed to be supervised continually, lest it burst into flames and destroyed the whole pile.

The charcoal-burner who remained did not conceal his delight at our visit. A former colleague of his associate had died recently and the latter saw him as an intruder. They hardly spoke to each other. Usually, no one came by for weeks on end. According to him most apprentice burners could not endure the boredom and the need for constant vigilance and did not last out a year. Two years was regarded as the critical period, beyond which you were incapable of doing any other work.

As scruffy as the Forest Ranger had described the breed, the charcoal-burner wore sandals, unlike his mate who had gone back to the hut unshod. I would wait until I was alone with the Forest Ranger before I asked how anyone could take the risk of walking about without shoes. I myself had at times run around barefoot as a boy and picked up thorns more than once. I recall the milkman who supplied Central High School, and his thick soles, impervious to any thorn, my school friends and I were certain.

We sat around on the ground and I listened to the two men talk, while wondering when we would have breakfast, which would surely not be as large as elsewhere.

We stayed with the charcoal-burner until late afternoon with only a snack at midday and had to wait until we were back at the cottage before being treated to a large meal of rice and fried chicken with that characteristic Guyanese taste of marinated flesh.

Each day we visited a different group, charcoal-burners, timber grant employees, and a balata bleeder who lived and worked alone. The night before the morning I planned to leave a storm broke while we slept and the Forest Ranger got up to close the shutters while I listened to trees crashing in the forest, brought down by a single giant which dragged everything around it to the ground. He warned that if the storm got worse we would have to sling our hammocks under the house, since it was the safest place to be should it collapse.

Tigers would hunt more assiduously than ever at this time, on the look-out for any monkeys that fell out of the trees. So he said, as calmly as if he were discussing arrears with a timber grant manager. Then, taking me completely by surprise, he asked if I had slept with his wife. Instinctively, I answered without hesitating, denying that we had been in any way intimate. He then went and rummaged in the pockets of his khaki jacket, pulled out a letter and handed it to me. My hands trembling, I protested that I could not read without light.

'No, it's not like fooping,' he said bitterly.

Later I recalled the guilt that overcame me on handling the folded paper and contrasted it with its absence at the time of the deed, when she floated over me with her necklace of wine-coloured beads. At the time I became jealous of the Forest Ranger, and by the end of the third day I was seized by the delusion that I was her husband and entitled to the banquet on which I had gorged. And whence the belated sense of guilt? If he were incapable of harming me would I have experienced the same guilt? These questions I asked myself long afterwards, back at work, where I could not bear seeing him again.

I cannot remember half of the things he told me that night when, even in a shuttered room, a lighted lamp would have blown out. But the sense of his words is still clear in my mind.

When they first met he was fascinated by her light skin and did not believe he could ever get near her. He confided in his aunt, who urged him to find a way of visiting her house, but on achieving his end he should show little interest in her. She told him the story about herself and Carver, her husband who, being no more than a shoemaker's son, treated her with great respect while they were neighbours but no more than acquaintances; yet she would rarely acknowledge his greeting when they met on the road. Sent off to the States as a student she was desperately lonely, unable to make friends, even among fellow students, who appeared to have no time for socializing. One afternoon she was walking through the snow on her way back to her apartment, thinking that she could no longer stand the cold or the loneliness, and half-resolved to write her parents for permission to come home. As she was turning into the road where she boarded someone called her name, 'Miss Elly?' Looking up she saw Carver, wrapped up in a greatcoat, a red scarf pulled tight round his neck. He asked if she did not recognize him. Of course she did, but being near to tears she did not dare speak. In Chicago she fell in love with the man she had despised in Georgetown. The Forest Ranger took heart from his aunt's story and went visiting. However, he had no need to dissemble because his future wife turned out to be uncommonly friendly, and in due course he asked for her hand in marriage, anxious not to lose her.

The Forest Ranger admitted a life-long feeling of being ugly, in spite of constant assurances to the contrary. Certain that his wife saw nothing in him and that she never forgave him for taking her off the shelf – she was twenty-seven at the time – he lost heart and tried desperately to please her, but without success. He saw their marriage go from bad to worse, helpless before her growing indifference. Then, an unexpected promotion from messenger at the Commissary Office to apprentice Forest Ranger undoubtedly saved him from some desperate act, and he came to look forward to his long trips in the bush, often prolonging them deliberately, to the chagrin of his wife who found all sorts of ways to humiliate him. But with every trip his independence from her became confirmed.

I never discovered the contents of his letter, but imagined it represented another gratuitous act of humiliation on her part, an attempt to punish him for what *she* had done.

While on the boat taking me back to town, I had time to dwell on her perversity, for so often I had heard stories of light-skinned women who waited for a 'suitable' man to come along only to settle later for someone they would not have otherwise chosen. Nor was the Forest Ranger's wife the first to turn her own fancied humiliation against a husband she appeared to welcome at the time of their courting.

CHAPTER 18

A Dream

A dream of the seventies recalls conversations with my pupils in a London school, who show an unusual interest in my life as a young man in Guyana and the fact that English is my mother tongue.

Shortwave, the 49 metre band; always shortwave. Spanish voices, interminable conversations, opportunities missed for learning Hindi and Spanish, a conspiracy of schooling which insisted on Latin, that Sanskrit was for babooman. Shortwave, Spanish, Portuguese, Spanish, Spanish, Cucutá on the border separating Venezuela from Colombia, another country, America exporting its vomit and distinguishing it with Academy awards. Spanish around the 49 metre band hemming in our local radio station. Clavelitos, clavelitos, clavelitos de mi corazón . . . Cucutá, Medellín. Georgetown, capital of the only English-speaking country in South America . . . Oh, for the Batacuda, minstrels wandering in the bowels of eloquent guitars, Brazil, where the maned wolf cannot live in captivity, like aboriginal Indians who died under the baleful stare of demons in dinner jackets. Forever travelling, brothers, towards our mothers and away from our mothers. 'The secret of life is that it is not worth living. Only then can you see the loveliness of this world.' 'Aren't you afraid of death, sir?' 'Ha, ha, haaa . . . !' 'Tell us about your childhood, sir!' 'My childhood? So long ago.' 'The 49 metre band, a mesmeric tango . . .' 'I loved dancing, boy.' 'Can you dance well, sir?' 'Well? We danced like gods, boy. We had to, because the women danced like goddesses . . .' 'I read a book, boy, called Strange Fruit. *So beautiful it made me weep. Thirty years later I re-read it . . . I almost couldn't finish it. I've lost the art of reading.' Swamp savannah, interminable hours drawing the map of our country while still at primary school.*

'*Why do you repeat the 49 metre band?*' '*I don't know . . . I see things.*' '*What things?*' '*I can't talk about them.*' '*Do you know, sir, that hundreds of years ago women in Paris wore masks when they went out, that the Muslim veil is no more than the perpetuation of a general custom?*' *Sometimes she covered her face, the Forest Ranger's wife; and to the question why she did so she only shook her head. Why this? Why that? I belong to a country and a continent. A pest on your Commonwealth! Children and dogs are afraid of masks. A child under analysis disclosed that he feared the dark and dogs, which the European analyst interpreted as evidence of hysteria! In our village all the children were afraid of the dark.* '*Why do you fret so?*' *Suddenly I am afraid of the incoherent in coherent speech, of the father in the mother, of the cold, of snow blowing upwards, of almond trees in flower, of convulsions at the dead of night, prevarications in structured stories and the gulf between laughter and terror.*

I will discover Chinese poetry and take fright at its beauty, in the same way I will become smitten by Japanese films. The rational in the irrational. Only then did I appreciate what my godfather had taught me and the power of the trickster figure who sleeps with one eye open. He might have composed the 'Roman de Renart'. Perhaps he did. Perhaps he did live in the twelfth century and waged war against the wolf, outwitted the bear and other animals trapped in their refinements.

At the age of seventeen and a half I gave up going to church, alleging that I could not stand seeing people attending on Sundays and reverting during the week to their immoral behaviour. Perhaps I was sincere, but I might have been pleading my own cause, for my strong feelings about moral issues did not prevent me from being drawn into a way of life which, by religious-moral standards, was far from admirable. Having solved the moral dilemma by giving up religious services I dared to judge others for standing on two boats at the same time. G., taking the opposite course, joined the Catholic Church. His parents, non-practising Hindus, had left him in a limbo in which he came to be more and more uncomfortable,

even exposed; and the fact that we never discussed religion and
that he joined the Church without even telling me I took to be
a gauge of his deep feelings of isolation in a predominantly
creole urban society. This took me by surprise, for I had
always conceded his superior strength, physical and intellectual. Nearly all the families who kept open house, displaying an
astonishing generosity to a large number of people, were East
Indian. And the young man who came into a substantial sum
of money and treated half a dozen friends daily in the Brown
Betty was Chinese. This, added to the fact that the benefici-
aries of their munificence were mostly creoles, was ample proof
of their efforts to buy their way into Georgetown creole
society. G., isolated from the influence of the Hindu masses,
educated into an admiration of Western values, chose to
become a Catholic.

I used to attend the Methodist church at the corner of High
and D'Urban Streets and retain many images of those years,
like that of the young man pumping the organ which my
Uncle Hubert played. An acquaintance and I would sometimes arrive at church late because we had been standing on the
other side of the road, watching the young man disappear and
reappear as he kept the organ going, streaming with sweat and
wearing the expression of a prisoner being whipped with the
cat-o'-nine-tails. Once he turned round, attracted by our
laughter, and threatening us with one hand he carried on
pumping with the other, the strenuous effort needed to
perform this feat accentuating all the more his expression of
torment.

Above the nave a gallery ran all round the church, which
must have been used in years gone by when attendances were
much higher; and even as a child the rows of empty seats above
our heads intrigued me, so much so that during the sermon I
would imagine there were hundreds of heads looking down at
us. I did not realize then that the falling off had begun with the
abolition of slavery and would continue for many years; that
the defection was part of a broad movement which would
follow the failing fortunes of an empire in crisis.

While still a small child I wondered why a tariff for the collection had not been fixed, and whether the verger did not pocket a portion of what he had collected. My godfather would surely not have missed such an opportunity. As a child I had many such blasphemous thoughts, even as I believed in the reality of hell and that all my transgressions against my mother must have been recorded in indelible ink on the lined sheet of a massive book.

In the years following my abandonment of religion I was all but overcome with fear about the inevitable emptiness that would follow. Nevertheless my loss of interest provided a sufficient guarantee for the success of my resolve; and when I heard that an acquaintance of mine could not find a church to bury his atheist father I was too far gone to change my mind, or even to reflect on the possible consequences of my godlessness.

Perhaps my religious faith died in town, the graveyard of all cultures.

CHAPTER 19

Appointment in Georgetown

A few days before my eighteenth birthday I received a letter of appointment to the civil service, assigning me to the Treasury, one of the most prestigious Government departments.

During those last few weeks at the Commissary Office I went around in a kind of delirium, overwhelmed by the certainty that from such and such a date I would be on the established staff. My future would be guaranteed. Besides, in four years' time I would be eligible for six months' leave on full pay, an advantage granted originally to European expatriates and later extended to civil servants born in Guyana. Mr U., who by now was treating me like a relation, did not conceal his delight, and insisted that I visit him more frequently. His son had passed his examination, and on the face of it I had no reason to look him up, believing that our friendship was best confined to the office, since his wife had not spoken to me once or even responded to a greeting of mine.

At this time – 1944 – he never spoke of his daughters, too pained, I am sure, by Betty's growing notoriety. Occasionally, in the midst of a discussion we were having in his drawing room, a slight sound from an adjoining room would cause a shadow to overtake his usual whimsical expression. I have often thought that some great secret lurked behind one of those blue partitions. Yet, whenever I got up to leave, prompted by a discretion that grew out of my respect for him, he would restrain me with a gesture, as much as if to say, 'If there's anything to be found out I trust you to take it no further.'

But more often than not our cordial arguments, which ranged from the existence of God to the crime of rape, were carried on without interruption.

His favourite instrument, the violin, he played with the trills and slides associated with the sitar and other Indian stringed instruments. Holding it on his lap he would lean forward like someone peering into an abyss, with the same posture of G.'s great-grandfather over his Sanskrit texts.

He played melodies evoking timeless images of the sky and the place where the land meets the sea, and often, while watching his mastery over an instrument, I wondered at his marriage to a lady so unstrivingly vulgar.

Mr F. called me into the office upstairs. He was acting for the District Commissioner, who had been on holiday for more than a week.

He did not look up as I went in, and I stood waiting without a word, sensing his anger and certain that he wanted to talk to me about my forthcoming transfer, of which I am sure he disapproved. He kept dipping his pen in the inkwell and wiping its nib on the edge, more often, I thought, than necessary. I could not help being preoccupied with the scribbling sound he made, and my attempts to recapture the scene sometimes give rise to the impression that he is writing on my flesh. He must have looked up eventually and spoken, yet all I can truthfully convey is his hostility and the act of writing, like some baleful occupation, and his calculated, petty conduct, that contrived to punish me for a fancied wrong. If he dared not make me kneel down on a grater he could at least take advantage of his status to keep me waiting. His authority, temporarily fortified by his position as acting District Commissioner, permitted him to behave as the District Commissioner never had.

Only a few months later I learned that Mr F. had gone into rapid decline, plagued with filariasis. But in spite of his pain and the afflicted leg, which he dragged after him, he took to treating the revenue runners like personal servants.

Naturally I spoke to Mr U. about my last encounter with Mr F. and he professed not to be surprised, because 'power does not corrupt; it reveals'. These words were the harshest I had ever heard him utter, he, who liked nothing better than plucking at his sitar for hours or engaging in a discussion about God with the gentlest of words. For me, Mr F. belonged to that ilk of monsters who march through life with a sword, hacking indiscriminately at friend and foe alike. Yet Mr U.'s view was much sterner, for, since we are all revealed by the exercise of power, the judgment is no less than a condemnation of mankind.

Mr U. lived in Georgetown, but for me he belonged, as well, to the West Bank and West Coast, their derelict houses, relationships long buried, spluttering candles used to soften the wax on registered letters, and the way time was regulated not by a clock face, but by the arrival and departure of ferry boats. I visualize devils and angels walking along the Public Road, one behind the other; myself as playwright and the play in a theatre with a strong resemblance to the Broodhagens' house where I lunched at midday and retired afterwards to a recess with a hammock and a profusion of books; parents who become more and more emaciated as their children blossom and flourish. I had grown stronger there, and there noticed the first intimations of a line running from my nose to my mouth. After one year and seven months I would step out of the cocoon in which my metamorphosis had taken place into the working world of Georgetown, only to discover a boredom that would finally drive me abroad.

All the Treasury officers had attended one of only three schools: St Stanislaus – a Jesuit secondary school – Queen's College and Central High School. This absurdity was compounded by yet another: no one seemed to see anything wrong with the preferential arrangement.

I began working in the Accounts section, separated from the Pension and Counter section by a polished wooden railing. A few yards along the covered walkway was the Income Tax Office, and yet further on the Customs. The Legislative Council Chamber with its ornate ceiling was directly above our section. The brick structure, one of the most elegant public buildings in Georgetown, lay on a greenheart raft, an ancient method of construction on swampy ground.

In a vault beyond the Pension section worked a dozen young women, as pale as nuns. From the moment they arrived at work they donned transparent gloves as protection against the effect of contact with old currency notes which they counted all day. No male outside the vault seemed to take any interest in them, as though their sojourn in the windowless vault had set them apart. Two men besides these young women worked in the vault, Mr Franker, their supervisor, and a young, taciturn man who stood at a machine with a treadle, destroying old notes the young women had already counted. Mr Franker himself did little else except read American journals on world affairs. One of his pale charges did eventually become a nun, no doubt as a natural progression from a condition of semi-internment to a more complete one.

We were required to call the accountant and those above him, 'sir'. In fact his superiors we hardly ever saw. The Deputy Treasurer occasionally came over to our section to find out how far behind the accounting schedules we were, while the Treasurer himself – the only creole to head a leading Government department – presented himself once a year to members of the department at a party he gave in his Kingston mansion.

The accounting section, in spite of its superior status, had the unenviable reputation of being unable to keep abreast of its work, and the awareness of this incapacity had become an obsession in the department. 'How far have you got?' 'Have you balanced the last one yet?' were questions we heard almost every day, so that, in spite of the surface calm, we were in fact a beleaguered section.

Vouchers representing money paid out at the counter were entered in the cash book and then passed to Accounts in a bundle. We were then required to enter them, in turn, in the schedules according to head and sub-head, building up thereby a profile of the expenditure of each department. Some departments, like the Public Works Department, kept their own accounts, being provided with their special 'imprests'.

My responsibility covered the post office schedule, in which were posted payments made at post offices throughout the country. The work, simple and monotonous, caused me to reflect on the uselessness of the algebra, geometry and calculus that had brought me so much distress at school.

I worked as I had never worked before, driven by some private demon which, until then, had not had any influence on me whatsoever. Had I believed I wanted to attract the attention of my superiors to my diligence I would have despised myself. But that was precisely its effect. One day the accountant called me to his desk to say how pleased he was with what I had been doing. I was a credit to my school. And with that single act my erratic demon became compromised. What, at that time, appeared an aberration on my part, I came to witness frequently in my teaching career. If some pupils needed encouragement, a small number reacted unfavourably to the faintest whiff of praise.

Having brought the post office schedule up to date I did just enough to avoid being conspicuous. I did not realize at the time that the schedule had not been up-to-date for years and, although it represented only a small proportion of the total accounts, my work was regarded as an achievement. A few months later I received an order transferring me to the main schedules. I had skirted a hill and was now expected to scale a mountain.

But I had already fallen into my old idleness and proceeded to do the minimum expected of our breed. If at times I appeared to be wedded to my table by the window with its two glass paperweights and piles of vouchers, for hours I would be absent, sitting on the Stabroek market wharf, peering into the grey, slow-moving Demerara River, about a mile from the point where it gave up its identity to the limitless ocean.

Hardly a year had passed when the first pleasure at being chosen for a post in the Treasury wore off, like a woman's make-up in a persistent downpour. I missed Mr U., Mr Ramoo, the coming and going of Public Works lorries, the month-end bustle when poor East Indians invaded the Commissary Office to put their thumb prints beside their names on the pension list, and the tension and humour of Crosbie days, like an animated version of a vast painting. What I had longed for many months ago had turned irretrievably sour. I had risen above the claustrophobic world of the home only to find another world of corrosive boredom. It is a curious thing, the way we are prisoners of a cultural code. The civil service as a career had not been *chosen* by me, or even by my mother, who had used her connections to secure the initial interview. Rather, it represented the ambition of a class, which saw in it a guarantee of material security, a second best when resources to study medicine, dentistry or law were lacking. I began to understand how my uncle *chose* a life in the bush, exercising a freedom apparently within everyone's grasp. The freedom I had longed for resembled an elusive horizon; and it seemed to me I had yet to grow up and embark on another apprenticeship, which had little to do with liberation from a mother or material concerns.

More than once Sophie reminded me how, when I was a very small child, when time and death were yet incomprehensible, I became obsessed with fire, and she would burn matches to bring my tantrums to an end. So she said. I would stare into the flame with the same rapt attention I brought to Hilton's magnified slides a few years later. But since matches cost a cent a box my mother did not approve, so punishment was introduced to our home as a substitute for fire. Was I now less a prisoner than in that far-off time? Presented with an opportunity to lead a richer life on the West Coast had I not rejected it in favour of something infinitely more sterile?

Not long after I took on my appointment at the Treasury Mrs Bourne – our next-door neighbour – died, no doubt from obesity. At one time I believed that all funerals were like my grandfather's, grand affairs, with the arrival of several mourning carriages and endless wreaths; but the few cars following the hearse caused no disruption to traffic; nor was there wailing among the women or any untoward incident.

Mr Bourne changed rapidly after his wife's death. To everyone's surprise he took up gardening and transformed his front yard into a large, flourishing bed modelled on Dr Bailey's garden at the corner of Princess and Ketley Streets. When his orchids failed to come up he placed a row of strange-looking objects on the paling staves to ward off the effects of envious eyes. My mother suggested that he consult the Agricultural Department, because many orchids only grew in association with a fungus. Her neighbourly advice was rejected with the accusation that she had procured the assistance of someone to kill his flowers. I could not believe this was the same Mr Bourne who had never tired of entertaining me with incidents from his life as a young man, who invited G. and myself to play cricket under his house and refused to let us go away before he had regaled us with cakes and a glass of lemonade. He no longer returned my greeting when, on arriving home, I caught sight of him at the window.

In the years that went by his demoralization became more and more evident. Paling staves were no longer repaired and his garden, overgrown with weeds, displayed the sad dereliction of an abandoned house. He himself shaved no more than once a week.

A year or so after his wife's death Mr Bourne's daughter married a young man who had been courting her for some time, but at the first disagreement with the couple he exiled himself to a makeshift bottom-house room, determined, it seemed, to complete his social isolation. I recalled the tenor of his stories, his sensitivity, which bordered on paranoia, even as a humble clerk. His wife, ailing, obese and decidedly plain, attracted others by her warmth; while he, in spite of his many advantages, became helpless when deprived of her level-headed support.

Both Mr U. and Mr Bourne were examples of a regime's inability, indeed unwillingness, to harness its people's talents. From the imperial point of view the function of a colony is to provide raw material for the imperial country's industry and to buy in turn its manufactured goods. Neither Mr Bourne nor Mr U. had a place in this scheme, a perfect prescription for a mediocrity which would ultimately destroy them. Mr U. was to undertake a number of trips to the United Kingdom in search of a cure for a stomach ulcer, although the doctors assured him he was perfectly healthy.

I began reading voraciously, following in the footsteps of G., who had been consuming pulp fiction from the age of fifteen. He as well had joined the civil service and worked at the Public Works Department. He no longer went to the YMCA, most of his spare time being taken up with courting. I felt let down, for my interest in games owed much to the competitiveness we each aroused in the other. One day he telephoned me at work to arrange a tennis meeting the following afternoon. Perhaps he had changed his mind about abandoning the game. But to my astonishment he turned up with his lady friend. Furious at this breach of etiquette – no woman ever crossed the threshold of that man's preserve except on special occasions – I decided to take advantage of his lack of practice and, brutally, relentlessly, set about the task of teaching him a lesson; in less than an hour I beat him 6–0, 6–0. What pleased me more than anything else was the expression on his face and her embarrassment. She had clearly been led to believe that he was the better player, which added to my satisfaction the quality of a consummation, so that I had the peculiar feeling of an entitlement to her body as a penalty for her presence.

G. and I did not see each other for months afterwards, not until I learned from his mother that he had contracted tuberculosis and was living for the time being with his aji – his paternal grandmother – in Albuoystown, on the edge of the city. I had been to the house several times, on the way to Clay, our favourite swimming haunt, on the canal which ran past her range yard. I found him lying in a bed which took up a good part of the single room which the shack boasted. His grandmother, who was busy in the kitchen in the yard, greeted me through the open door when she heard my voice.

G. told me how he had caught the disease, in those days a killer that haunted people's minds more than malaria. His lady's brother had died six months before of tuberculosis, but the family had neglected to have the room fumigated. It was there that he and she made love regularly.

It would be difficult to convey my feelings at this moment. An era had come to an end, it seemed, for I had considered in my heart of hearts that G. was invulnerable, since whatever he did he did well, overcoming all obstacles people thought to be insurmountable. After the year he had missed school he recovered lost ground without much difficulty and laughed at my desultory attempts to resume my studies in French, the subject I liked best.

We spoke of earlier times, of our escapades at various cinemas, my good fortune at paying half price two years after my fourteenth birthday; but we said nothing about school or our homes. He told me about the man living next door in a tumbledown shack, who appeared in vaudeville with Madame O'Lindy and adorned his jacket pocket with a red handkerchief. He had never spoken to G. until he fell ill, but now showered attentions on him and entertained him with amusing stories to cheer him up. G. promised to invite him over if he came home from work early, so that he could relate the story of the man who was buried 'in a coffin with a chimney'. I insisted on hearing it right away and in the end he gave in.

A man in his fifties took a young wife, who made frequent calls on him. Sometimes she would even wake him up at two in the morning and demand that he fulfil his marital obligations. In his desperation the husband consulted a healer, who sold him a concoction so effective that it endowed him with a permanent erection. Neither the healer nor the doctors the man consulted were able to bring him relief and, too embarrassed to go out, he lost his job and eventually his wife, who complained of his abnormal potency. When the poor man died a few years later he was buried in a coffin with a chimney-like device to accommodate his erect penis.

There was a false note in our laughter and to avoid succumbing to a sentimental weakness I had always taken great care to conceal, I went outside to speak to his grand-mother.

'You don' go to Clay no more,' she said.

I told her I had never learned to swim properly, not like G. and his brother. I had given up swimming.

She was putting the finishing touches to her new mud stove. How rich she was, I thought. And how rich G. was, with his two grandmothers! Whenever we agreed to meet he would specify the address: behind the alleyway in Lombard Street, at his parents; at his mother's mother in James Street, in the centre of Albuoystown, or at his aji's on the edge of town, where the Punt Trench, boundary between town and country, carried sugar-cane-laden punts drawn by giant mules. He professed to envy me the social advantages of my class, whilst I concealed my own envy, confirming my godfather's assess-ment of my character.

In Aji's presence I saw much about myself as false; and the shame at my glee in beating G. in a game of tennis, at the fragile things that shored up my pride, overwhelmed me with the need to plead that my envy was part of a deep affection. I watched her scooping mud from a bucket and applying it to the unfinished stove, marvelling all the while that she had little need for conversation.

I reflected on the grand tombs of slave masters in the Bourda Cemetery, on the street names in blue enamel preserving the memory of pompous men, and the plain wooden boards destined to encase the spot where Aji would be laid to rest.

Her bucket emptied soon after the sun went down and I followed her into the room, where G. lay reading by the light of a kerosene lamp.

Aji accompanied me to the unlit street and asked when I would be coming back.

'Soon,' I answered.

George recovered within a matter of months on his regime of eggs, milk, molasses and rest. But, he absorbed in his studies, we saw little of each other after that. Our ways had diverged at a point which began with his illness and a determination to become a scholar, and in my attempt to evoke our friendship the trivial things appear more clearly etched: my first public haircut in a barbershop to which he had introduced me, the faces of beggars after a meal in his mother's restaurant, a novel he recommended – *The Headless Horseman* – when I still found reading a burden; my partiality for mirrors to which he became indifferent; his incomprehension at my love of old photographs and our identical views on the characters of people we met. He became a scholar and made long journeys between the covers of books.

CHAPTER 20

The Great Fire

One afternoon in February 1945 while standing at an eastern window of the Public Buildings I noticed a thin column of smoke rising above the surrounding buildings about half a mile away. I went back to my schedules, but, unable to concentrate, took up my post at the window once more, like someone who had been ordered to keep watch. The column, no thicker than before, hardly swayed in the absence of a breeze; yet I saw in it something menacing, even portentous. I made the trip between my schedules and the window several times, until the placid figures of cyclists and pedestrians coming from the direction of the smoke convinced me that nothing unusual had occurred in the area.

I had witnessed the early evidence of the most disastrous fire in Georgetown's history. It had broken out in a Booker's back shop, and when I went back to the window I saw a huge pall of smoke hanging over the rising column, now dense and shaking as it sucked in the air around it.

As I was about to announce that a fire had broken out someone at the telephone shouted out that Booker's drugstore in Main Street had burned down and the fire was spreading rapidly.

Immediately after work we all rushed to the scene of the conflagration. From a position east of the burning buildings there was no great heat, yet telephone wires on the other side of the street were bursting into flames mysteriously, after spluttering like ineffectual matches. Gripped by the fascination of destruction we could only watch as some of the oldest and most attractive buildings in the capital succumbed to the flames. A man riding past on a cycle lifted a clenched fist and shouted, 'Let it burn! Let it all burn!'

Suddenly, recalling that Avis's workplace was the *Daily Chronicle*, next door to the Booker's drugstore, I hurried up High Street only to find the building untouched next to the black ruins of the drugstore. Its position to the windward had saved the premises. I realized I was agitated now because a member of my family might have been a victim, while, until then, I could only see the beauty and destructive power of the conflagration.

Having lost my taste for the spectacle I decided to go home, when, skirting the crowds, I saw the Post Office Tower engulfed in yellow and orange flames while the iron-pillared insurance company, only two doors away, stood unscathed in the midst of the disaster.

At home I joined Avis at dinner and she related how Mr Delph – manager of the newspaper – who had ordered the evacuation of the building, had gone to a friend's house, unable to stay and see his home and possessions consumed. In the event he and his family lost nothing.

My mother arrived soon afterwards and joined us at table. I told them what I had seen. Avis, like her employer, had come home immediately after the evacuation.

All Georgetown south of the *Chronicle* and west of High was threatened, but my mother refused to go and watch with us and 'gloat', as she put it. It was Avis and I who went out together, late at night, for the first time, as I recall, as if some force had kept us apart until then. We first went to see the *Daily Chronicle* to make certain that it had indeed survived. There it stood, marking the northern boundary to a visible, yet incomprehensible, devastation, while charred ruins stretched far away, interrupted here and there by an iron or brick structure. We made for Water Street where the fire still raged, watched by thousands assembled; but there was no weeping, no wringing of hands. Indeed, at one point the crowd burst into laughter when an old man ran out of a building with his shirt on fire, and disappeared up the road screaming, followed by another man who wanted to help him.

I invited Avis to a meal in a downtown restaurant, only to find that we had grown so far apart we had little to say to each other. The gentlest of my mother's children, she bled with some secret pain which caused her death in her forties, leaving a husband and five young children. My mother said that in her last year she wanted to come and see me in London and 'talk things over'. Yet here we sat opposite each other, in my view separated by the gulf of an untended relationship. I told her how Sophie used to pacify me with burning matches, and all she could say was, 'you were always like that,' in her soft, endearing voice.

The psyche, like an ancient book whose pages rustle at night and disturb our sleep, is as unknowable as the suspended stars. Hindu philosophers would have the world welded together and encased in an egg, but might they not be speaking of the psyche, in an arresting image? Whatever metaphor we use to describe it would be accurate, for it is all things; yet false, since it is nothing. If my mother is to be believed my elder sister and I were not separated by a gulf, but a bridge, and because it lay submerged under the fluctuating waters of a lake on which our family lived I had been unaware of its existence.

People were curiously quiet the day following the disaster, as though the fire had consumed more than the burnt-out buildings and their contents which, after all, would be replaced at some time in the future. I could not help thinking that it signified the end of an epoch, like Grandfather's death many years back, and that all our lives would be irreparably changed by it. The man who had shouted 'Let it burn!' had done so with a passion suggesting some hidden meaning which would almost certainly have eluded investigators aiming to discover its causes. (Indeed, the physical cause of the conflagration – a drum of overheated alcohol – had been disclosed over the radio at the height of the disaster.) His clenched fist, his almost ecstatic expression, and the – seemingly – tacit acquiescence of many in the watching crowd, revealed clandestine feelings like the undertow beneath a placid river surface. I am certain Mr Bourne would not have condemned the gesture or its accompanying words; nor would Godfather or the reluctant militiaman; nor the umbrella menders, nor Norma's mother, nor God-knows-who among the deprived who sat in the nether pews of official churches. Indeed, I can see the militiaman standing in the midst of the charred ruins intoning a litany against the living dead who would tremble before the fires of a mythical hell while ignoring the reality of a hell in which their lives were played out.

'*A thin column of smoke . . . I went back to my schedules.*' But if people in Charlestown are to be believed, at the same time, stray dogs began whining and, tails between their legs, made for the safety of the river, displaying an enviable sensitivity in a city where terror had silenced most of us. I was only aroused to deep concern when I remembered that Avis was working in a building that might have been destroyed. If, as a child, I felt I belonged to a larger group than the family immediately around me, as a man my loyalties had lost scope and even shrunk, having been preyed upon by a growing selfishness. My godfather and my mother had tried to instruct me about myself just as the militiaman had warned me about taking a narrow education too seriously. But I followed the precepts of the latter enthusiastically while those of the former proved too unpalatable even to contemplate.

The buildings that began to go up on the burnt-out lands where attractive wooden structures once stood were for the most part made of concrete. One of the first, Barclays Bank in Water Street, is a low, featureless construction that set the tone for the others, all, apparently, hastily designed, and none which could be described as Guyanese. If the Great Fire signalled the demise of the old style in Georgetown's business quarters, the reconstruction that followed it dragged us into a modern age dominated by a cold display of glass and concrete. And this soul–loss – at least in the Water Street area – seemed an apt commentary on our colonial condition.

About two weeks after the fire a Muslim gentleman who once had a vegetable stall in La Penitence market and opened a wholesale shop in Water Street more than a year before the fire burnt it down, came to ask my mother for a reference in connection with drawing money from a loan fund set up to help destitute businessmen. He had failed to renew the insurance on his shop in time and his claim had been disallowed. Some years back, while I was still at school, he had threatened to sue my mother for money which, she claimed, represented goods in excess of what she had ordered. He only desisted when she countered that she would call the maid to testify in court on her behalf.

I came home one evening to find the shopkeeper and my mother in earnest conversation in the gallery. He greeted me effusively, adding that he had often seen me going past his house in High Street and would deem it an honour if I would drop in and see him. Unable to recognize him, I looked enquiringly at my mother who, from her expression, would have preferred not to introduce us. 'Yes, I now remember him,' I said, following the briefest of introductions. Tempted to add that he should have kept away from our house, I asked in jest if he had come to dun my mother for debts she had not paid. And, embarrassed by what he believed to be an expression of disapproval of his past conduct, he insisted that he had acted honourably and, in fact, my mother still owed him money, although he had no intention of claiming it because she used to be his most decent customer before he branched out into the wholesale trade, which had brought nothing but sorrow.

'Mr M.'s come for a reference,' my mother said, breaking into his protestations, '. . . as to his character.'

No event showed more clearly how my mother's financial

position had changed, what with my two sisters and me now contributing to a household that had known straitened circumstances for more than a decade and a half. There she was, facing her past, as it were, with the tables turned, and enjoying the luxury of talking money without begging for it, without pleading her widowhood, being her proud self, as she could afford to be since her children had become adults.

I wanted to say what I thought of him, to savour the vengeance welling up in me, but, in spite of my mother's severity, I could not, for I was now a calmer person. Besides, the idea of making a fuss over money was abhorrent to me at a time when I was earning well. What is more, ours had never been a 'money' house; none of us was capable of rousing ourselves over it, considering it no more than a means of security.

'Give it to him, ne,' I said to my mother.

But she turned away, perhaps feeling far more strongly about the matter than I did.

I sat down at table in a recess of the drawing room, now used as a dining area – the dining room had gone out of fashion in the thirties – and began eating my evening meal, left on covered plates by the maid before she went home. I could see the heads of my mother and her guest across the large drawing room – their bodies were truncated by the piano. And the sight of their disembodied heads made me think of the man I once knew as a boy, presiding over the musty-smelling stall in La Penitence market with his Muslim headdress, taller and more self-assured than he was now. His spine must have begun to shrink, as if to emphasize his loss of financial stature.

I was mystified by my mother's reluctance to give him the reference he came for, and get rid of him as quickly as possible. But they talked on and on in hardly audible tones, perhaps long after I had finished my meal, taken a shower and left on my evening round of pleasure.

One day – perhaps the same week – he called to me from a window of his High Street mansion as I was riding by and invited me to come up and meet his wife. I climbed the long staircase to the landing, where he waited for me, smiling broadly.

'Your mother is a good woman. A good woman.'

His wife, standing behind him, waited to be introduced, and with gestures as extravagant as her husband's welcomed me in turn, before offering me a seat among the numerous chairs scattered about the drawing room. He, as loquacious as the revenue runner Mr Hanif was taciturn, showed her the greatest deference, while she, the picture of a dutiful wife, seized every opportunity to demonstrate her hospitality. She fetched a platter with sweetmeats and cakes of different colours, tried to make me eat continually, and would hear none of it when I declined to have a drink.

Not a single picture on the walls! No studio photographs, no wedding photographs, no representation of any kind, an abomination had this been a creole home, where the head of the family invariably looked down from his exalted position between polished frames on a blue partition; or a Hindu house with its idealized evocations of deities illustrating stories from the Vedas.

Mr M. disclosed that my mother had not given him the reference he had asked for; and my reaction must have been plain to see, because he assured me that the matter was not in the least important.

Then why did he invite me up? I wondered. But I never found out, even though, overwhelmed by his hospitality, I was tempted to ask.

Mr M. had lost his stock in the fire and did not have enough capital to reopen another shop. But the La Penitence market beckoned and, according to his wife, might prove just right for his old age.

'God would have it so,' his wife said. 'I tell him he was happier with the market stall and all the people he get to know. He's like that. He like meeting people.'

Perhaps the conflagration was a bearable disaster which gave him the opportunity to abandon business on a larger scale. But he remained unconvinced by his wife's comforting words.

She went on to remind him that their children had grown up and that their striving was no more than a habit. After all, if they fell on hard times their children would support them.

'I right about the money, you know,' he said.

'What money?' I said.

'The money your mother owe me. I don't make mistakes about these things.'

According to him, my mother's servants ordered things for themselves and charged them to her account.

'How you think those young women live on the wages they get?'

I did not give him the satisfaction of agreeing with him, but his version made sense to me, accustomed to the maids' constant demands for more money.

He told me of a similar accusation made by another woman, who, as it turned out, suspected that her maid was making unauthorized purchases, but preferred to accuse him rather than her employee, hoping that the young woman would take fright at the rumpus and cease the raids on her account.

'I am the wronged one, Mr Heath,' he declared with vehemence. '. . . No matter, she was a good customer. Your mother was a good customer.'

His wife, embarrassed at the turn the conversation had taken, remarked that misunderstandings were as much part of life as anything else.

All of a sudden Mr M. seemed uncomfortable at the tension he had brought about by his brief outburst, out of the blue, you might say, although the feelings that created it must have been lurking just below the surface from the moment he called me up from the street and welcomed me with effusive gestures as if I were a long-lost Muslim brother who had made the pilgrimage to Mecca with him.

Throughout the rest of our conversation he felt obliged to remind me what a good customer my mother had been, how she had visited his stall behind the wrought-iron bars of La Penitence market on her way to the school in Mocha, a village which he had only visited once, not to dun anyone, but to buy mangoes which grew on heavily laden trees by the graves in the church next to the school where my mother taught. He was trying to make amends, I could tell, and he should have been able to judge from the way I looked at him that his efforts were unnecessary, since I did not discount his version of my mother's indebtedness to him. In the end the strenuous attempts to justify himself had the effect of reducing the enormity of the wrong he had suffered.

Now, recalling my visit to the shopkeeper I am certain his wife advocated openly what he wished for unconsciously, namely, to set up shop in the La Penitence market once more, where he had run a small stall for so long he was unable to get the experience out of his system, and to recover the ardour of the old days when the children were growing up and their life resembled the East Coast train with its purposeful journey to Rosignol.

I never once spoke to my mother about my visit or the shopkeeper's version of her indebtedness to him, understanding the need to preserve her private myth of struggling for survival against a harsh world ruled by rapacious men, launched at the time of my father's death when, eight and a half months with child, she stayed away from his funeral, fearing that my unborn sister would be harmed by him as he was being let down into the bowels of Mother Earth.

CHAPTER 21

The Treasury

Not long after I began work at the Treasury Mr Franker was transferred from the vault to the Accounts section, and it soon became clear that he was out of his depth, for, with little knowledge of accountancy, he frequently had to consult junior officers about basic matters. Furthermore, his new exposed position in a section where his every gesture could be seen and judged by fellow officers meant he dared not read his magazines or sit dreaming at his desk. Mr Franker did not conceal his unhappiness at a promotion he had not sought.

Because of our mutual interest in music he and I took to discussing our views on recitals we had both attended or heard on the radio, and I soon discovered that he did more serious reading at home than his American magazines suggested. But he lacked the fire of those men I once strove to emulate and more often than not I listened politely to his conventional views without attempting to put forward my own.

Once I showed him a comic piece I had written and he offered to send it off to the *Daily Chronicle*, but I declined. The very thing that would have given me great pleasure – publication of something I had written – I hesitated to seek, held back by an inexplicable reluctance to expose myself.

As I began to take an interest in philosophy and saw myself floundering in a mass of gratuitously obscure words, I despaired of ever acquiring the abstract vocabulary I believed essential to my understanding of the world around me and my growing torment about my place in it. It is probable that the

appearance of what has been termed my 'ruthless will' dates
from this period, when I set out, systematically, to acquire an
adequate fund of words.

Now it became clear to me that G.'s path and mine, having
diverged at some point in the last year, could not possibly join
again, and all that remained of our long association, nurtured
during eight years of competitiveness in games, visits to
picture houses and endless conversations, was a mutual
sympathy and respect. Our interests, apparently identical over
that fertile period, turned out to be very different now, for he
wanted to be a scientist, while I, having no idea where my
ambition lay, had become obsessed with the power of words.

Towards the end of my second year an unusually gifted youth
began working at the Treasury. I had a nodding acquaintance
with him through my mother, who had spoken of his family.
Hubert's father, one of the first creoles to own a motor car in
the twenties, had lost his job when the national railway was
taken over by the Government and spent more than a decade
attempting to sue the colonial authorities for wrongful
dismissal. Unable to secure a petition of right from the Crown
– a prerequisite to bringing a legal action against a Government department in those days – he nevertheless persisted,
while his legal costs mounted. His experience may well have
had an influence on Hubert, who himself later took up studies
for the Bar. A compassionate young man, he possibly thought
he could reform this most medieval of professions, whose
members enjoyed the unique privilege of protection against
legal process for professional incompetence.

Remarkably – according to my mother – Hubert's family
maintained its dignity throughout this time when the children, still at school, were being brought up on a shoestring.
Their extraordinarily correct manners, their carriage and
generally admirable conduct provided a model for the whole
penniless middle class during the Great Depression, whose
children took loving care of a single pair of shoes, even to the

point of renouncing the traditional pleasure of an evening stroll.

Hubert had learned a great deal from his father about international affairs. In the habit of holding forth at table during the midday meal, the old man had passed on his knowledge to those of his children who cared to listen. Hubert listened hungrily. Yet, in spite of his background, I failed to understand how someone so young could speak authoritatively on an esoteric subject like the Indonesian struggle for independence against Holland, and state confidently that the United States of America had been selling arms to Holland as well as to the Indonesian freedom fighters. How did he know? Whence his interest? I had no inkling of a war that raged in Indonesia, or even of the existence of a Dutch Empire. I knew that Guyana had been ruled by the Dutch for a longer period than it had been a British colony. But a Dutch East Indian Empire and a war of independence!

Hubert practised weightlifting in the afternoons and suggested that I do as much, remarking bluntly that I could not carry my thin frame with me through life. Alas, I was beyond caring. I had brought it this far and intended travelling through life with it, a decision that did not prevent me from taking an unusual interest in the 'before' and 'after' Atlas advertisements for gaining weight. I also found myself hurrying past those yards where, late in the afternoon, young men stood around waiting their turn to hoist a long bar with weights at its ends over their heads, legs apart and eyes bulging with concentration. Intellectual though he was, Hubert admired the pneumatic physiques of weightlifters featured in specialist magazines to which his brother subscribed. I could not make him out. I could not reconcile his undoubted intellectual vision with his predilection for gross images of masculine display. He, who liked thumbing through these magazines, would predict the end of the Soviet-Chinese alliance and suggest that the only guarantee of individual freedoms enshrined in the Soviet constitution were elections based on a multi-party system.

A brother of Hubert's, slightly older than he and entirely different in temperament, was as happy-go-lucky as Hubert was restrained and, as I discovered later, frequented the kind of night haunts and company in which I was now irretrievably embroiled. Once we met at a rum shop and drank until early morning; and I learned during those hours of carousal, when we ended up at his East Indian mistress's home in Robb Street, that what I believed to be an unusual way of life which risked bringing disgrace to our families was the road more than a handful of young men from our milieu had chosen to cope with their frustrations.

Hubert and his brother were chalk and cheese; yet, in spite of this and their two-year difference in age, they got on exceedingly well, each admiring the other for some quality he lacked. I could not help comparing them with Sonny and myself.

Sometimes after work I would ride with Hubert to his home, or he to mine, and we would talk about anything which came into our heads. I had become something of a legend for my laziness and was often reminded how I once took my cycle *to cross the road* in order to buy stamps at the General Post Office – a temporary establishment erected opposite the Treasury to replace the one burnt down in the Great Fire. On my way back the windows were all occupied by fellow officers laughing and applauding. One of them greeted my return with, 'You must be exhausted!' Hubert enquired whether my reputation did not bother me, to which I replied that once my work was done properly I could not care less what others thought of me. Puzzled by my indifference to the opinion of those with whom I worked and especially to those in authority, he gave the impression that he saw it as his duty to save my soul. Would I stay at the Treasury? What else could I do, I asked. Go abroad and study. Since leaving school he had conceived the idea of studying abroad and considered the civil service as a staging post on the road towards an eventual career

worthy of his talents. Impressed by his enterprise I asked him
how he would go about it and, in answer, he initiated me into
his plan. He would save for five years, go away on the six
months' paid leave entitled to civil servants after four years'
service, register with an Inn of Court in London, and so on.
To practise in Guyana he would have to study English law at
an English institution! I listened to him, agape. He went on to
explain the Guyanese legal system which, until twenty-nine
years before based on Roman-Dutch law, had now been
replaced by English Common Law. (Even today the sale of
land is regulated by Roman-Dutch law, which requires
advertisement, a court process and, finally, registration.) All
this he had learned from his father, giving him a decided
advantage over the young men amongst whom he worked.

I promised to reflect on the idea of going abroad to study,
though it certainly would not be to study a soulless discipline
like law. A thought that had long since settled in my mind, but
with little chance of thriving, had suddenly achieved the
stature of a plan, albeit a plan with no specific subject in mind
at this stage. My secret wish was to go to Brazil, but I would
have needed a permit to work there if, at the end of my leave, I
had decided to stay.

Without a tradition of studying in my family and the
stimulation of another's ambition it is unlikely that my vague
desire to go away would have vaulted to the point of fruition
as a project with definite, realizable steps. Like the aboriginal
Indians I could not make up my mind readily; but helped by
Hubert, who himself had been instructed by his father, my
wish had latched on to his; and in the manner of a remora on a
shark's back, I could travel with him, plan with him and
follow his example in saving systematically.

The war in Europe had come to an end and the news,
announced to vast crowds gathered in and around the Public
Buildings, was welcomed with a great roar. But in the year
that followed people gradually came to appreciate the great

change that had taken place in the country's fortunes as a result of Germany's capitulation. Imports flooded into the country once more while purchases of bauxite to feed the Canadian aluminium factories were reduced. Furthermore, the American air base closed and the Americans returned home, leaving shopkeepers, the administration and all those depending directly and indirectly on their dollars, disheartened. Most of those who had worked for them could not find suitable employment and like the employees of the Control Board – it had been wound up by the authorities as an unnecessary indulgence, since the emergency had come to an end – they turned their eyes to opportunities abroad.

Meanwhile, the traditional haven for emigrants from the Caribbean – the United States – had imposed severe restrictions on immigration. Only with the passing of the British Nationality Act of 1947, a statute with the specific aim of swelling a labour force not up to the demands of British industry, did workers from Guyana and the Caribbean islands find an alternative to American emigration. Clerks, linotype operators, engineers, diamond-cutters and other skilled and semi-skilled workers besieged the passport office.

I was to be part of this exodus, a fact that has often prompted me to reflect on my motivation for leaving the country of my birth. Although I did not lack a strong personal motive – my feelings of intense frustration – I belonged to that mass of people seeking to take advantage of opportunities not available in Guyana. Of these two reasons, the individual and the collective, was one the cause and the other a pretext? Or were they both aspects of a complex cause I did not fully understand?

If I never got to the bottom of this problem I was to have an experience which brought matters to a head so swiftly, I wondered afterwards at the prevarications that, until then, had accompanied the long process preceding my decision. It involved Sonny, my brother, and B., a young woman I had met at a dance and taken out only a few times over the previous two years, but whose home I began visiting regularly some weeks before.

Soon after I began going steady with B. I had a nightmare, which recurred a week or so later. I dreamt I had stolen something from my brother Sonny, who would not recover from his illness until I had restored what had been taken from him. The dream wounded me all the more, since I had idolized him as a boy.

When the dream had been all but forgotten I related it to B., and the very night I let her in on my secret it recurred, throwing me into a state of agitation. Eager to let her know what had happened I went to her house the following evening, a dingy, one-bedroom cottage in one of those side streets made up with rough-hewn stones which lurk behind the pitch roads of Georgetown. I hardly knew her parents, a couple with the ability to dissolve into the woodwork whenever I arrived and to make less noise than the insects circling the single, unshaded electric bulb of the piece that served as sitting room and dining room. But that evening her father was waiting at the foot of the stairs for me.

'Goodnight,' I greeted him with what must have been surprise in my voice.

He asked me outright if I had a brother in the Berbice asylum and reacted sharply to my answer that I had. I minded little what he thought or did, since my discomfiture at visiting his house had been growing.

'You said nothing to us,' he objected.

I confessed I had had no idea what to say, since I hardly ever saw him or his wife. Besides, I only took into my confidence those who were close to me. Quietly, he replied that he understood, but I could not come to his house again.

Later, I learned that his anger was due as much to what he called my 'arrogance' as to my connection with Sonny. But then, determined to conceal my own outrage at his high-handed behaviour, I left him and made for the cake shop in which I always ate a snack on my way home at eleven o'clock.

I stood under the radio which, unlike those of other cake shops, always played softly. The proprietor, an East Indian – unusual in those days for that kind of establishment – had taken to telling me about his money affairs and we often talked for a good half-hour before I went home to bed. That night my expression must have betrayed my unwillingness to have our nightly chat, for he gave me my change and went back to the rocking chair he and his wife occupied in turn. I remember only too well my almost irresistible urge to take him into my confidence and disclose what had just happened; and above all to speak of the dream that would not give up its secret.

Looking back on that night I can only think that I missed G., with whom I had shared so much in those momentous years that spanned the period from childhood to early manhood. Why else should I want to confide in an acquaintance, hardly more than a stranger? And what would I have said to him? That I had been excluded from a house I did not care to visit anyway? He was consumed with worry about the profits of a business that could not guarantee his survival over the next year. Having bought it at a price that reflected business generated by the circulation of American dollars at the time, he was now caught in a general slump, and fed his conversation with his obsessive concern over money. How trivial my problems would seem to him!

Mr U. had said time and time again that once we find a solution to our material wants we will have penetrated the forest only to be faced with the desert. Could he have been right? I had managed to save nearly a thousand Guyanese dollars and found myself in the enviable position of being able to dress like a dandy and attend every function that took my fancy. The image of a desert stretching before me, expanding year by year, obliged me to consider anew my plans for the future.

I went over to the counter and engaged the proprietor in a conversation which would, predictably, end in a discussion about money he could not accumulate to keep his shop going and to pay for his girl-child's dowry.

During our desultory exchange, interrupted now and then by a customer, his wife came out of the back shop, sat down in the rocking chair he had vacated and began suckling their infant.

The tranquillity of that cake shop reminds me in some ways of the West Coast, except that this was an island in George-town, a night stop, an image at once public and domestic, consisting of glass cases with platters of seasoned braised steak, mauby jars, an infant asleep, a polyglot radio and a counter where every month end the proprietor and I argued amicably about the credit I had run up.

He said that his brother, who owned and hired out a launch at Bartica, used to stuff wads of dollar notes in his trouser pockets without counting them.

'Only two years ago!' he exclaimed. 'Now . . .'

In the event I said nothing about myself and was soon caught up in his money talk and endless intrigues between brothers, sisters and in-laws. Not for them 'uncles' and 'aunts' by association, as with creoles. Blood and marriage remained the only source of those desperate bonds that carry with them obligations of a lifetime.

I left when he began putting the shutters in place. And on my way home I saw that other shopkeepers had already done the same, so that their establishments were now masked by flat, anonymous boards which proclaimed their identity only by the colour of their paint.

Unable to relieve myself of my preoccupation with a theft I had not committed I was determined to find out what Sonny thought of the matter. I travelled to New Amsterdam one Saturday morning and went to see him.

The hospital, in its attractive setting of flowering shrubs and spacious grounds, might have been the home of a wealthy landowner. But I had heard so many stories about the administration – like the pilfering of patients' food parcels – I was not kindly disposed to those who worked there.

A nurse took me up a staircase and asked me to wait in a gallery overlooking the well-maintained yard while she

fetched Sonny. During the whole of my journey from Georgetown I had tried to concentrate on my first meeting with my
brother after more than seven years, without success. I tried to
think why I had made the journey only once before, but found
my thoughts drifting away as though they had a will of their
own. Now I tried again, but before I could find a reason I saw
Sonny coming towards me in the company of the nurse. She
stood looking at the two of us with an ambiguous smile, then
turned away to disappear down the staircase we had taken.

I gave him the chocolate I had brought, overcome by guilt
that he was confined, while I was free to go whenever I
decided. The thin figure whom I had idolized would not even
look me in the eye, but stared into the distance in the direction
of the sea.

'Would you like me to come again?'

'No,' he answered promptly.

'Would you like me to bring some more chocolate?'

'Yes.'

Convinced that I would extract no more than monosyllables from him, I said I dreamt I had stolen something from him,
but did not know what it was. In my surprise that he bothered
to give me an answer I did not catch the meaning of his words.

'What'd you say?' I asked eagerly.

Then, for the first time, he turned and looked at me.

'I said you know what you stole!'

Astonished at the implied accusation I could only stare at
him. What had I stolen? But terrified of receiving an answer
that might disturb me I did not question him further.

I searched for something to say, unable to escape the
conviction that I must know what I had stolen since he did.
Could I be lying to myself? He seemed to have shrunk since he
left home. And this absurd thought, as absurd as the questions
I wanted to ask, urged itself to the fore and prevented me from
inventing something sensible to ask.

'Why not eat your chocolate?' I asked.

And, as if obeying an order, he tore the wrapping paper
from a bar and began eating greedily.

I could no longer look at him and felt I was capable of sobbing endlessly for those shadowed afternoons when the sun set precipitously on our games.

Twenty-odd years later when I saw him again all his teeth had been extracted. He would not even allow me the courtesy of monosyllables and entrenched himself behind a silence as palpable as his erstwhile contempt for my claim to be considered as a person in my own right.

'I have to go now,' I said, expecting and receiving no reply.

But I remained with him, reflecting on the powerlessness of words.

I took a bus to come back to Georgetown, partly because I did not wish to wait for the afternoon train. But more than anything else, I could not bear to view the landscape from a passenger compartment. Yet, during the first part of the journey, I hardly paid any attention to the landscape, being absorbed in the brief – and as I thought – last meeting with my brother. Childhood was over, as was the age of youthful friendship; and now I had entered the realm where we stand alone. Everything I had done until then had been performed in a kind of dream, dotted at intervals with illuminated signs bearing words at the time illegible: admiration, envy, competitiveness, egoism, the longing for adulation.

The bus drove along the coastal road past the endless coconut groves of Mahaicony, past squatters' houses built where the sea came onto the land unhindered by a wall, past the wreckage of cars by the wayside beyond which white egrets followed the browsing cattle. Where would it end, this interminable journey?

My pride would not allow me to forgive the man who barred his house against me on account of Sonny. Unable to bear the tension my dislike for him had aroused I decided to have it out with him at the first opportunity.

The next time I saw his daughter – we had continued meeting – I told her how I felt and she readily agreed to speak to him.

He telephoned me at work and we fixed a date and time to see each other in the billiard hall of the Tower Hotel, where he knew I was in the habit of playing.

Reflecting on the impending meeting the absurdity of my behaviour did not escape me. I had never enjoyed being in this man's house and had no desire to go back there! Why then this stubborn wish to have it out with him? I felt that something else lay behind my wounded pride. Perhaps it was my anxiety to demonstrate at all costs my loyalty to Sonny, who had been offended by a man who did not even know him. Having 'stolen' something from my brother I owed him a heroic defence which, at the same time, would alleviate my feelings of loss and guilt.

I arrived first and sat down to watch a game of volunteer snooker. I remember thinking that the balls were not ivory, like those used on the number one table at the YMCA; I could tell from the sound they made on contact with each other. In this, one of the more superior hotels in Georgetown, the balls were not ivory. At that age I was unable to reflect for long on a single subject, yet here, exceptionally, I could concentrate on the sound of composition balls for several minutes on end. The muted thrill I experienced at a collision of round objects, and the pleasure of knowing that they were inferior to the ones used at my club, had ousted more serious thoughts so effectively that when my friend's father stood before me I could only look up in surprise.

I offered to buy him a drink, and we retired to the adjoining lounge with its wickerwork easy chairs. For a time we exchanged meaningless talk, observing the tacit rule that circling one's opponent was a matter not only of prudence, but of honour.

'Well, why you wanted to see me?' he asked eventually, with a bluntness which, although familiar to me, offended none the less.

'I don't like the way you spoke about my brother.'

He shook his head, indicating with a simple gesture that I was unreasonable.

'I don't like the way you treat my daughter,' he said in turn.

I protested, but before I could put my objection into words he apologized, saying that he knew we got on well. However, he had been told I would not marry her because I intended going away. After years of association I wanted to escape my obligations. I let him speak, feeling that a burden had been taken from me, since my expulsion from his house had been an act of revenge and, apparently, had nothing to do with Sonny's illness. If only he understood the irony in his protest at my apparently callous behaviour towards his daughter, who had in fact escaped the trap of marriage with someone entirely unsuited to domestication! We had both taken up absurd positions only to satisfy our outrage at an imagined offence.

But when I objected, saying that B. knew of my intention not to marry very early in our friendship, he became angry. He had heard of my 'other women'. Had I told them the same thing?

'That's none of your business,' I countered.

'No,' he said calmly.

Then, deliberately, in a tone calculated to have the maximum effect, he said, 'Whether you stay or go abroad you'll end up like your brother.'

Stunned by the provocation I searched my mind for the most effective way to repay him.

'Mr . . . what's your name again?' I asked.

He stared at me, full of hatred.

'Well,' I went on, 'whatever it is, I'm told . . .'

With unexpected swiftness he knocked the drink out of my hand before I could finish. And almost at once the snooker players looked in, attracted by the sound of breaking glass.

I took a two-dollar note from my pocket and gave it to the barman in payment for the drink and the glass. My heart thumping, I was hardly able to see for my confusion. I made my way between the tables, past the snooker players, through the hall and out of the door, convinced that all eyes were on me.

Once out in the sunlight I could only think, I must get away! The very next day I would put in for my six months' leave. More than five years in the civil service and almost two with the Control Board should earn me a quick, favourable decision. If not I would resign. Hubert, who had already been granted leave, had booked his passage. He would no doubt assist me in the search for accommodation when he arrived in Britain.

I had begun working at sixteen, and now, not quite twenty-four, the first part of my working life had surely come to an end.

CHAPTER 22

The Final Round

As I anticipated, permission to take my six months' leave was granted fairly quickly – late the following month, and a fortnight or so after Hubert's departure. I lost no time in writing him at the London address he had given me before he left, urging him to find me a room.

Even today I recall the thrill at my impending liberation from the civil-service chains that bound me, all the more dangerous because of their promise, nay, guarantee of security. Although I was not going to Brazil I was going *away*, away from the stifling rule of parochial norms.

My Aunt Lena thought me foolish to harbour intentions of staying away for good when I had no specific subject of study in mind, and when things were getting better in Guyana. 'Better?' 'Yes, better.' I dismissed this apparently eccentric view. But in fact there was much truth in what she said. The political turmoil that had begun with riots at Enmore on the East Coast had been maintained, and meetings of the People's Progressive Party under the lamplight at street corners were attracting growing crowds.

But there were subtler changes as well. Few people remarked a reduction in daily funeral processions, and fewer still the dwindling number of vultures circling overhead. Yet these two phenomena had an identical cause, the sustained DDT campaign which had rid Guyana of its malarial pest. If more people were surviving longer, the insecticide which saved them from an early death also spoiled the eggs of vultures, which were at the top of the food chain. They fed on dead animals whose bodies carried the insecticide. Those who noticed the vultures' fall in numbers did not regret it, for the birds were associated with cowardice and death. Small children liked throwing stones at them and seemed mystified that they never managed to hit their targets, whose languid, evasive half-flight conveyed something witch-like and mysterious. No one had any idea where their nests were to be found, but we knew they would appear between nine and ten at morning riding on air currents which took them up to a height from where they could survey the landscape for carrion.

The afternoon before the day I was to take a plane to Trinidad, on the first leg of my journey to the UK, a crowd gathered in front of our house to stare at a vulture impaled on our fence. The extraordinary sight – I had never once seen one of these birds dead, nor had anyone, to my knowledge, a fact attested to by the silence of the people congregated before our house – would have been enough to earn us a reputation for practising obeah, had not local people been aware of my mother's reputation as a Christian with the highest credentials and the long shadow of her de Weever forebears, respectable people who, although their credit was on the wane, still exerted a certain influence beyond their resting place. At least that is what my mother would have me believe when she arrived home.

I told her of the set-to with my lady friend's father and my belief that he was responsible for the dead bird, and took her silence to mean that the bad company I kept was bound to prejudice the family in some way sooner or later. She had never had an enemy in her life. I said that I, unlike her, had enemies and, to demonstrate my humility, asked her to pray for me while I was abroad.

I imagined her kneeling beside her iron bed invoking my transgressions and begging God's favour for her boy-children in a language shorn of all embellishment.

I offered to throw the bird into the same trench at the bottom of the street where we had disposed of our last dead dog, whose distended bowels were on the point of bursting;

but she implored me not to touch it. Tomorrow, after I had gone, she would pay a passer-by to dispose of it on the municipal rubbish heap beside the road.

She came with me to look up my uncles and aunts on this, the eve of my departure for a country Guyanese believed to be paved with gold, and we went from house to house, proclaiming that all was well, that I needed nothing. So many 'relations', so many people come down in the world! Some had abandoned all pretension to status and entertained us under electric bulbs so weak they failed to illuminate the corners of the room, while others flaunted their opulence in drawing rooms with polished floors and fans discreetly placed between ferns disposed at intervals under the casement windows. We went as far as the outskirts, where the cicadas fell silent and street lamps grew brighter beneath buttressed trees and thick algae covered the trenches.

'You're going to a country where visiting is in bad taste,' one 'uncle' told me in a hardly audible tone.

All the windows in his drawing room were closed and nearly every square foot on the walls covered in pictures or furnishings, its spectral interior inviting comparison with the forest where, too, voices are muffled.

'Always ring before you go anywhere.'

Once he must have been a man of substance, for the crockery in which his wife served us Mazawatee tea and corn pone was as delicate as his hands. It turned out that he had been the favourite pupil of my grandfather's, about whom my mother had spoken several times. She had attended his examination for the diploma and recalled how the visiting examiner, moved by his performance of the first movement of Beethoven's Appassionata Sonata, made him repeat it while he, the examiner, stood gazing at the floorboards. According to my mother passers-by would stop in front of his house when he began playing late at night with all his windows open. I recall his closed windows and the musty smell of linen.

I had spent August holidays with nearly every one of these families, eking out the respite from school in brief excursions

and vigils at the window while longing for home. Now, a
grown man, I was at a loss to identify a number of them, either
out of vengeance for those wasted months or because time,
like some malevolent insect, had dug trenches in their
coarsened features.

My mother and I ambled through the streets, stopping from
time to time when she pointed out places where she had
lodged as a young lady away from her Essequibo home. And
she talked with uncharacteristic verve to hide her disbelief that
I was going away.

She spoke of most of the things she had begun confiding in
me since I passed my Senior Secondary examination and, as it
were, acquired the key to adulthood, elaborating on them in
the way a carpenter constructs an extension to some ancient
cottage. Yet not about my dead father, already firmly
established as a model for me, nor about the future, which
hinged on my performance in further exams. I learned that I
had lived for a while with Ethel Carew and her husband, who
had all but adopted me in the early years, soon after my
father's death, confirming long-felt intimations of abandonment. Instead, it was Sonny who went to Grandfather's and
embarked on his descent into a twilight world. I learned that
my grandfather, Peter Moses, in spite of his liberal ideas on
education, maintained a strict segregation between his children and the delinquent boys at Onderneeming; that Lynette,
my youngest sister, began speaking at such an early age, the
first servant girl – before Sophie's time – left our household on
the grounds that such precociousness boded ill for those
associated with it.

'You didn't ask me to help you pack,' she said, changing her
tone of voice. 'You're too proud!'

I answered nothing, indifferent to remarks that would have
roused me a year or two before.

That night I placed my luggage by the back door and lay
down on the bed on which I had been driven to near
distraction with insomnia. Eyes closed, I listened to dance
music from the old school in lawyer Peter's yard, as I had done

on countless Friday nights when I came home and found the house asleep. And everything that seemed so ordinary then, the latticework overlooking Drysdale Street, my open window, the strains of an unfamiliar piece from the hall, would take on a magical significance in the years of exile.

The book is now closed, bound with leathery inflorescences, bearing images of death and laughter, fire and time, of autumn rains when rice is planted in flooded fields and memories fade against screens dividing rooms in long yards, and the rainbow spans the river.